THE AMERICAN
PRESIDENCY
FOR BEGINNERS®

THE AMERICAN PRESIDENCY

FOR BEGINNERS®

Written by
Justin Slaughter Doty

Illustrated by
Kwadwo Amo-Mensah

Foreword by
Neal Monroe Adams

FOR BEGINNERS®

For Beginners LLC
30 Main Street, Suite 303
Danbury, CT 06810
www.forbeginnersbooks.com

A For Beginners® Documentary Comic Book
Copyright © 2017

Cataloging-in-Publication information is available from the
Library of Congress.

ISBN # 978-1-939994-70-7 Trade

Manufactured in the United States of America

For Beginners® and Beginners Documentary Comic Books® are
published by For Beginners LLC.

First Edition

10 9 8 7 6 5 4 3 2 1

Contents

For Christopher Slaughter Doty and Dawn Reshen-Doty,
the earthly authors of my blood and the most
magnificent parents in the world.

For all those who have given me the gift of knowledge,
friendship and the will to never stop challenging myself:

Neal Adams
Barrie Adedeji
Bill Gross
Merrilee Warholak
Henry McNamara
Kwadwo Amo-Mensah
Nicholas Liotta
Anni Cecil

For the greatest paramedics in the world:
Frank Signorelli and Amber Mitchel
Novi Ayivorh
Alex Buenaga
David Clarence
David Dixon
Byran Evans
David Jacobs
Tavish O'Connor
Scott Shannon
Lindsay Thoumire

"Stay the Course"

Foreword

If, in truth, all the world is a stage, and men and women the players upon it, then the American presidency is indeed great theater. The theme of the play has been American history itself and the cast a remarkable assemblage of genius and mediocrity. There have been moments of high drama, deep tragedy, alarms of war, inspired mission, farce, humor, deceit, shame, and treachery. On occasion, the role of president revealed hitherto undetected wellsprings of talent; at other times, the leading players were driven from the stage amid catcalls and hisses. Great deeds were performed and eloquent speeches given, sometimes from surprising quarters. The Civil War was won and the Gettysburg Address written by a man who had experienced less than one year of formal schooling. On the other hand, a "third-rate burglary" unraveled a skein of wrongdoing and bad acting that culminated in the disgrace of another. The performances of some presidents shall be remembered as long as we honor courage, intelligence, patriotism, eloquence, fortitude, and mercy. Others, however, were but "poor players who strutted and fretted their hour upon the stage and were heard no more."

While the role of president brought a measure of fame and notoriety to all those chosen, we remember best those whose characters and actions illuminated and defined the role itself. In this regard, our thoughts naturally turn to George Washington. "First in war, first in peace, and first in the hearts of his countrymen," as Lighthorse Harry Lee put it, he was also the first to play the role of president. Washington was so consummately suited to the part, so universally respected and trusted, and so thoroughly uncorrupted by temptation or jealousy, that the office of president he did so much to create and shape was synonymous in the minds of many with the man himself. In short, he was a hard act to follow. Washington was the natural choice for the part because he embodied those timeless qualities of leadership which the framers of our government had studied in their classical educations. Although the following words were written by Thucydides some 2,500 years ago to describe Pericles, they might also have been penned by one of the Founding Fathers to describe the first president:

> Powerful by his influence and ability, and manifestly incor-

ruptible by bribes, he exercised a control over the masses, combined with excellent tact, and rather led them than allowed them to lead him. For since he did not gain his ascendancy by unbecoming means, he never used language to humor them, but was able, on the strength of his high character, even to oppose their passions. That is, when he saw them unweeningly confident without just grounds, he would speak so as to inspire them with a wholesome fear; or when they were unreasonably alarmed, he would raise their spirits again to confidence. It was a nominal democracy, but in fact, the government of the one foremost man.

This is indeed the stuff of which heroic roles are made!

Washington's successors in the role of president have, each in their own time and way, portrayed the full range of human emotions and experiences. One can only imagine Lincoln's agony as he issued orders that forbade the further exchange of prisoners of war, knowing as he did that his directive might shorten the war but would certainly condemn thousands to death. We remember how Theodore Roosevelt's ebullience in the presidency (the "bully good pulpit" as he called it) contrasted starkly with Franklin Pierce's sadness and misery. McKinley's diffident hesitation when asking Congress to declare war against Spain in 1898 strongly differed from Truman's unhesitating decision to employ the atomic bomb against Japan in 1945. Television showed the world Kennedy's buoyant optimism upon assuming the presidency in 1961 and Nixon's desperate sadness upon leaving it in 1974.

Certainly, the presidential drama has had its moments of victory and defeat: think of Truman's relief and joy when announcing the unconditional surrender of Germany and Japan, and Wilson's agony when United States membership in his League of Nations was denied by the Senate. Indeed, for so many presidents their hour upon the stage was a wild rollercoaster ride careening between victory and defeat, success and failure. Lyndon Johnson's "Great Society" represented one of the most remarkable *tour de forces* any chief executive ever displayed, addressing as it did civil rights, health care for the elderly, and the environment among other concerns. Yet, his Viet Nam policy as well as the dogged, self-destructive determination with which he pursued it was nothing if not Greek tragedy. How greatly he wished to bequeath to future generations a legacy of peace and human progress, yet, in the end, so many said of him, as Lord Byron wrote of Napoleon,

> With might unquestioned, the power to save,
> Thine only gift hath ben the grave.

Occasionally, presidential drama enmeshed the leading players in forces beyond their control, that is to say, required the actors to possess qualities and skills they unfortunately lacked. In this regard, the other Johnson (Andrew) comes to mind: temperamentally unsuited to the role, he could not cope with the cast of characters with which he was required to work; the demands of the turbulent Reconstruction period were simply too much for him. Although Johnson's impeachment has been largely dismissed as the product of political passion, opportunism, and skullduggery, the critics have yet to judge that he acted with much skill. On the other hand, John Adams did play his part correctly, but nevertheless, found the audience to be unappreciative of his efforts. Adams split the Federalist Party over the issue of war with France, an action he felt necessary, yet one which cost him a second term in the White House. While later historians have praised what he did as courageous statesmanship, for John Adams the applause came too late.

Of course, other presidents were overwhelmed (or undermined, as the case might be) by their own fecklessness, naiveté, arrogance or other personal weakness. Grant and Harding proved to be mere cat's-paws in the schemes of ingratiating sycophants and other persons in whom they foolishly placed their trust. Shortly before his death in office, Warren Harding remarked in anguish and sorrow that it was his "friends," not his enemies that cost him sleep at night. Although Nixon, who, it seems, willingly permitted himself to be ensnared in the coils of the Lacoön, certainly learned much about the

> ...tangled web we weave
> When first we practice to deceive.

Yet, one must wonder whether he (or anyone else, for that matter) truly ever understood the dark forces that ultimately destroyed him.

However, presidential tragedy was occasionally relieved by a measure of farce. For example, on a somewhat "lighter" note, William Howard Taft certainly knew what had trapped him. One night, while on a 1911 tour of western states, the rotund chief executive (he weighed more than 300 pounds) found himself hopelessly wedged in a Colorado hotel bathtub. His predicament was quickly solved, however, through the ministrations of a bunch of burly cowboys hastily recruited for the job. After a few shouts of "OK, boys, altogether now!" out popped the President! No doubt, those guys dined out on that story for the rest of their lives.

Of course, as can be the case in any play, presidential drama has sometimes been greatly heightened by the players' entrances and exits. Nominating conventions have occasionally seen the emergence of minor characters from obscurity to fame (the so-called "dark horses"). James K. Polk and Warren Harding were good examples of this phenomenon. Although he never made it to the White House, William Jennings Bryan's "Cross of Gold" speech at the 1896 Democratic convention transformed him into the most famous "also ran" in American presidential history. Some elections were truly "cliffhangers." In 1800, Jefferson and Burr actually tied in the Electoral College balloting (which led to the passage of the 12th Amendment) and, in 1960, Kennedy triumphed over Nixon with less than .25% of the popular vote. In the elections of 1876 and 2000, the losing candidates (Samuel Tilden and Al Gore, respectively) earned more popular votes than their opponents (Rutherford Hayes and George W. Bush, respectively); in both cases, the methods employed to resolve the disputed outcomes remain controversial. In 1968, Nixon's victory over Hubert Humphrey was so narrow (less than 1%) that the results were not certified until late the next day. Is it possible that Nixon's repeated trials and tribulations entering the stage may have aggravated an innate sense of insecurity and thus contributed to his later tragic exit?

The timing of an actor's exit from the stage can be even more critical than the circumstances surrounding his entrance. Certainly some presidents were dispatched before their time, before they could fulfill their potential. Here, one naturally thinks of Kennedy, but perhaps James Garfield was another good example. Others lingered too long or attempted ill-advised comebacks. Theodore Roosevelt's 1912 run on the Progressive Party ticket had the unforeseen consequence of transferring the ideas of that movement from the Republican Party (where TR hoped to see them accepted) to the Democratic Party 20 years later under the leadership of his distant cousin.

Nevertheless, in certain cases, it seems that the hero was carried from the stage at the moment most propitious to his historical reputation – when his best work was behind him and nothing but disappointment and frustration lay ahead. In this regard, Lincoln and FDR come to mind; both exited the stage at the dramatic climax. We shall never know how well Lincoln might have managed the challenges of

Reconstruction. However, given the divisions within his own party and the excruciating task of leading four million people from slavery to citizenship, it is reasonable to conclude that the attempt would have done little to enhance Lincoln's immortal image of martyred Great Emancipator. FDR's sudden death on the very cusp of victory in World War II 80 years later presented a similar situation. Winston Churchill, who possessed a fine sense of theater, remarked that he truly envied the timing of his wartime colleague and friend's passing. Death at the very climax of his dramatic performance spared the four-term president the passion and paranoia of the postwar period, (domestic and foreign) the ravages of age, and the inevitable invidious comparisons between earlier triumphs and later frustrations.

Be that as it may, no one can gainsay the fact that the drama attendant to a president's death in office exercises a profound effect in shaping his historical reputation. Not every president who died in office, even those who were murdered, was subsequently the recipient of a much-inflated reputation, but Lincoln and Kennedy certainly were. Indeed, so pronounced was this phenomenon in their cases that all too little remains in the public mind of the real men. The emotionally-charged and mystical images that continue to emerge remind us of Ariel's song in Shakespeare's **The Tempest:**

> Nothing of him that doth fade
> But doth suffer a sea-change
> Into something rich and strange.

In fact, even some presidents who lived long after they left office and died peacefully in their beds have had their posthumous reputations exaggerated and distorted – for mercenary reasons, of course. Parson Weems was the first to discover that "there was gold in old George's bones" and invented whole-cloth those silly stories about chopping down cherry trees and throwing silver dollars across the Potomac River. The tradition continues today with endless torrid tabloid headlines, magazine articles, books and movies purporting to tell us at last the whole truth about JFK and his family. One thing is certain: the final curtain in presidential drama certainly does not come down at the grave.

As in all plays, presidential actors have had understudies and villains. Occasionally, an actor waiting in the wings would be called to take the star's place upon the stage – thanks to the actions of villains. Those assassinations were high drama themselves, "plays within the play," if you wish. The villains and lunatics that committed those acts earned their infamy by being critics of the most extreme sort. John Wilkes Booth, who happened to be one of the most successful actors of his day, made certain that he played his scene stealing performance for maximum dramatic effect. He actually shot Lincoln in a theater and then leapt from the presidential box to the stage shouting, **sic semper tyrannis!** Booth has been accused of many faults and deficiencies, but lack of dramatic sense is not one of them. Furthermore, it is strange and ironic to contemplate that if it had not been for the heinous crimes of Booth, Charles Guiteau, Leon Czolgosz, and Lee Harvey Oswald, the names of Andrew Johnson, Chester Arthur, Theodore Roosevelt, and Lyndon Johnson might survive only as footnotes in history.

Finally, no historical sketch of presidential drama would be complete without some mention of those who auditioned for the part but were never given the opportunity to "tread the boards." Sadly, it can be said that some of those estimable aspirants were more talented, experienced and worthy than many of the individuals who were ultimately chosen. At any rate, the lives and contributions of such leaders as Henry Clay, Winfield Scott, William Seward, James Blaine, William Jennings Bryan, Robert Lafollette, Alfred E. Smith, Adlai Stevenson, Hubert Humphrey, and Al Gore deserve to be remembered as well. Bryan, who ran no fewer than FIVE times, deserves some sort of award—if only for persistence. In fact, one of the many curious conclusions that may be drawn from a study of presidential drama is that superior talent, intellect, integrity, experience, even desire for office, have not always guaranteed success.

So, the stage is now set, the lights are going down. Let the play begin.

—Neal Monroe Adams

Neal Adams taught US History for three decades at John Jay High School in Katonah, New York and later served as Upper School Headmaster at Wooster School in Danbury, Connecticut. He graduated with a B.S. in Education from the University of Vermont and obtained a Masters of History at Wake Forest University. He also did doctoral work at Duke University and specialized in the history of the British Empire.

Currently, Neal tutors at the Brookfield Learning Center and teaches piano. He is the Minister of Music at the Newbury Congregational Church in and lives with his wife, Linda, in Brookfield, Connecticut. They have three grown children and three grandchildren.

The Evolution of the Presidency

The Presidency was not born overnight; it was the product of the evolutionary culmination of intellectual minds over hundreds of years. How could a government obtain and preserve an independent executive that was strong, but not overbearing, while guaranteeing that the executive could not be eternally controlled by one man or one family? That question would eventually be settled by compromise when the constitution was ratified in 1789. However, before ratification the Presidency was a topic of lively debates among the Founding Fathers.

What contributed most to the establishment of the Presidency was the government of the Articles of Confederation which was in place until 1789. The Articles were incredibly weak; there was one legislative chamber of government—a large House of Representatives with a weak "President" who acted more or less like the Speaker of the House—which was unable to govern efficiently and nearly brought the newfound republicanism of America to its downfall. However, at the Philadelphia Convention, where the Founding Father's debated a new form of government to replace the old articles, James Wilson voiced his support in the creation of an independent executive. The idea came from a careful study and understanding of history. James Wilson, as well as the other Founding Fathers, knew a great deal about societies of the past, their structure and also of the great works of men such as John Locke, Plato, Niccolò Machiavelli, Montesquieu, and William Blackstone.

The famous Republics of old—the Roman Republic and to a certain extent, Athenian Democracy in Greece—were both a guide and a warning on how to create the new Republic that would govern the states. The Roman Republic had led to the rise of a brutal and crippling tyranny that ultimately led to Rome's destruction. However, the restricted and hierarchical governments of modern Europe—riddled with monarchy—brought with it egregious corruption, restriction of individual liberties and property while providing little stability. The Founders had to find a happy medium between a weak Republic and an overbearing monarchy.

The Founders found help in writings.

Plato had written of monarchy and democracy,

> "there are two mother forms of states from which the rest may be truly said to be derived; and one of them may be called monarchy and the other democracy.... Now, if you are to have liberty and the combination of friendship with wisdom, you must have both these forms of government in measure.... No city can be well governed which is not made up of both...."

Machiavelli wrote of classical Republics

> "the customary proceedings of republics are slow, no magistrate or council being permitted to act independently, but being in almost all instances obliged to act in concert one with the other, so that often much time is required to harmonize their several opinions; and tardy measures are most dangerous when the occasion requires prompt action."

Montesquieu wrote of checks and balances and divisions of power,

"Here then is the fundamental constitution of the government we are treating of. The legislative body being composed of two parts, they check one another by the mutual privilege of rejecting. They are both restrained by the executive power, as the executive is by the legislative."

These three powers should naturally form a state of repose or inaction. But as there is a necessity for movement in the course of human affairs, they are forced to move, but still in concert.

As the executive power has no other part in the legislative than the privilege of rejecting, it can have no share in the public debates. It is not even necessary that it should propose, because as it may always disapprove of the resolutions that shall be taken, it may likewise reject the decisions on those proposals which were made against its will..."

John Locke wrote of natural rights,

"There is another power in every commonwealth which one may call natural, because it is that which answers to the power every man naturally had before he entered into society. For though in a commonwealth the members of it are distinct persons, still, in reference to one another, and, as such, are governed by the laws of the society, yet, in reference to the rest of mankind, they make one body, which is, as every member of it before was, still in the state of Nature with the rest of mankind, so that the controversies that happen between any man of the society with those that are out of it are managed by the public, and an injury done to a member of their body engages the whole in the preparation of it. So that under this consideration the whole community is one body in the state of Nature in respect of all other states or persons out of its community."

William Blackstone complimented Locke in saying:

"The public good is in nothing more essentially interested, than in the protection of every individual's private rights."

It was up to the Founding Fathers to find a way to create a Presidency which would guard the natural and individual rights of the people through a healthy relationship with the other branches of separated government, and they were divided on how to accomplish this. Many Founders proposed that a council be created instead of one executive. James Wilson argued for an independent executive that served only one term, Alexander Hamilton proposed a Monarchy nearly the same as in Britain but all these ideas were voted down. Instead of drawing up a totally new office for the executive, the Founders began searching for existing models that could be replicated on a larger scale. The best model was the Governor of New York, an indefinitely electable executive who was Commander in Chief, had veto power and had the ability to pardon.

The Founders also looked towards existing governments that did not have monarchy. During the debates over the new constitution few governments existed that were not monarchial, but the governments that were operating free of monarchy—Switzerland, Holland and Poland—were not exactly bastions of freedom nor nations that could boast that they had societies with a high quality of life. Poland had an elected monarch, however the Polish nobles had seized power from the electorate thus nullifying the monarch's power, creating corruption and bickering among nobles. Jefferson personally believed such a monarchy to be just as bad as the English monarchy.

Ultimately, a President with very limited power was settled upon. The President was agreed to be eligible to run for office as many times as he wished as well as have the power to veto legislative bills, the power to pardon, the power of appointments, dominance of diplomacy and treaty as well as having the role of Commander in Chief. For many of the Founding Fathers, this was too much power guaranteed to one person, yet many of the Founders agreed to these provisions because they knew George Washington would be the first President and they trusted him. And so the stage was set for American Presidency in 1789.

George Washington
(1789-1797)

"I hold the maxim no less applicable to public than to private affairs, that honesty is the best policy."

Introduction

So much has already been said about George Washington that when introducing him it may be best to let his own words speak for his character. After the constitution was ratified and the United State was formed, the first internal rebellion broke out in 1782. Revolutionary War veterans were revolting against Congress, which had refused to pay their promised dues. The rebels called on Washington to lead them again and to storm the congressional halls. Speaking to the group of men who he had lead during the revolution Washington took out the list of their grievances from his pocket. Before reading the paper he explained to the room of rebels, "Gentlemen, you will permit me to put on spectacles. For I have not only grown gray but almost blind in the service of my country." He then quickly dismissed their points and told them that he would never lead a revolt against the country and against the ideas that he had given every inch of his being for.

George Washington was born on February 11, 1732 in Westmoreland Virginia. His dream was to become a General and to have an illustrious military career. By 1755 Washington had already begun building himself a career in the English military. In 1756 he fought in the Seven Years War, gaining invaluable leadership skills and knowledge of the battlefield. That knowledge would be vital in 1776, when he led the colonists to victory in the Revolutionary War, breaking away from the country he used to serve.

When the Revolutionary War broke out, Washington was a respected choice for Commander in Chief of the Continental Army. His moderate, methodical and systemic thought processes, combined with his revered military career made it easy for people like John Adams to promote him during the Second Continental Congress's meeting.

Returning to his home of Mt. Vernon after the war, Washington, heeding the call of his nation once again, presided over the ratification of the constitution in 1788–1789. Soon after, he became the President of the United States.

It is no coincidence that Washington is the icon of the United States, as he led the nation through many of its incredible hardships. When he became President of the United States, the first in history; he forged the template that every President would follow.

A Presidency, not a monarchy

In 1789 all of Europe was watching as the new young country called the United States elected its first leader. The United States had rejected the European system of absolutism and kings, but how long would the new system last? Surely the first leader of America would eventually become a king if America was to survive in the world. Wrong. George Washington was satisfied to be president, elected by his peers and often at the mercy of the house and senate as all future Presidents are. Washington could have very well accepted a crown in the same fashion as Caesar and become the first king of the United States, but instead he upheld the power of the people of new Republic, turned down a 3rd term, created a judiciary system and rejected the tyranny of political parties.

Creating stability and dealing with indecision

The United States had made a change in 1789 and created a new constitution and a presidency in order to leave behind the weak Articles of Confederation. Therefore Washington, as the first President, had to make sure that the new system did not have the same fate as the old one. Washington's administration was highly focused on moving the country towards a path of stabilization and peace. Ideology, while extremely important to most of the Founding Fathers, was far less important to Washington then pragmatism. This struggle between the two is best characterized by Washington's cabinet. The first President surrounded himself with brilliant men, many of whom were at odds with one another. This was especially true of his Secretary of State Thomas Jefferson—a firm believer in absolute Republicanism—and Secretary of the Treasury Alexander Hamilton who was much less inclined to always go with the Republican values of the day.

More often than not Washington would side with Hamilton on issues of policy. Hamilton was not afraid to advocate for the creation of banks—seen by Jefferson as giving the government too much power—and for the levying of taxes. And in the case of taxes Washington, who was in charge of a nation that had debt up to its eyes, agreed to levy a tax on whiskey. However he quickly learned though that the American spirit had not changed much since 1776, and a rebellion erupted. When faced with the challenge of the Whiskey Rebellion, Washington was able to successfully quell the uprising and proved that the new presidency had the power to bring stability where the old Articles of Confederation could not.

Just as important as quelling rebellions was the ability of the new administration to solve economic problems of the time. George Washington was a general, not an economist and therefor he used the tried and true tactic of delegation to deal with economic problems relying on his two closest advisors, Hamilton and Jefferson. Hamilton advised Washington to establish a national bank to encourage domestic production while Jefferson rejected those ideas and believed that a bank and a focus on domestic production would bring corruption and the death of the agrarian lifestyle. Washington sided with Hamilton and supported his program. While the Hamiltonian innovations had many positive effects, more important was the fact that Washington dealt with indecision and acted rather than doing nothing at all. Moreover, Washington's choice affirmed the power of the cabinet, showing that a strong cabinet can sometimes make a strong presidency. Hamilton and Jefferson were not his only strong choices either, Henry Knox—the Secretary of War—and Edmund Randolph—the Attorney General—were capable men handpicked by Washington to fill positions that he created.

The following labels appear on the map within the illustration:

NH 6
VT 3
12
MA (16)
RI (4)
15
CT (9)
NJ 7
DE 3
MD 8
21
4
12
8
4

☐ Washington
▥ Territories

The Diplomacy of neutrality, legalism, and alliance

We may be all too familiar with the concept of world policing in today's Presidency but in the era of Washington such an idea was not even conceivable. However, when the French Revolution erupted with the storming of the bastille a great deal of pressure was on Washington to come up with a policy stance toward the French. Federalists in the United States—those who aligned themselves with the policies of Alexander Hamilton—wanted neutrality with the French while Republicans—those who found favor in Jefferson and liberalism—wanted to aid the French in their struggle.

To the dismay of Thomas Jefferson, President Washington decided to remain neutral during the French Revolution. Once again Washington sided with his advisor Hamilton who said the United States should not get entangled with France causing his other greatest advisor, Jefferson, to resign over the matter. How did Washington remain neutral with an ally who assisted the Americans in their revolution? Legalism. The United States was bound to aid France by the "Treaty of Alliance," a treaty established after the American Revolution with the French who

had helped the colonists defeat the British. Washington's close advisor, Hamilton masterfully manuevered away from the obligation by pointing out that the French regime that had ratified the treaty no longer existed after the French revolution. The leaders who had agreed to the treaty had been executed or imprisoned and the government dissolved, thus, in the eyes of Hamilton, dissolving their Alliance treaty as well.

Despite his concern regarding engagement with France, Washington was convinced that diplomacy could be proactive and used to defend the United States. Such diplomacy during the Washington era led to the Jay Treaty—negotiated by John Jay—which settled disputes with Britain over questions of trade and the damages of the revolutionary war. There was also the Pinckney Treaty with Spain which strengthened America's relationship with Spain and defined Florida's borders. Washington reinforced the security and stability of the United States through diplomacy and averting war, a tactic that many Presidents would replicate after him.

So Long, Farewell...the writing and final thoughts of Washington

Often the most remembered part of the Washington administration is his farewell address, which was not an oral one. The speech was written at what many professors consider to be PhD level and preached the wisdom of neutrality and independence from political parties. It was published in a Philadelphia newspaper as Philadelphia was then the temporary capitol. Washington spoke his mind about the corrupting influence of the party system and to this day is revered for it. His speech writing—which was assisted by Hamilton—has been admired as well, however such a level of writing was only possible due to Washington's electorate. Washington was addressing an educated ruling class, the only people who could vote at the time. Presidents that followed in the future—now with an electorate that is not as enthusiastic about hearing a thesis—have tried to channel Washington's eloquence but rarely have as much success. However Presidents such as Lincoln who could harness the power of Washington's speech but use simplicity at the same time are the most remembered today.

Washington returned to his home in Virginia and retired, turned down a third term and enjoyed the rest of his days in peace.

John Adams
(1797-1801)

*"Abuse of words has been the great instrument
of sophistry and chicanery, of party, faction, and
division of society."*

Introduction

John Adams was one of the most important and central figures of early
American history. Born in 1735, in Braintree, Massachusetts, Adams
lived the one of the most modest lives of the early Presidents. Raised in
a small house built by his father, life was challenging in his youth, but
with the support of his family Adams eventually left home to attend
Harvard.

Adams became a lawyer soon after he finished his work at Harvard in
1755 and received great fame and notoriety for defending the Red Coats

that had participated in the Boston Massacre in 1770. With a strong belief in justice and common decency, Adams successfully defended the Red Coats and got all but two acquitted. "It is more important that innocence be protected than it is that guilt be punished, for guilt and crimes are so frequent in this world that they cannot all be punished."

In the prelude to the Revolutionary War, Adams slowly drifted to the side of the Sons of the Revolution. When war finally broke out, he served in the First and Second Continental Congresses. With Thomas Jefferson and Benjamin Franklin, he worked on editing and promoting Jefferson's Declaration of Independence. Venturing on his own writing path, he released his *Thoughts on Government*, expressing his ideas for how government should function – greatly influencing the system of government that would surface after the war.

Serving off and on as a minister, both during and after the Revolution, first to France, Holland and then to Britain, Adams found himself more concerned with issues of his own country than the foreign ones. He returned to the United States in 1788 and authored the Massachusetts state constitution, one of the first to ban slavery.

And so by 1789, Adams was a respected man, both for his intelligence and his love of country. Minutes before Washington was inaugurated President, Adams took the oath of office for the Vice Presidency himself, a position that would lead him to becoming the second President.

NH 6
VT 4
12
MA 16
14
RI 4
CT 9
20
NJ 7
DE 3
MD 7 4
4
11
3
8
4

☐ Jefferson
▨ Adams
■ Territories

VICE PRESIDENT
$1
PRESIDENT

Prepared for Peace

When John Adams stepped into Presidency he did not have many allies. Adams was a naturally independent man who had little time for political parties and power seekers. Like Washington, Adams was determined to keep the United States stable. He envisioned a presidential agenda that would prepare the country for the inevitable conflict and resolution on economic and foreign policy issues. His first act was to create a navy. The British Empire had maintained control all around the world by having the strongest navy and Adams knew that if the United States was to be taken seriously in the world and be able to defend its trade routes it needed a navy as well and was perhaps Adams only noncontroversial act as president. Both Federalists and Republicans agreed with him completely.

The creation of the navy came just in time as relations with France quickly dissolved as Washington left office and Adams stepped in. War broke out between France and England around the time of the election of 1796 and the French began to seize American vessels at sea, taking their resources and men. Northern Federalists—who relied on sea trade—demanded the president do something while avoiding war to disrupt trade. Prominent Federalists—including Alexander Hamilton—wanted Adams to begin building up the military and establish a standing army. Adams did not agree and was not in favor of a standing army. However he also got no relief from Republicans. They wanted the United States to aid France despite the violence and cruelty taking place in the country. Adams would not have that either.

Courage in Crisis

Following Washington's example Adams chose to first begin with diplomacy. In an attempt to seek peace with France, John Adams sent three American diplomats to negotiate peace. Diplomatic veterans John Marshall, Elbridge Gerry, and Charles Pinckney traveled to France to negotiate with the French Foreign Minister, Charles Maurice de-Talleyrand. To the Americans surprise, three French agents, called by "X," "Y," and "Z" in the American press demanded bribes and goods before any negotiations could begin. Although bribes were somewhat common in European diplomacy of that time, Marshall and Pinckney were outraged and refused to play ball. Because of the lapse

in negotiation between the United States and France after the X, Y, Z affair, the United States entered into an undeclared "Quasi War." The Quasi War, essentially meaning an undeclared war, was bad news for the United States. French naval vessels became aggressive at sea, and although the United States had a navy, it was hardly ready to deal with one of the major European powers. Thus peace with France became Adams main goal throughout his presidency.

The Revolution in France had its droplet effect as well. Other nations including the United States and Great Britain feared revolution coming to their shores. A few radical Republicans in the United States, as well as the rebels that formed in Pennsylvania against the new taxes, had called for a Revolution similar to that of the Reign of Terror in France—where thousands of politicians and members of the aristocracy were slaughtered. With pressure from the Federalists to do something about revolutionary sentiments and with fear of legitimate revolution starting, President Adams enacted the Alien and Seditions Acts. They consisted of four acts, the Naturalization Act, the Alien Act, Enemies Act and finally, the most controversial of them all, the Sedition Act. The acts restrained immigration and attempted to censor free speech in the public forum, which made many politicians feel that they were at risk of being imprisoned for simply speaking their mind. Adams, who up until the Alien and Seditions Act had remained independent from the federalists made a grave mistake and alienated the electorate, especially the Republicans who were outraged and believed the acts to be unconstitutional.

Ultimately Adams' policy of diplomacy began to work despite the protest of the political parties. Elbridge Gerry, one of the original diplomats during the XYZ affair who had stayed in France, finally returned in 1800 to alert Adams that the French wanted peace. The Quasi War ended at the Convention of 1800 where American and French diplomats negotiated an end to the fighting on the seas. President Adams achieved his main goal, peace with France by remaining independent of party influence—an action which doomed Adams but saved the country.

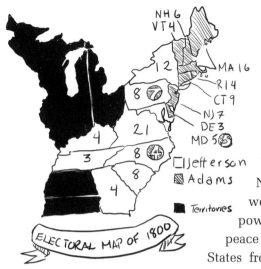

NH 6
VT 4
1 2
MA 16
R 14
CT 9
NJ 7
DE 3
MD 5
8
21
4
3
8
8
4
□ Jefferson
▨ Adams
■ Territories

ELECTORAL MAP OF 1800

Final Days in Office and the first peaceful transition of power

As John Adams left the capitol and let Thomas Jefferson take the reins of power there was no doubt that Adams left behind an important legacy. Not only did he show the entire world that men could relinquish power, but the realization of a peace with France saved the United States from devastation. A war with a European adversary, fought so soon after the Revolutionary War—with hardly a military or Navy to demonstrate strength—could have ended badly had Adams not used diplomacy. In fact, Adams even said "I desire no other inscription over my gravestone than: Here lies John Adams, who took upon himself the responsibility of the peace with France in the year 1800." Adams also proved the power of keeping an independent mind while in office. Party is not everything. By standing firm and refusing to cave in to Hamiltonian Federalism for the majority of his term in office—while also remaining fairly independent of his cabinet—he proved that independence in politics is often beneficial. From the creation of a navy (which would be vital in the War of 1812 as we shall later

see) to establishing a lasting Peace with France, Adams' Presidency marked an administration capable of bringing about great diplomacy and future insight for preparedness in war.

Adams greatest weakness was that he did not clean out the cabinet upon his entry into the White House and instead retained Washington's appointees—an error many Vice Presidents who ascend to the Presidency make. He was surrounded by federalist loyal to Hamilton and he led astray when it came to policies such as Alien and Seditions. He also appointed John Marshall to the Supreme Court, an appointment that is now referred to as the "midnight judges' appointment." The "Midnight Judges" got their title because John Adams appointed them in the final weeks of his presidency. The myth is that President Adams appointed many of them at midnight before Thomas Jefferson took over the Presidency, but in truth, Adams appointed them over a time span of three weeks. Marshall was responsible for Judicial Review and was one of the longest serving Justices in legal history. The Adams administration is the prime example one term presidents that can be just as important as or even more important than those presidents who obtained two terms.

Thomas Jefferson
(1801-1809)

"If a nation expects to be ignorant & free, in a state of civilization, it expects what never was and what never will be."

Introduction

Studious from a young age and naturally intelligent, Thomas Jefferson, was born on April 13, 1743, and was tutored at his home, Monticello. Jefferson's father, Peter Jefferson, died when Thomas was a young man, bequeathing Monticello to him. Jefferson left home for William and Mary College at sixteen, finishing in two years. In 1759, while at William and Mary, a favorite professor of his introduced him to the philosophies of three men whose portraits are still hanging in Jefferson's home today: John Locke, Sir Francis Bacon, and Isaac Newton. These men sparked

Jefferson's interest in Republicanism and democracy, ideologies which Jefferson would hold close to his heart for the entirety of his life.

Jefferson was admitted to the bar in 1767. He practiced law for five years, but switched law for his true passion, politics, when he joined the Second Continental Congress in 1775. Although he had left academic life, he never gave up academics. It was there that Jefferson wrote The Declaration of Independence, severing the colonies from Britain and engaging King George III in Revolutionary War.

As the war was being fought, Jefferson returned to his home in Virginia and became a delegate. Shortly after becoming a delegate, in 1779, Jefferson became Governor of Virginia. After serving two terms, his wife passed away in 1785. Leaving the United States to grieve and to find himself, he became Minister to France. When Washington became President, Jefferson was made Secretary of State, eventually reaching the vice presidency when Adams became President.

Warning others about the growing power of the federalists in the government during Adams' presidency, Jefferson authored, alongside James Madison, the Kentucky Resolutions in opposition to the controversial Alien and Seditions Acts. By the end of the Adams administration Jefferson was determined to run for president again and in 1800 represented the antithesis of federalist ideas.

For Jefferson, the pen was mightier than the sword. Jefferson's writings and views on government would forever change the world, sprouting republicanism across the entire planet. Monticello, his home, is the testament to his brilliance. Filled with thousands of books, paintings and scientific inventions, Jefferson's intellect still exists in our world today, physically and intellectually. Although sometimes harsh and unforgiving, Jefferson respected his adversaries. And while strong on his values, Jefferson was able to compromise on both a political and intellectual level.

Conservatism and the Presidency

Before delving into Jefferson's presidency it is important to first discuss the role of conservatism in the presidency. In our modern political environment we often evaluate and analyze our presidents simply by what legislation they enacted or how well they used the presidency to vocalize messages in the political pulpit. Rarely do we analyze the importance of maintaining what we have. Even rarer is it to see appreciation for the quiet presidents who let the people be. Now I bring this up not because

Jefferson did not accomplish many things, in fact it is the opposite. As you will see Thomas Jefferson did accomplish a great deal, more than most Presidents. However there is another piece of the presidency that must also be taken into account, especially when it comes to presidents who are more conservative than others. That consideration is what the president did *not* do and did *not* say. Thomas Jefferson and many of the men who believed in classical liberalism were happy to keep things static. Many of them believed that the best way to preserve the yeomen farmer and the agrarian lifestyle which they so greatly valued was to limit government to only ensure safety and public good. Moreover, the classic interpretation of the presidency was that it should be a limited role with a primary focus on management over theatrics. Jefferson was the embodiment of the classical view of the presidency.

Stretching the Limits for Louisiana

Thomas Jefferson was revered by many Americans, both those from the north and the south. However he had a special reputation with the south as a grand defender of the agrarian lifestyle which the south was accustomed to. The agrarian culture was one which Thomas Jefferson wanted to spread as he believed it was the cornerstone of maintaining a Republic and the values for which the United States stood for. So when Emperor Napoleon of France hinted that he was willing to sell the territory of New Orleans, Thomas Jefferson handpicked James Monroe to be his negotiator in order to acquire the territory. This was initially all the land Jefferson intended to purchase, but Monroe quickly realized that by 1802 Napoleon was ready to sell the majority of the French Louisiana Territory.

Napoleon, who had been working on plans for an invasion of England, needed money and he was more than willing to sell all of the territory. Monroe jumped at the opportunity to acquire the territory of Louisiana when Napoleon offered it up for a lower price than they intended to pay for only New Orleans. Fearing that Napoleon would retract his offer at any time, Monroe agreed to the deal and Jefferson went through with the purchase.

Domestically, members of Jefferson's own party—such as John Breckinridge—raised questions about the constitutionality of the treaty. Breckinridge and others claimed that a constitutional amendment would be needed before the treaty could be accepted. A vote to nullify the purchase nearly passed, losing passage only by two votes. Jefferson circumvented adding a constitutional amendment by quickly passing the treaty before much debate could occur. This has caused historians to debate the constitutionality of the purchase, and whether or not Jefferson was being hypocritical by going against his conservative values. However, few people have questioned the immense benefits of the purchase.

Promoting the Public Good

Once the French territory was purchased by the United States, the question of what do with the land became the talk of the day. Jefferson believed that the exploration of the territory could be bolstered by the government and so he commissioned the two famous explorers, Lewis and Clark, to travel across the Louisiana Territory and the Western portion of what would eventually be the United States. They began the exploration on Mississippi River, trekking all the way to the end of the Oregon territory.

The Lewis & Clark expedition provided great amounts of new information for the scientific and economic realms of academics. In addition, they helped the United States begin planning on further westward expansion, as well as gathering more detailed information

on the Native Americans living in those territories. Both the territory purchase and the expedition made Jefferson very popular after the constitutionality question blew over. With a congress full of newly elected Republicans, there was even more of an advantage for Jefferson.

He used his political capital to repeal many of the taxes that Washington and Hamilton had put in place, abolishing the internal revenue service. He also managed to pay off a majority of the national debt by making large cuts in the Navy and in getting rid of unnecessary government expenditures. Moreover Jefferson followed through on a promise made during his campaign and repealed the federalists Alien and Seditions Acts.

Jefferson's presidency was not all smooth sailing though. The issue that forever plagued Jefferson's life and legacy, slavery, would come up during his presidency as well. Before we go into slavery in the early 1800s during Jefferson's presidency we should step back and visit the constitutional convention again. When the Founding Fathers convened and began debating the constitution back in 1789 the majority of those present ended up settling with slavery, even the men from the North. Why was this? Well, many of the Founders who opposed slavery did not advocate for an amendment banning it because they believed that slavery would eventually die out on its own. Many also felt that if they tried to ban slavery the constitution would never be ratified.

Jefferson, a slave owner but also the man who proclaimed that "all men are created equal" desperately wanted to see the next generation of Americans rid the country of slavery. Feeling that little progress was being made he called for the ban of the international slave trade in 1808.

The Embargo, a lesson of cause and effect

Even more difficult than the issue of slavery was the foreign policy tensions with Great Britain. By 1807 Great Britain had been stopping and seizing American vessels, enslaving thousands of American sailors and disrupting trade. Jefferson, not wanting to respond with military action, decided to wage economic warfare against Great Britain believing that an embargo would hurt English industry and force the English to rethink their policy of impressment.

Unfortunately, the Embargo had an adverse effect. Since England was still able to trade with France and many other nations, the loss of the United States as a trade partner was not as damaging as Jefferson envisioned. Additionally, the embargo hurt the United States more than anyone else, ruining the northern economy. Even worse, Jefferson—the great promoter of agrarian life and ethics—actually spurred industry to develop in the north by forcing businesses to start manufacturing at home instead of relying on foreign goods. The embargo was repealed in the last days of Jefferson's presidency because of protest from both northerners and southerners.

A President, Not a Spectacle

One of Jefferson's most lasting changes to the Presidency was the change in style of Presidential image. He wasted no time, starting his reforms to presidential image immediately after his inauguration by walking to the white house. He changed the way addresses concerning the state of the union were delivered to Congress. From Jefferson's Presidency to the presidency of Woodrow Wilson, the state of the union was written via letter and announced by a handpicked speaker in Congress by the President. This change in the President's speaking and personality role, one of many by Jefferson, came about because Jefferson felt that a President coming to Congress to present a state of the union was like the English King going to parliament. While strengthening the

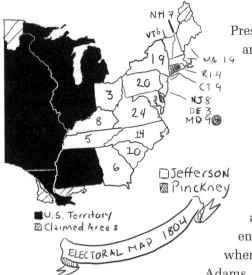

NH 7
VT 6
19
MA 19
RI 4
20
CT 9
3
NJ 8
24
DE 3
8
MD 9
5
14
10
6

☐ Jefferson
▨ Pinckney

■ U.S. Territory
▨ Claimed Areas

ELECTORAL MAP 1804

Presidents power as Commander and Chief and the Presidents influence over diplomacy and legislation, Jefferson also greatly decreased the role of the President as a presence in people's lives. His conduct with other politicians was also very different from Washington and Adams. Washington had enjoyed his political gatherings where everyone dressed up. Adams was happier enjoying a solitary evening with his wife and books. While Jefferson still enjoyed social occasions he would often answer the white house door in his nightgown or robes and rarely put on a show for guests. All the pomp and grandeur was thrown out, no more presidential carriages, court appearances or formal rituals with foreign visitors. There was always expensive wine—as this was one of Jefferson's loves—but the White House in Jefferson's time was modest and many believed him to be a champion of the common man.

While Washington and Adams set the standards for the Presidential administration, Jefferson set the standard for Presidential image which would carry on for nearly 100 years, interrupted only once by Civil War, and then changed during World War I with Woodrow Wilson's administration.

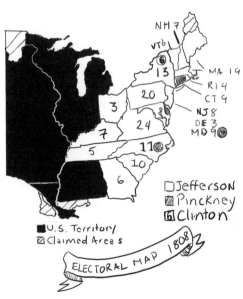

NH 7
VT 6
6
13
MA 19
RI 4
20
CT 9
3
NJ 8
DE 3
24
MD 9
7
11
5
10
6

☐ Jefferson
▨ Pinckney
▣ Clinton

■ U.S. Territory
▨ Claimed Areas

ELECTORAL MAP 1808

James Madison
(1809-1817)

"Knowledge will forever govern ignorance; and a people who mean to be their own governors must arm themselves with the power which knowledge gives."

Introduction

James Madison, born March 15, 1751 at Port Conway, Virginia, was bright and active at a young age. During his youth, he was privately tutored under the guidance of Donald Robertson. By sixteen, Madison was off to attend the College of New Jersey, what is now Princeton—graduating in 1771.

During the Revolution Madison jumped into the world of Virginia politics. Working with Thomas Jefferson, Madison became increasingly talented in the realm of compromise and mediation. Alongside Jefferson, he aided in the passing of the Virginia Statute for Religious Freedom and in writing the Virginia constitution.

During the years of rule under the Articles of Confederation, Madison became a vocal critic of the weak form of government. Leading a crusade for a new Constitution, he and Alexander Hamilton as well as John Jay authored *The Federalist Papers*, arguing for a stronger government. Just as important was Madison's effort in helping to draft the Bill of Rights. Madison was so elegant with his persuasive arguments for ratification of the Bill of Rights that when he gave a speech in favor of the bill in New York, they named the avenue he stood on "Madison Avenue."

Madison worked in the House of Representatives from 1789 to 1797 after the ratification of the constitution, aiding George Washington and even initially working with some Federalists. But nearing the end of the Washington Presidency, Madison became a fierce opponent of the federalists, and began working with Thomas Jefferson on forming the Democratic-Republican Party. Co-authoring the Kentucky Resolutions during the Adams administration, which practically called for secession, Madison would never again be on good terms with Federalists.

When Jefferson won the Presidential election of 1800, Madison became his secretary of state. Having given invaluable advice to Jefferson during the early years of his administration, Jefferson called on Madison to help him with an issue that would evolve in *Marbury vs. Madison*. At the end of Jefferson's second term, Madison was a likely successor as President to his best friend and partner in politics.

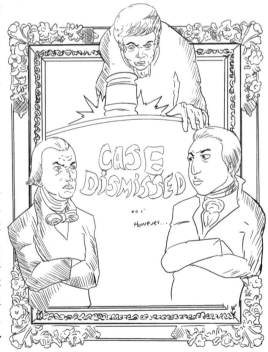

Tidying up domestic policy

By the time James Madison became president he had proven to the world that he was his own man. He had, at times, found himself in agreement with the federalists and democratic-republicans. He had argued for stronger

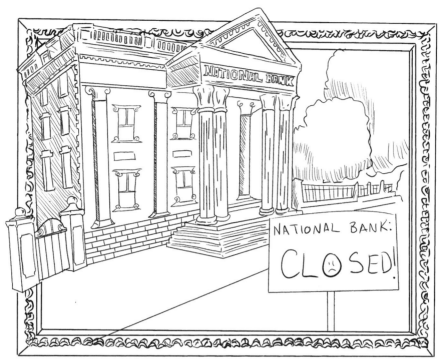

government and weaker government. With Madison, nothing was partisan, every issue was different and required open mindedness. Faced with the tumultuous final years of the Jefferson presidency, Madison brought his analytic mind to the field of domestic policy.

With the National Bank up for reauthorization, Madison—believing that it was unconstitutional—vetoed the re-charter of the National Bank. Thus, the Bank expired and was forced to close, ending the First National Bank of the United States. Madison was then faced with the issue of the Embargo Act which Jefferson had signed into law. Madison accepted its failure and repealed the remnants of it. The repeal met little to no opposition, as the embargo was extremely unpopular.

War of 1812

With the failure of Jefferson's Embargo Act of 1807 to end British impressment of American ships, conflicts between the two nations continued to escalate throughout Madison's presidency. To make things more difficult for Madison, the election which had made him President also gave congress new members made up of very young representatives, many of whom became "War Hawks," promoters of a fight against Great Britain.

War Hawks

The War Hawk faction was led by Congressmen and Speaker of the House Henry Clay from Kentucky. Clay—who was such a brilliant orator that he was elected Speaker on his first day in the house—commanded the support of Western and Southern states. The trade hungry Northerners tended to be "doves" fearing war would disrupt their economy.

Clay became the famous Congressmen that we know him as today because of his knack for comprise, but he initially gained fame in government because he was an early War Hawk. Clay pressured Madison to go to war and received support on that issue from another famous statesman, John C. Calhoun. Eventually Clay got his way despite some protest from Madison. After many private conversations with Madison, Clay and the rest of the War Hawks pressured the president into delivering a war message to Congress. Madison, unsure of a better route to take, declared war on Britain, hoping to bring an end to impressment.

Madison faced a difficult challenge. He had to deal with preparing an army and navy to fight the war after eight years of reduction in armed forces because of Jeffersonian policy. The war also came close to home, the British army, some of whom were Canadian soldiers, were able to burn down the White House during the conflict. Meanwhile, northerners were at the brink of disunion, fearing that they were being forced into war by the West and South.

As time went by, members of the House of Representatives called for attacks on Canada, battles at sea and extra western defenses against the plains Native Americans who were supported by the British. The sea battles went well for the United States, and later into the war General Andrew Jackson and William Henry Harrison had decisive victories in the Western territories. During this time Madison carefully held together the nation by working with both the War Hawks and the federalist opposition. With no precedent for presidential war time leadership Madison was on his own, but the nation stayed together throughout the many battles.

However, the battles on the Canadian border did not bode as well as the naval ventures because the Canadians were able to successfully defend their nation. Some of the House members—whose motives for attacking Canada were for the United States to annex the whole territory away from the British—had destroyed their chances of gaining new territory in Canada. After the Canadians defended themselves, a cold shoulder was turned to the United States for many years.

The final major battle of the War of 1812 actually took place after the Treaty of Ghent was signed, but due to slow transportation of messages, both General Andrew Jackson and the English armies were unaware that peace was declared until after the battle. The English army attempted to capture New Orleans as well as much of the Louisiana Purchase territory, but General Andrew Jackson fought them off in one of the greatest land victories in United States history.

Hartford Convention

The Federalist Party was growing more and more enraged by Democratic-Republican policy, including the Embargo Act, the War of 1812, and further complications in United States relations with Britain. In response to all the chaos they gathered in Hartford, Connecticut to discuss the future of New England and the party. Some radicals proposed secession from the union, others wanted peace with Britain, but the radical shouting was drowned out by the more moderate federalists. The moderates preferred to focus on getting a repeal of the 3/5 clause, which allowed slaves to count as 3/5s of a person in a state's population, which gave southern slave states a popular edge over New England, resulting in larger control of the House of Representatives. Ultimately, nothing came out of the convention, as the end of the War of 1812 soon ended after the convention began, embarrassing the Federalists.

Treaty of Ghent

In an effort to have peace between Britain and the United States, President Madison sent a party of three diplomats to make peace: John Quincy Adams, Henry Clay and Albert Gallatin. They met the English diplomats at Ghent. Quincy Adams and

Clay began the talks of peace in disagreement over the terms of Ghent, but eventually the American diplomats came to a consensus with the British diplomats. The Treaty of Ghent restored the nations to the *status quo ante bellum* (the state before the war) bringing borders back to their original prewar formations. In addition, the English concluded their policy of impressment of American ships.

Internal Improvements and the American System

With the War of 1812 resolved, and peace upon the seas realized, Speaker of the House Henry Clay called upon members of Congress to join him with his American System. The American System called for internal improvements by way of an active government. Clay and National Republicans put forward bills that would construct canals, bridges and roads. While some of Clay's proposals passed, Madison vetoed much of the internal improvements, including a bonus bill that both Clay and John C. Calhoun championed. Madison did not believe that the Constitution allowed for such improvements to be funded by the federal government—such improvements in his view had to be left up for the states to fund. Madison quickly became the first president to regularly exercise his veto power. Unlike much of the work of his predecessors, Madison wanted things done by the book, and was not afraid to stop what others saw as "progress" to keep all laws and legislation in line with the Constitution.

During this time Madison also advocated converting the Native

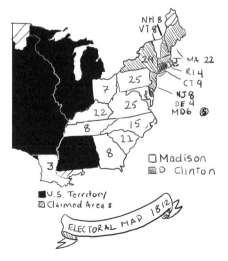

Americans from tribal and hunting based tribes to agrarian farmers. Madison told his generals to not attack the settlements, but Generals such as Andrew Jackson disregarded the President's order and continued persecutions of Native Americans.

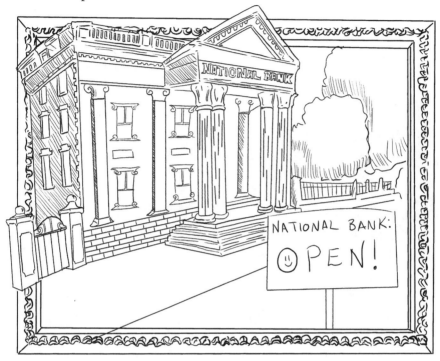

Nearing the end of his presidency he did finally find common cause the Clay and the war hawk allies. The War of 1812 was a realization for President Madison that a National Bank was necessary for the survival of the nation. Although he let the First National Bank expire early on in his presidency, Madison chartered the Second National Bank of the United States believing that the vacancy of the first bank hampered the government's ability to fight the War of 1812 as effectively as it could have.

James Monroe
(1817-1825)

"National honor is the national property of the highest value."

Born April 28, 1758, Monroe was not born into the elite of Virginia like many of his future peers. Tutored by his mother until age eleven and then sent to a preparatory school for college, Monroe was adequately prepared when he attend William and Mary. He enrolled at the College of William and Mary in 1775, but before he attended, his father died and subsequently Monroe inherited his father's land.

Monroe dropped out of school to serve in the Revolution. Taking part in the Battle of Trenton, Monroe was shot and wounded in his left shoulder. After the war was over and after he had recuperated,

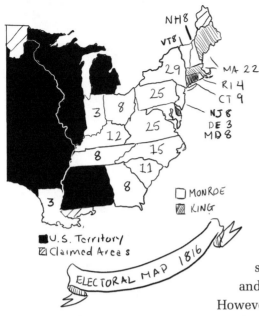

NH 8
VT 8
29
MA 22
RI 4
CT 9
25
3 8
NJ 8
DE 3
12 25 MD 8
15
8
11
8
☐ MONROE
3 ▨ KING
■ U.S. Territory
▨ Claimed Areas

ELECTORAL MAP 1816

Monroe studied law under Thomas Jefferson. While he became proficient in law, Monroe never returned to William and Mary to get his degree.

After studying law, Monroe entered into Virginia politics. He fought successfully for Virginia to ratify the constitution, but did not have the same success in his run for Congress and was beaten by James Madison. However, Monroe recovered from the defeat and won a seat in the Senate.

Rising through the ranks, Monroe became Minister to France in 1794. He successfully freed American prisoners being held there, even saving and bringing home Thomas Paine—the author of *Common Sense*. However, Monroe quickly left his post due to harsh feelings towards Presidents Washington's foreign policy with France.

Home again, Monroe was governor of Virginia for two consecutive terms. When Jefferson became President, Monroe became Minister to Britain. Returning to Virginia once more, he served another term as governor in 1811. When Madison became President, Monroe became Secretary of State once his governorship ended in Virginia, then Secretary of War later on during Madison's tenure. He advised Madison throughout the War of 1812 and eventually was drafted to run for President himself.

Good Feelings:
The limits of early presidential power
and the price of compromise

After the War of 1812 the Federalist Party collapsed and Jefferson's Democratic-Republicans surged in the election of 1816. This set the stage for the "era of good feelings"—the period best known for encompassing James Monroe's tenure in office. It was a time when everyone was a Republican, but not everything was harmonious.

Factions split inside the Republican Party. Such divisions occurred between men like Henry Clay who believed in a more active government and others like John Randolph or John C. Calhoun who were protectors of states' rights and advocates of minimal government. Monroe often sided with the National Republicans such as Henry Clay and advocates of the American System, however, he did veto toll collecting on the Cumberland Road and some internal improvements. Rarely were any issues so hot that fighting broke out between the two factions, for that would come later with the debate over slavery. During this time, the Erie Canal was built, universities were sprouting up around the United States and businesses prospered.

Monroe also embarked on a two year political tour of the nation that was a political success, his visits to Boston and much of the North East swayed unsatisfied Federalist over to the side of the Democratic-Republicans. However harmony was threatened when economic conditions began to worsen in 1819. In 1819 the economy collapsed when the first panic during peace time in American history occurred. The collapsed was caused by a mixture of credit contractions by the National Bank as well as overproduction of agricultural goods by farmers. There were long-lasting effects of the 1819 panic, which sowed the seeds for harsh feelings against the national bank that would become polarizing in later years. However the panic was over by 1821 and an era of economic expansion and growth followed.

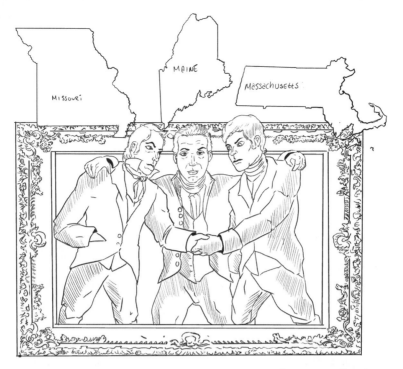

Missouri Compromise and Jackson's Florida Mishap

The only major political battle in Monroe's tenure was over what to do about the entrance of Missouri into the Union. Missouri's entrance into the Union would undo the balance of free states versus slave states, and so a deal was made to physically divide Massachusetts—which originally encompassed all of Maine along with modern day Massachusetts—and allow the entrance of Maine along with Missouri to keep the balance in check. In addition, any state above the 36°30 parallel line that entered into the Union after the compromise would be free, and below it would be a state that allowed slavery.

Monroe also had a battle with his general, General Andrew Jackson, who decided to ride into Florida claiming he had orders to take the land. Moreover, he claimed the orders to have come directly from President Monroe. President Monroe claimed to have never ordered Jackson into Florida and was disturbed by Jackson's lie and actions in the territory. Monroe and his Secretary of State, John Quincy Adams, had been attempting to make a deal with Spain to purchase Florida territory, and so Jackson's interference was unwelcome. Jackson withdrew by 1819, however, Jackson was nearly tried for committing an unlawful invasion. John Quincy Adams defended Jackson and got him off the hook for the attack.

Monroe Doctrine

By the time of Monroe's Presidency, the European presence in South American nations was at its most limited. Many South American nations were in revolt and had begun fighting for their independence, which many Americans supported. Fearing further European meddling in the affairs of South American nations, President Monroe and his Secretary of State John Quincy Adams worked on crafting the Monroe Doctrine. Quincy Adams wrote the Doctrine stating that any European nation's imperialistic presence in the South Americas would be seen as an act of War against the United States. However, this doctrine also applied to nations such as Russia, who were making claims on American territory on the pacific coast. So while keeping European colonial powers out of South America, the Doctrine was additionally able to stop Russia from encroaching on American land.

This was the United States' first experience flexing its relative power, and it was successful. Quincy Adams' proclamation would be used by many Presidents that followed Monroe, including: Abraham Lincoln, Theodore Roosevelt, Woodrow Wilson, and Lyndon Johnson.

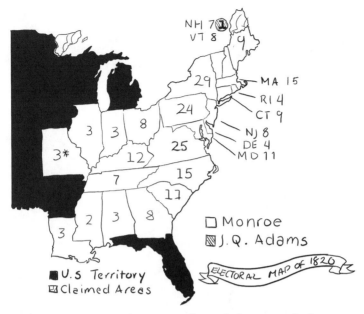

NH 7
VT 8
9
29
MA 15
24
RI 4
CT 9
3 3 8
NJ 8
DE 4
25
MD 11
3*
12
15
7
11
2 3 8
☐ Monroe
3
▨ J.Q. Adams

■ U.S Territory
▨ Claimed Areas

ELECTORAL MAP OF 1820

However Monroe's foreign policy did not end there. American relations with Spain were rocky, especially after Andrew Jackson's questionable advances in the Florida territory. Initially, it didn't seem that the United States could acquire the Florida territory from Spain, but through the work of John Quincy Adams, Monroe was able to conclude the Adams-Onis treaty, which defined the borders of Florida and welcomed Florida into American territory.

John Quincy Adams
(1825-1829)

"Always vote for principle, though you may vote alone, you may cherish the sweetest reflection that your vote is never lost."

Introduction

John Quincy Adams, the son of President John Adams, was brought up by his father to be a great statesman and scholar. Born July 11, 1767 in Braintree, Massachusetts, John Quincy Adams became a diplomat by his eleventh birthday. Accompanying his father to France, the Netherlands and around the United States, Quincy Adams learned the art of diplomacy from a young age. By the age of fourteen, Quincy Adams was a secretary on a diplomatic mission to Russia. In Russia, Adams learned to speak Russian, read Shakespeare and the history of all the nations he could get his hands on. However, out of all the things

Quincy Adams learned about in Russia, nothing was more important in shaping his life than witnessing Russian serfdom with his own eyes. His years spent in Russia lit the flame that led Quincy Adams to fervently oppose slavery and encourage him to run for office later in life.

Returning home to the United States, Quincy Adams enrolled at Harvard. By his twentieth birthday, Quincy Adams had graduated and begun an apprenticeship to become an attorney. Adams despised the two years of apprenticeship and was happy to be done with it in 1789, finally passing the bar in 1791.

Leaving his quiet life in Massachusetts, Quincy Adams accepted President Washington's offer of a role as minister in the Netherlands. Quincy Adams was back into diplomacy, where he would stay for the majority of his adult life. Adams later became minister to Portugal under Washington, and later Minister to Prussia when his father, John Adams, was President.

With his father's loss in his bid for reelection in 1800, Quincy Adams fell out of politics due to his unpopular federalism. Although he was able to become a state senator in Massachusetts, he lost his run for the House of Representatives and became unpopular in his home state for sympathizing with Jeffersonian expansion. Quincy Adams left politics again to pursue teaching at Harvard.

However, his time as a Professor would not last long; he accepted an appointment as the first Minister to Russia when President James Madison gave him the opportunity. Quincy Adams was held with high regard in Russia, even liked by Tsar Alexander Romanov. But when President Madison called Quincy Adams to negotiate the Treaty of Ghent which would formally end the War of 1812, Quincy Adams left Russia to return to work. Alongside Henry Clay, who Quincy Adams bickered and fought with over the terms of Ghent, peace was achieved among the United States, Britain and Canada. Quincy Adams took on another role as minister to Britain before holding his famous tenure as Secretary of State for James Monroe.

From 1817–1825, Quincy Adams became the one of the most successful and revered Secretaries of State in American History. Quincy Adams acquired Florida, wrote the Monroe Doctrine and developed the role of the Secretary of State as chief diplomat of American Foreign Policy; setting a precedent for all Secretaries of State who succeeded him—even to this day. His stellar role as Secretary of State brought him to becoming President of the United States.

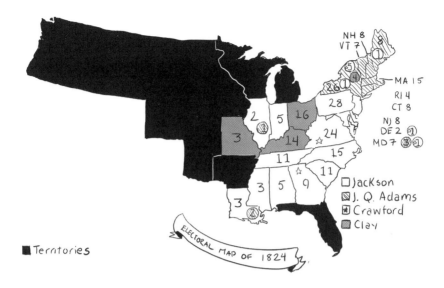

NH 8
VT 7
MA 15
RI 4
CT 8
NJ 8
DE 2
MD 7
28
2 5 16
3 14 24
11 15
3 5 9 11
3

Jackson
J. Q. Adams
Crawford
Clay

Territories

ELECTORAL MAP OF 1824

Election of 1824

In a four way election between John Quincy Adams, Andrew Jackson, William H. Crawford and Henry Clay, John Quincy Adams won the presidency—but not through popular vote nor through electoral vote. Andrew Jackson won a slim majority of both the popular and electoral vote, however, by the rules of the twelfth amendment a candidate must win a clear majority, which for Jackson would have been 131 electoral votes. Unfortunately for Jackson, he only had 99. Thus, the election was thrown into the House of Representatives, where it is alleged that Henry Clay made a "bargain" to make John Quincy Adams President if Clay received the position of Secretary of State. Correspondence between Adams and Clay seem to prove that this accusation is untrue.

Throughout the election, Quincy Adams held the support of James Monroe and much of the Democratic Republican Party, while Crawford was chosen by the Republic caucus to run. However, the elitist and corrupt caucus was not well received by the voters. It didn't help that Crawford also had succumb to a stroke by the election, which rendered him incapacitated. Clay decided to run against the Republican caucus, but was not popular enough with constituents outside his Western states. Jackson was seen as the man of the people, and easily won the popular vote with his fame from the Battle of New Orleans and his charismatic posture.

Old Man Eloquent

Although Quincy Adam's father was often bombastic and terse, Quincy Adams was very different in his approach to politics while in the White House. He was known by his fellow statesmen as "Old Man Eloquent" and led with a calm and cautious character. However Quincy Adams did have a good deal in common his father, he was strong headed and had a specific vision for the United States—one that was close to Whig's hopes for the United States but just different enough to cause complications.

His first move while in office was to promote internal improvements. This took place in form of canals, bridges as well as National Universities and encouragement of the art and sciences. Adams met strong opposition in the House of Representatives and could not get much of his vision for internal improvements passed. A few of Quincy Adams proposals were accepted, such as completing the Cumberland Road in Ohio as well as infrastructure in what would become Michigan, but no passed legislation ever surfaced on the topic of universities and encouragement of the sciences.

Despite the opposition on internal improvements John Quincy Adams did have success in other places. He vigorously sought to decrease the national debt, which he successfully did more so than any other President in United States history, decreasing the debt by over 68%. The debt was $16,000,000 at the beginning of Adams presidency and by the end of his term it fell to $5,000,000.

Finally, one of Adams' most controversial acts at the time was his pursuit of more peaceful relations between the Americans and the Native Americans. Quincy Adams' administration was the most kind towards Native Americans. Modifying the policy of previous Presidents, Quincy Adams often defended Native Americans, such as the Cherokee, when their domains were threatened by settlers of the West or even in the Deep South. In Georgia, as well as in many Western Territories, the federal government supported the Cherokee over Georgians, which practically caused an armed rebellion against the Quincy Adams administration.

Congressional Coup and the Abominable Tariff

In an effort to exploit the political benefits in publically exposing Congressmen who supported John Quincy Adams, the Democrats, who had an allegiance to Jackson, drew up a protective tariff that would disproportionately favor the North over the South. The idea was to use the political issue to bolster support for Jackson in the upcoming election. John C. Calhoun, who was at the time Vice President, as well as many other politicians, assumed that the tariff was strictly political and that it would not pass. They were wrong and Northern and Midwestern representatives passed the Tariff. Quickly it gained the reputation and title of "Tariff of Abominations" because it drove up the prices of goods in the South. The reaction was negative towards Quincy Adams and the Republicans, as many Border States started to lean Democratic in opposition to Quincy Adams' perceived favoring of policy that benefited the North.

The Quincy Conundrum

John Quincy Adams is typically seen as a better statesmen than a president. However, Quincy Adams did have some success in office. Quincy Adams brought the national debt to its lowest level, acknowledged the rights of Native Americans and set forth a vision of the United States which encouraged education and the development of infrastructure. His greatest flaw was that he did not evolve with his times. Quincy Adams acted as the Presidents before him did, when he actually presided over a time of an evolution in politics. The Era of Good Feelings was over and Jackson supporters could often be ruthless and hostile. Where Quincy Adams expected common decency and compromise, he received attacks and vicious ad hominem. The new political climate which revolved around two major parties—the National Republicans and the Democrats—was just something Quincy Adams could not and did not want to adapt to. Quincy Adams was happy to leave the Presidency, but upset that the wild and ruthless Andrew Jackson replaced him.

The rest of Quincy Adams' life was almost like a completion of his unfinished presidency, nipped in the bud by Jackson. Quincy Adams devoted the rest of his life to opposition to Free Masons and slavery by becoming a member of the House of Representatives. He defeated pro-slavery measures, ended the gag-rule that banned talk of slavery in Congress and brought a resolution to the nullification crises when Jackson was in the White House. Quincy Adams, a friend of man, free and slave, inspired people like Abraham Lincoln, whom Quincy Adams met in the 1840s. Quincy Adams passed away on February 28, 1848, after having a stroke in the House of Representatives.

Andrew Jackson
(1829-1837)

"It is to be regretted that the rich and powerful too often bend the acts of government to their own selfish purposes."

Introduction

Born March 15, 1767, Jackson was born on the border between the North and South Carolina territory. At the young age of thirteen he joined the local militia. His role was as a courier, a better fate than his brother, Hugh, who died while fighting at the Battle of Stono Ferry. While on courier duties Jackson was caught by the British, along with his brother Robert, and imprisoned. In prison, the boys were barely fed and treated inhumanely. The brothers contracted smallpox and only Jackson survived. He was eventually released from prison through efforts by his mother, Elizabeth. After saving Jackson from prison she joined a volunteer nursing service where she fell ill and passed away. Andrew Jackson, by the age of fourteen, was an orphan.

Taken under the wing of his uncles, Jackson studied law as he grew older. Without much money or a strong family name, Jackson had to build his credibility on hard work and merit. His career in law eventually paid off, financially and politically, as Jackson was elected as a delegate to the Tennessee constitutional convention in 1796.

After the ratification of the Tennessee constitution, Jackson served as a member of the House of Representatives and then as a Senator. However, Jackson only served a year of his senate term. Thus, after his short political tenure, Jackson worked on building his home and fortune. He became a skilled land speculator and also made much of his money from his plantation and slaves.

Having become commander of the Tennessee militia in 1801, Jackson was first tested as a military leader in the War of 1812. His two most famous battles were the battles of Horseshoe Bend and New Orleans. Horseshoe Bend was a victory and secured Jackson a promotion to major general. The Battle of New Orleans, where Jackson defeated 7,500 English soldiers with only 5,000 Americans, was the crown jewel in his military background and secured him a national reputation among Americans.

In 1817, Jackson invaded Florida and was able to capture a significant amount of Spanish posts. The government protested, as they were trying to conduct diplomacy with Spain. However, John Quincy Adams, the Secretary of State, defended Jackson. The United States was quickly able to obtain Florida and the acquisition was completed in 1821.

Jackson, with all his fame from New Orleans to Florida was told that he should run for president. Initially waving off the idea, Jackson was convinced to jump back into politics and easily won a Senate seat. During the 1820s, Jackson worked with Martin Van Buren, who had established a Democratic Party machine in New York to gain national support for his run for president. In 1824 Jackson ran for president, but lost—despite receiving the majority of popular votes. Determined to eventually win the presidency, Jackson ran again in 1828, that time victoriously.

MA 15
RI 4
CT 8

NJ 8
DE 3
MD 6(5)

☐ Jackson
▨ J.Q. Adams

▪ U.S. Territory
☑

ELECTORAL MAP OF 1828!

Jacksonian Democracy

During the early period of United States history, from the Washington presidency to the Quincy Adams administration, only white males with wealth and land could vote. Although radically democratic for its time, voting rights were limited to a tiny percentage of the population. Around the time Jackson stepped into the White House this started to change. Although Andrew Jackson never pursued any federal legislation to combat the restriction of voting for white males, Jackson was an advocate of liberty and the expansion of democracy to the populist class. During this era of American history, expansion to Western United States allowed a new brand of voters to be born. The traditional voting requirements of property ownership and wealth broke down as middle class farmers were able to meet voting requirements by simply settling new land. Northeasterners quickly demanded a lessening of voter restriction, seeing that the middle class in the West could vote. What resulted was the disintegration of the old oligarchy which ruled politics, introducing a new generation of politicians and voters.

Fumbling the Affair and Spoiling the System

Jackson's presidency had a rocky start. Jackson's Secretary of War was caught in a scandal over an affair which forced Jackson to shake up his cabinet. This happened just in time for the creation of the spoils system. The spoils system meant that political appointments to government offices were to be based on party membership and loyalty instead of merit and experience. Jackson dismissed over 20% of Federal employees and recruited Democrats to take their place. This often led to loyal members of parties—with little to no experience in government—taking jobs they were unfit for and the problem of party patronage would be an issue in politics for over half a century following Jackson's presidency.

Bank Wars and bringing politics straight to the people

The first decisive political battles in Jackson administration were over the banks. The banking issue would soon establish a permanent hatred between Democrats and the Whigs (a new opposition party formed by Henry Clay). Jackson had an almost surreal hatred of banks ever since he was a young man. However, as president Jackson had no intention of destroying the Bank of the United States when he first stepped into office. Moreover, he understood that the population was very content with the Bank, even the conservative James Madison had eventually endorsed it. The panic of 1819 had done some damage to the banks reputation but there would still be an uphill battle to take up the issue of destruction of the Bank if Jackson chose to do it.

Jackson's close friend and advisor, Roger Taney, who would later be Jackson's appointee to the Supreme Court, told Jackson that regardless of public feeling he should speak negatively about the Bank in his state of the union address. And so Jackson began his presidency with quite a stir over banking, denouncing the institution in its entirety.

Henry Clay and Daniel Webster, National Republicans who would soon be leaders of the anti-Jackson Whig party, decided that it was best to run against Jackson on the issue of reauthorizing the Bank of the United States. Believing that the people would rally behind the Whigs and stay loyal to the Bank, which had brought considerable prosperity to the land, Clay fired back. While Clay's perception of the Bank's popularity was correct, he underestimated the fact that Jackson was an able politician. Jackson immediately called on his Senate Democrats to boisterously oppose the Bank. Thomas Hart Benton and James K. Polk (future President) launched investigations into the conduct of the Bank. They faced little opposition to the investigation, believing that anyone who blocked the investigation would look as if they were corrupt. Polk's report was a firebrand of shaky information and red meat that made the Democrats rabid about destroying the Bank.

In 1832, in a masterfully drawn up message to Congress, Jackson vetoed the re-charter of the Bank. And by 1833 Jackson was withdrawing the funds of the Bank and delivering them safely into the coffers of pet banks across the United States—an act that was most likely unconstitutional. In response to the act which the Supreme Court warned Jackson not go through with, Whigs, led by Henry Clay, censured Jackson in the Senate for what they saw as an unconstitutional act. However the censure was not effective in turning popular opinion and by 1836 the National Bank had been defeated and destroyed. Circumventing the Supreme Court and turning public opinion to his side, Jackson defeated Clay and Bank sympathizers. This was truly one of the first times a President used the strategy of bringing an issue directly to the people and using a grass roots effort to get his way.

ELECTORAL MAP OF 1832

NH 7
VT 7
LO
42
MA 14
RI 4
CT 8
30
5 9 21
NJ 8
4 23 DE 3
MD 5 3*
15 15
4 7 11
5

☐ Jackson
▨ Clay
▧ Floyd
▨ Wirt
■ U.S. Territory
▨ Claimed Areas

Henry Clay, unsatisfied with the old fractured Republican party of the Madison-Monroe days, sought to form a new opposition party with other statesmen who were opposed to Jackson. Modeled after the Whigs in England, who sat in opposition of the majority government, the Whigs were the antithesis of Democrats. Henry Clay quickly became one of the more prominent Whigs and de-facto leaders, alongside Daniel Webster, and fought relentlessly against Jacksonian policy.

Nullification Crisis

The tariff of abominations, which was passed during John Quincy Adams presidency and used by Jackson to win the election of 1832, had caused an uproar in much of the United States—this being especially true in South Carolina. The South Carolina legislature believed that

the Tariff of Abominations was unconstitutional which allowed the state to nullify it. In fact, Jackson's Vice President, John C. Calhoun, resigned and ran for the Senate to assist in defending the ability of a state to nullify. Jackson signed into law a new tariff, the Tariff of 1832, which was a compromise between Northerners and Southerners. Although hailed as a great achievement of compromise in many states, South Carolina still believed that the Tariff of 1832 was just as bad the Tariff of Abominations and continued to pursue nullification.

South Carolina mobilized a militia to fight off federal forces from the federal government, fearing war could break out over the issue. Meanwhile, John Quincy Adams—now a congressman—was authoring a compromise tariff to diffuse the situation. Congress passed a force bill while Quincy Adams worked on the compromise, which Jackson could use if all else failed. However, Quincy Adams' compromise passed. With the tariff lowered and the President threatening force, South Carolina backed down.

Indian Removal Act

Jackson pursued a policy of "Indian removal" throughout his Presidency, which is now referred to as the "trail of tears." Jackson forced tribes to move west, into Arkansas and Louisiana. The trips were brutal, entire tribes of Native Americans perished and soldiers killed and beat thousands of their people. Over 45,000 Native Americans were forcibly removed, making it Jackson's most controversial action as President. It is worth noting that there was not much opposition to Jackson's policy. The populace was generally for the removal of Native Americans, believing most of them to be savages who were ready to kill any white man.

Roger Taney

Jackson's Attorney General, close friend and closest advisor, Roger Taney, was appointed to the Supreme Court by Jackson. Taney, a defender of states' rights and Jacksonian democracy was one of the most controversial Chief Justices in American history. His future decisions regarding things such as Dred Scott v. Sanford and rulings on the Missouri Compromise left a lasting impact on the United States leading up to the Civil War.

Martin Van Buren
(1837-1841)

"The government should not be guided by temporary excitement, but by sober second thought."

Introduction

Born in Kinderhook, New York, on December 5, 1782, Martin Van Buren was the first president to be born a citizen and the first president to have English as a second language. Growing up in a Dutch speaking family, Van Buren learned English after already being proficient in Dutch. Having received a basic education at fourteen Van Buren switched his studies to law. He passed the bar in 1803 and began practicing law.

At the age of 29 Van Buren won an election to the New York State senate as a Democratic-Republican. It was there that he joined and eventually led the "Albany Regency," one of the first political machines in politics that held onto power through the spoils system.

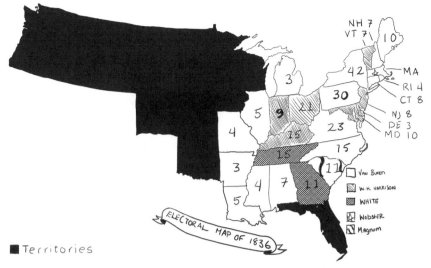

NH 7
VT 7 10
42
MA
RI 4
CT 8
3
30
NJ 8
DE 3
MD 10
5 9 11
4 15
23
3 13
15
4 7 11 15
3 11 Van Buren
W. H. HARRISON
5 WHITE
Webster
Magnum

ELECTORAL MAP OF 1836

■ Territories

Van Buren quickly rose through New York political ranks, becoming state attorney general in 1816 which carried him to the United States Senate in 1820. Eight years later, Van Buren became Governor of New York and began working on the political machinery that would not only get Andrew Jackson elected president, but bring Jacksonian policies to realization through Van Buren's Democratic Party. For his political genius, Van Buren earned his title the "Little Wizard."

Resigning his governorship only two months after winning it, Van Buren joined Andrew Jackson's cabinet as Secretary of State. A divide quickly disrupted Jackson's cabinet over the Eaton Affair. Van Buren secured favor with Jackson by resigning his post and settling the Eaton Affair, which got him a position as Minister to England. However, his ratification for that position was rejected by the Senate, largely due to John C. Calhoun. Jackson, still respecting his good friend, helped him receive the Vice Presidency, launching Van Buren's track to the presidency.

The Crutch of Image

Just as Van Buren entered the White House, the economy collapsed in 1837. With the breakup of the Bank of the United States, the decentralized banking around the country led to large amounts of inflation. This was followed by a great deal of unemployment that lasted for nearly five years. Van Buren had no real options to deal with the economic crisis, as the president had little power at that time to deal with the economy. Still, Van Buren, although innocent of causing any of the economic damage, was blamed for it and received the nickname "Martin Van

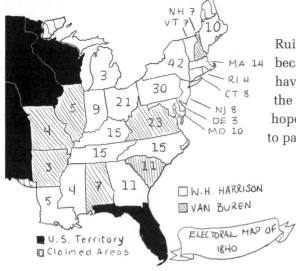

NH 7
VT 7
10
42
MA 14
RI 4
30
CT 8
NJ 8
DE 3
MD 10
3
9 21
5
4
15
23
15 15
3 11
4 7 11
5

☐ W.H. HARRISON
▨ VAN BUREN

■ U.S. Territory
▧ Claimed Areas

ELECTORAL MAP OF 1840

Ruin." Van Buren quickly became the first president to have serious image problem, the people saw him as a hopeless leader due largely due to party politics.

Making the best of a tough situation

Van Buren was determined to accomplish as much as he could while in office despite his image problem. He started his agenda by championing an independent treasury. The independent treasury was to be a system that was separate from that of the private and central banking systems. It allowed the government to have bonds and pay credit in specie. Moreover, the treasury allowed the government to hold tax money in federal treasuries instead of in private banks. The treasury, which was supported by many moderates, was able—when it was finally established in 1840—to heal some of the economic woes. Unfortunately for Van Buren it was too little too late. By election time, the economy was still in a condition where winning re-election would be difficult, if not impossible.

His efforts didn't end with the treasury though. Nearing the end of Van Buren's term, the government had accumulated a staggering $1,500,000 surplus. Van Buren refused to spend any of the money on public works to potentially alleviate the depression, as he, as well as most Democrats, felt that public works projects were not something the federal government should have a role with. Martin Van Buren's final confrontation in office was over slavery. He was personally appalled by slavery, but felt that constitutionally he had no power to solve the problem. As President he attempted to stop the spread of slavery by vetoing Texas' admission into the United States, but allowed slavery to persist in the District of Columbia.

William Henry Harrison
(1841)

"I contend that the strongest of all governments is that which is most free."

Introduction

William Henry Harrison was born on February 9, 1773 in Charles City County, Virginia. His father, Benjamin Harrison, was a successful planter and even a signer of the Declaration of Independence. Harrison went off to attend Hampden-Sydney College. However, he quickly left school to pursue a career in medicine. Unfortunately, when Harrison was only eighteen, his father passed away. After his father's death, Harrison decided to join the army instead of finishing his medicinal studies. His military career began with his service under General Anthony Wayne. During his time serving under Wayne he gained experience fighting in the Midwestern Plains, something which would prepare him for his future career in the military.

When Harrison was 22 he married Anna Symmes and became a Captain. From this point on, Harrison quickly rose through the ranks. By 1800, Adams made him the territorial Governor of Indiana, a position he held for twelve years. However, Harrison was not a popularly recognized figure until 1811 when he won the battle of Tippecanoe —a battle against the Shawnee in Indiana—that would become synonymous with this his name throughout American history. Harrison's victory led to the acquisition of nearly 3,000,000 acres of land. He went on to fight bravely in the war of 1812 and after the war, retired for a short period of time. In 1816 he filled a vacant Congressional seat and by 1825, after serving one term in Congress and multiple terms in the Indiana state senate, he became a United States Senator.

In 1828, before leaving office, John Quincy Adams made him minister to Columbia. However, Harrison's role as minister was short lived, President Jackson recalled him and replaced him. Harrison once again retired until 1836. Receiving the Presidential nomination, Harrison lost in 1836 due to Jackson's popularity which Martin Van Buren used to secure a victory. Four years later he made a political come back and won the Presidency in 1840.

Inaugural and Death

On March 4, 1841, William Henry Harrison gave the longest inaugural address in presidential history. Unfortunately, Harrison gave the address in the rain under frigid temperatures and contracted pneumonia from doing so. Harrison died on April 4, 1841, thirty-two days after taking the oath of office, making his Presidency the shortest in history.

John Tyler
(1841-1845)

"I was called from my farm to undertake the administration of public affairs and I foresaw that I was called to a bed of thorns."

Introduction

John Tyler was born in Charles City County, Virginia, on March 29, 1790. Born in the same county as William Henry Harrison, Tyler had a similar upbringing. Born into a strong political family, Tyler's father, John Tyler Sr., was a wealthy planter and Governor.

When Tyler was seventeen years old, he attended William and Mary. By nineteen, Tyler had studied law and passed the bar. Only two years later his political career began when he was elected to the Virginia legislature. Then, in 1813 Tyler married Letitia Christian. Not too soon after, at twenty-six years old, Tyler won a seat in the United States Congress. He quickly rose through the ranks of politics, becoming a Governor at thirty-five and then winning a Senate seat at thirty-six.

Before becoming President, he was best known for his career in the Senate. Tyler supported Andrew Jackson in the elections of 1828 and 1832, however, he abandoned Jackson after Jackson opposed nullification in South Carolina. In fact, Tyler was the only Senator to not vote for the Force Bill, which allowed Jackson to assume powers that could have suppressed nullification in South Carolina. Furthermore, during Jackson's tenure in the Senate, Tyler was told by Virginia Democrats to expunge Jackson—he resigned in protest.

The Whigs—after seeing Tyler's disdain for his own party—chose Tyler to run as the Vice Presidential candidate in 1836. Although Tyler lost in 1836, he jumped right back into politics by getting elected into the Virginia legislature. Soon after, in 1839, the Whigs re-nominated him as the Vice Presidential candidate when he and Harrison won the 1840 election.

His Accidentency: Problems of legitimacy

John Tyler was the first president to ever assume the office by the death of a former president, which bestowed upon him the title of "His Accidency." Having no historical precedent, Tyler was put into a tough position and was unsure of how to handle his newfound power. There was even some debate over whether Tyler was actually President when he first stepped into the office.

Whig Dissatisfaction and the weakening of presidential power

John Tyler's ascendancy to the presidency had been based on his balancing North vs South; he had been put on the Whig ticket to keep the South happy. But how would he act now that he was President? To the Whigs dismay, Tyler broke ranks with the mainstream Whigs and supported Southern causes. Tyler vetoed Henry Clay's attempt at reestablishing a national bank as well as some of his plans for internal infrastructure improvements. Moreover, Tyler vetoed two Whig protective tariffs. However, facing a depletion of federal funds, Tyler caved in on the third Whig Tariff. The Whigs were still unhappy, as Tyler, after nearly his entire cabinet resigned, appointed conservative Democrats to fill all the positions.

It was to this end that Tyler was thrown out of the Whig party and not nominated to run again in 1844. As political divisions grew, so did

Tyler's attitude toward being President and by 1844 Tyler had become very unhappy with his position.

Tension was so bad that Tyler was almost impeached after vetoing one of Henry Clay's bills. In one of the first attempts at impeachment in U.S. history, John Tyler went through impeachment proceedings after vetoing Henry Clay's tariff. Tyler was accused by the Whigs of abusing his veto power. However, nothing ever surfaced past the first proceedings; Tyler remained in the White House and during his last week in office fought to bring Texas into the union.

James Knox Polk
(1845-1849)

"No President who performs his duties faithfully and conscientiously can have any leisure."

Introduction

James K. Polk was born on the frontier of North Carolina on November 2, 1795. Polk did not stay in North Carolina for long, by the age of ten Polk moved with his family to Tennessee. In Tennessee, Polk's father, Samuel, became a prosperous land owner. Thus, at age nineteen, Polk was able to attend College in the state in which he was born at the University of North Carolina.

After graduating in three years, Polk began studying law with Felix Grundy who was a friend of Andrew Jackson and an eventual Attorney General for President Van Buren. Under Grundy's tutelage, Polk passed the bar exam and also developed an interest in politics.

Polk's first entry into politics occurred in 1823 when he ran and won a seat in the Tennessee state legislature. His ability to give grand speeches and his short stature secured him the nickname of the "Napoleon of the Stump."

By his 30th birthday, Polk won Andrew Jackson's Congressional seat in Tennessee. People began to see Polk as following in Jackson's footsteps and his nickname changed to "Young Hickory." Polk's congressional tenure was impressive, it began on the most powerful congressional committee—the Ways and Means committee—and he eventually became majority leader and then Speaker of the House during the end of Jackson's second term in office.

Leaving Congress in the midst of Van Buren's presidency, Polk won the Tennessee Governorship in 1839. However, Polk met political hardship when he was defeated in his re-election race and in his last attempt to take back the governorship in 1843.

His career seemed to be over, but Polk—with his political prowess and perfect timing—secured the Democratic nomination and became the dark horse candidate in 1844.

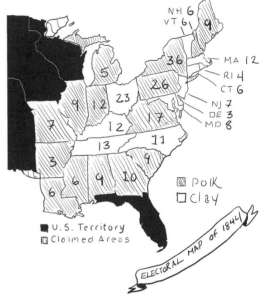

Setting Goals

From the onset Polk stated that he would complete four goals during his Presidency. The first was the reestablishment of an independent treasury. The second was the reduction of the tariff. The third was the acquisition of all or some of the Oregon territory. And finally, the fourth, was the acquisition of land that would eventually become California and New Mexico—all which he promised to complete in one term.

Mexican-American War and 54-40 or fight!

Polk came into office with a big problem—Mexico. His predecessor, John Tyler, had annexed Texas and made it a state. Polk reaffirmed Texas's right to exist in his inaugural address and that of course angered the Mexican government. Polk, interested in further acquisitions from Mexico in the California and New Mexico regions, sent John Slidell

to negotiate the purchase of the territory. The Mexicans refused Slidell after hearing that they would receive no compensation for the loss of the Texas territory. Polk, set on holding Texas and acquiring California—which was partly possessed by Mexico—sent General Zachary Taylor to the land between the Nueces River and Rio Grande territory contested by both the United States and Mexico. Taylor crossed the Rio Grande and occupied a piece of Mexican territory. In response, the Mexicans retaliated and killed eleven American soldiers. Polk, although already prepared to ask Congress for a declaration of war, now had an easier job doing so.

Polk put the blame entirely on Mexico, claiming they had attacked the United States. Freshmen congressmen and Whig, Abraham Lincoln, challenged Polk's version of the story, taking the house floor to voice his opposition to the war. However, Americans were convinced that Polk's side of the story was true and thus the Mexican-American war began. Although a quick war, Polk was often too political during the conflict. He appointed a man with little military experience, Franklin Pierce—a future president—as a colonel for political purposes to a military post which unsurprisingly led Pierce to becoming injured and unable to lead his troops.

However, General Taylor had a series of victories throughout the Mexican-American war and by 1848, Mexico was ready to come to peaceful terms. They signed the Treaty of Guadalupe Hidalgo, increasing United States size by over a third. Polk achieved more than his original goals outlined and acquired territory that would become California, Nevada, Utah, Colorado, New Mexico, Wyoming, and parts of Arizona.

Polk's acquisition of land didn't stop in Mexico. The Oregon territory which Polk had promised to acquire was controlled by Great Britain.

Boundary disputes over the Oregon territory had been plaguing the country for some time and Polk, promising the acquisition of all the Oregon territory below the 54°40 north parallel line, initially would not accept any deal below the full amount of land. However, after negations with Britain, the Americans were able to acquire the Oregon territory at the 49th parallel. Fearing a two front war, one with Mexico and one with Britain, Polk decided that this was an adequate settlement and brought the Oregon Treaty to ratification in the Senate. Although some Democrats were angry over the compromise, many Americans were relieved to finally end the disputes. With peace achieved, Polk brought the independent treasury system back and quietly left office.

Zachary Taylor
(1849-1850)

"I have no private purpose to accomplish, no party objectives to build up, no enemies to punish—nothing to serve but my country."

Introduction

Zachary Taylor was born in Orange County, Virginia on November 24, 1784. Before his second birthday, his family moved further west to Kentucky. They settled near Louisville, where his father, Colonel Richard Taylor, received a great deal of land for his service in the Revolutionary War.

Taylor received his education from private tutoring, as the unsettled Kentucky was barren of schools. At 23, with help from his powerful and respected relative, James Madison, Taylor enlisted and became a Lieutenant. In 1810, Taylor married Margaret Smith and was promoted to Captain.

During the War of 1812, Taylor successfully defended Fort Harrison in Indiana. For his efforts he received a promotion—temporarily—to Major. However, after the war was over, his rank was revoked and

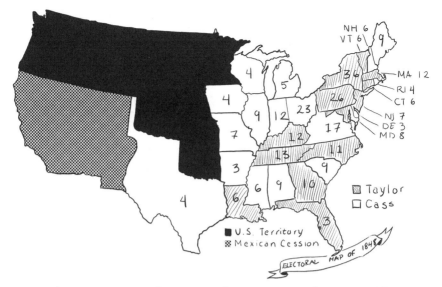

reverted to Captain. Taylor resigned in protest and was quickly given back the rank of Major.

Taylor continued to rise through the ranks and in 1819 received another promotion to Lieutenant Colonel. From 1820 to 1832, Taylor fought the Black Hawk tribe of native Americans in the Black Hawk War. In 1832, the leader of the Black Hawks surrendered to Taylor, earning him the rank of Colonel.

In 1837 Taylor fought the Seminoles in Florida, becoming Brigadier General. Soon after, in 1841, Taylor became Commander of the Southern Division and settled down in Louisiana. He purchased a planation, slaves and started his new southern life.

Taylor was once again called to take charge in 1845 to defend the Rio Grande in the Mexican-American war. He did so successfully and became very popular. President Polk became quite jealous of his new found popularity and began shifting military power to General Winfield Scott. However, when Taylor defended himself and his 5,000 troops against 20,000 Mexican troops, his fame only increased— backfiring Polk's plan. By 1848, Taylor was so popular that the Whigs adopted him to run without even knowing his stance on the political issues of the time.

Much to do about territory

Taylor, initially indifferent towards slavery in the expanded territory of the United States slowly drifted to favoring admittance of the new territories as free states. This change of opinion was thanks to correspondence he had with Whig ally and friend, William Seward, a man who would later be Abraham Lincoln's Secretary of State and closest friend.

Senators Clay and Webster, the main authors of the Compromise of 1850, feared that Taylor may have vetoed their effort to avert war. However, we will never know if he would have or not.

Death

Taylor died in 1850, of what, historians are still not sure. Most likely, Taylor died of cholera, which caused dysentery which was very common in the United States at that time.

Millard Fillmore
(1850-1853)

*"An honorable defeat is better than
a dishonorable victory."*

Introduction

Millard Fillmore was born on January 7, 1800 in Cayuga County, New York. Fillmore, one of nine children, was born to a poor farming family. He worked on the farm for most of his early life until he turned fourteen and became an apprentice cloth maker.

At nineteen years old, Fillmore met Abigail Powers whom he fell in love with. She was a school teacher and inspired him to take up education and to leave cloth making. Fillmore bought a dictionary and his freedom from apprenticeship—which cost him $30—and began to teach in school.

After picking up teaching, Fillmore befriended a local county judge and began learning law and by twenty-three Fillmore was admitted to the bar and opened a law office. Three years later he married Abigail.

Fillmore leaped into politics in 1828, securing a seat in the New York State Legislature. His proud accomplishment in the legislature was passing a bill that eradicated imprisonment for debtors. After his first term in the legislature, Fillmore left Cayuga in 1830 and moved to Buffalo, New York, the ever-expanding political sector of New York State.

In 1832, now in Buffalo, Fillmore won a Congressional seat as a Whig. While losing re-election in 1834, Fillmore fought and retook his seat in 1836 where he stayed until 1842. While in Congress, Fillmore became chair of the Ways and Means Committee where he championed high tariffs—two of which were vetoed by Whig President John Tyler. However, Fillmore did eventually get the tariff raised on his third try.

Fillmore retired from Congressional politics in 1843 and failed to gain the Whig vice presidential nomination in 1844. Worse off, Fillmore lost the election for New York Governor to Democrat Silas Wright. For three years after his political defeats he returned to practicing law. After reconnecting with many of his political ties, Fillmore won the New York State Comptroller election in 1848. And when in 1848 the Whigs needed to secure New York in the Presidential Election, they choose Fillmore as their vice presidential candidate. The rest, as they say, is history— President Taylor died in office and Fillmore rose to be president.

Strong succession and the Compromise of 1850

Millard Fillmore unknowingly made one of the best moves a vice president can ever do when taking office. He cleaned out the Taylor cabinet and appointed his own men. As you will find out with later presidents, the thing that usually destroys the administrations of vice presidents who become presidents by way of death is retaining the old cabinet. Fillmore would benefit greatly from this action as his administration would be tumultuous, starting with the Compromise of 1850.

Newly acquired territories of the United States, claimed during the past administrations, began applying for admittance into the union during the late 1840s and early 1850s. This caused battles in the Senate and the House over whether or not they should be admitted as free or slave states. It's important to note that the time surrounding the Compromise of 1850 highlights a time in American history when the power of government was all but centered in the Senate. Fillmore was largely unable to do anything but sign the Compromise, which was put into place by the Triumvirate of the three most powerful senators:

The Triumvirate

Henry Clay

(Millard Fillmore)

John C. Calhoun

COMPROMISE

Daniel Webster

Clay's initial plan was to pass a gigantic compromise that would settle the balance of free and slave states. It failed to pass, as radicals on both sides of the aisle did not wish to sign their name to such a bill. Clay decided that it would be best to split the bill up into four separate acts, which he could more easily pass. The plan worked with help from Daniel Webster in the north and John C. Calhoun representing the slave holders interests in the south.

Although often seen as simply delaying the inevitable Civil War, the compromise gave the United States extra and vital time to prepare for fighting that would ensue only a decade later. Clay, Webster, Calhoun and by process, Fillmore, all share part of the responsibility of the Compromise, which was invaluable to the survival of the Union. The compromise was not perfect though; the darkest aspect of the bill was the fugitive slave act which allowed federal marshals to find and recapture escaped slaves.

While we should not forget the terror that the Fugitive Slave Act inflicted upon blacks in the nation, the compromise was an absolutely vital piece of compromise legislation that would, in the long term, save the United States. Unfortunately for Fillmore and his fellow compromise-oriented Whig associates—primarily Clay and Webster—their reputations were tarnished by the compromise. Fillmore was not nominated for reelection by the Whigs. Daniel Webster was called a "fallen star" and Henry Clay was disgraced and accused of caving into the South. Despite the commentary of the time, Fillmore, Clay and Webster—as well as John C. Calhoun—actually saved the Union from disintegration.

Franklin Pierce
(1853-1857)

"If your past is limited, your future is boundless."

Introduction

Franklin Pierce was born in Hillsborough, New Hampshire on November 23, 1804. One of nine children, Pierce was the son of a prominent father. Benjamin Pierce was a revolutionary war veteran, a successful farmer, tavern-keeper and the leader of the Democratic-Republicans in New Hampshire.

Pierce attended private school in his youth, preparing him to leave for Bowdoin College by the age of fifteen. After graduating, Pierce studied law and was admitted to the bar in 1827. That same year, his father became Governor of New Hampshire.

Pierce opened a law office in 1827 but quickly decided to jump into politics. In 1829, the same year that his father won another term as governor, Pierce won a seat in the state legislature. Pierce had a successful tenure in the legislature, winning reelection three times and even becoming speaker of the lower house.

In 1833 Pierce joined national politics by securing a seat in Congress as a Democrat. He became a loyal Jacksonian which won him great favor within the Democratic Party. In 1834 he married Jane Appleton and by 1836 he had become a United States Senator. However, Pierce's wife, who had frail health and stayed in New Hampshire instead of Washington, eventually convinced him to resign national politics and to return to New Hampshire. Pierce returned to state politics, becoming the leader of the New Hampshire Democrats.

In 1846 President Polk offered Pierce a seat in his cabinet as Attorney General which Pierce declined. Instead, he accepted Polk's commission in 1847 to appoint Pierce a Colonel in the Mexican War. Pierce became a Brigadier General and fought with General Winfield Scott. However, Peirce was injured early on in the battle from falling off his horse. His health deteriorated to the point where he would faint repeatedly, raising questions over his leadership ability in war. Nevertheless, Pierce returned to New Hampshire and survived the war.

Pierce again kept himself out of gubernatorial politics and only took political action in the revising the New Hampshire State Constitution— biding his time for the election in 1852.

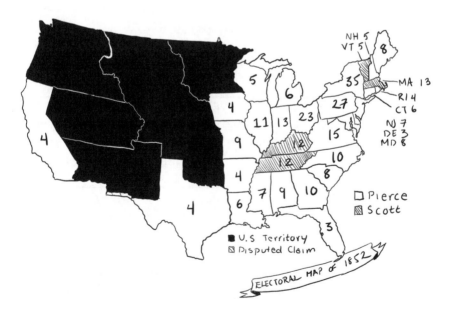

Personal Loss

Pierce's presidency started out with a frightfully sad turn of events. During a train ride after his victory, his car overturned and his wife and a son, the last surviving of three children, were killed. Pierce fell into a state of depression; his mourning lasted throughout his presidency.

Kansas Nebraska Act

The Kansas-Nebraska Act, passed in 1854 with Pierce's signature, brought the territories of Kansas and Nebraska into existence. Alongside the acquisition of territory, it repealed the Missouri Compromise of 1820 and allowed popular sovereignty—the right of the residents of the states to decide whether slavery should exist in the state or not—to become the deciding factor in the question of whether to make states free or slave. Another polarizing part of the Pierce administration was the Ostend Manifesto—a document that contained the reasoning for acquiring the territory as well as what to do if Spain wouldn't sell. The Manifesto revealed that the Pierce administration was ready to have war with Spain if the offer to purchase Cuba was rejected.

Dissolution of Pierce's presidency and the Whigs

Franklin Pierce's presidency was born in chaos—with the death of his family—and went downhill from there. Pierce, unlike the compromisers before him, decided the Northern abolitionists and anti-slavery moderates were not worth worrying about. Through the Kansas-Nebraska Act, Pierce and the Democrats brought slavery to the forefront of politics, igniting the issue like it had never been ignited before. Furthermore, the Ostend Manifesto proved to the North that the issue of slave power was only becoming stronger, not weaker. Threatening war with Spain over the issue of Cuba, a region which would only be exploited by the slave holding class, made northerners were less inclined to compromise.

However, Pierce was an able politician in some respects. He held on to every single cabinet member he appointed throughout his first term. He also had a few achievements in office: he reduced the national debt from $60 million to $11 million and spurred the construction of the transatlantic cable. However, with violence and anarchy breaking out all over Kansas due to the Kansas-Nebraska act, Pierce could not secure re-nomination from the Democrats and was forced into retirement.

The fate of the Whig party was jeopardized as well. It was in shambles by the end of Pierces term. Two of their Presidents had died in office, John Tyler had turned out to be more of a Democrat than a Whig and Fillmore was neither wanted by the Whigs nor did he care for them anymore. Daniel Webster and Henry Clay, the titans of the Whigs, had both died in 1852. The Fugitive Slave Act brought slavery closer to home in the North then it had ever been which made the room for compromise fall apart. Republicans, who were tired of Whig concessions to Democrat slave owners, were beginning to sweep the North. While the north was not completely abolitionist, the fugitive slave act persuaded enough northerners to vote for an antislavery ticket. With all these events occurring, the Whigs base slowly disintegrated and eventually morphed into the Know-Nothing Party and Republican Party.

James Buchanan
(1857-861)

"Whatever the result may be, I shall carry to my grave the consciousness that I at least meant well for my country."

Introduction

James Buchanan was born in a log cabin in Cove County, Pennsylvania on April 23, 1791. Buchanan's father, who moved the family to Mercersburg, Pennsylvania when James was six, was a businessman. James worked in his father's trading post until he went off to school at Dickinson College. However, Buchanan nearly came home from college due to expulsion, but after begging for a second chance and promising to study, he was allowed to stay. He graduated with high marks when he was eighteen.

He studied law after graduating and began practicing law in 1812. But when the War of 1812 broke out, Buchanan decided to volunteer to fight. He helped defend Baltimore from the British which gave him some military glory. His reputation easily secured him a seat in the state legislature as a federalist where he served two terms before taking up law again.

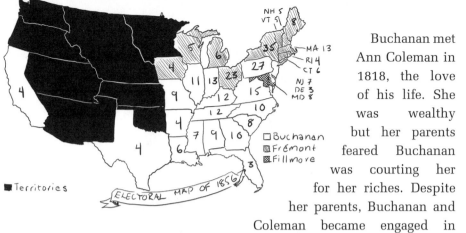

NH 5
VT 5
MA 13
RI 4
CT 6
NJ 7
DE 3
MD 8

☐ Buchanan
▨ Frémont
▧ Fillmore

■ Territories

ELECTORAL MAP OF 1856

Buchanan met Ann Coleman in 1818, the love of his life. She was wealthy but her parents feared Buchanan was courting her for her riches. Despite her parents, Buchanan and Coleman became engaged in 1819. Coleman started to believe rumors that Buchanan only wanted her for her money and broke the engagement with a letter—devastating Buchanan. She died soon after and Buchanan never married and remained melancholy over the relationship for the rest of his life.

He returned to politics after Ann's death, winning a congressional seat in 1820 as a federalist. During his time in Congress he became an ardent Jackson supporter, eventually switching to the Democratic Party. His loyalty to Jackson got him a position as Minister to Russia, a job he handled very well. He negotiated the first trade treaty between the United States and Russia. After that success, he returned home and became a Senator in 1834. He chaired the foreign relations committee and was one of the most prominent conservative Democrats and always supported the southern slave power interests.

In 1844, after campaigning for James K. Polk, Buchanan was given the position of Secretary of State. After serving in Polk's administration, he retired from office and hoped to gain the nomination for president. He lost both nominations in 1848 and 1852. However he eventually received the position of Minister to Britain when President Pierce took office. Buchanan's reputation soared in the South when he helped author the Ostend Manifesto and attempted to expand the slavery even more by purchasing Cuba from Spain. By 1856, amidst bloody violence in Kansas, he was seen as the best choice for the Democratic nomination.

Dred Scott

After a decade of battling in courts, the Dred Scott v. Sanford decision was settled in 1857 by the Taney Court. The Supreme Court ruled that blacks—whether slave or free—could not be United States citizens and therefore could not sue in federal court. However, in an *obiter dictum*, the court also ruled that Congress could not regulate where slavery could and could not exist, effectively nullifying all of the compromise that was achieved in the four decades leading up to the decision.

Buchanan, before and after he was inaugurated President, had improper correspondence with multiple Supreme Court justices including Roger Taney, possibly influencing the decision in Dred Scott. Southern Democrats praised the ruling, Republicans were appalled and Dred Scott only furthered the divisions that the issue of slavery produced in the country. Buchanan dealt with even more controversy a few years down the road when there was also a major division between the federal government and Utah during Buchanan's administration. In 1859, Buchan received reports that Mormons attacked Federal employees. Buchanan reacted by calling them rebels and sent troops into Utah. A peace was brokered with the Mormons and a provisional governor was again appointed the Utah territory.

Kansas

After Dred-Scott, Buchanan attempted to admit Kansas into the Union. His efforts would break apart the Democratic Party. His main opposition came from Senator Stephan A. Douglas who firmly believed that Kansas should be dealt with by popular sovereignty.

Buchanan wasted almost all of his political capitol on weakening Douglas, as Buchanan wanted Kansas to be admitted as slave state and not given popular sovereignty. The political division over how to admit Kansas bolstered the civil unrest and anarchy which had broken out in the Kansas territory under President Peirce. Ultimately the pro-slave forces in Kansas lost and in 1861 Kansas was admitted as a free state.

Fort Sumter, John Brown and the shadow of war

The year 1855 was a turbulent one for the union. John Brown—an evangelist abolitionist—led a raid on Harper's Ferry and slaughtered numerous slave owners. For his crimes, he was hanged. The South became fearful of more violent abolitionist aggression while the North was appalled by his execution.

In 1859 and 1860, Southerners began preparing for Civil War. Many Democrats, including leading Democrats in South Carolina, began building up a military and preparing for secession should a Republican be elected in 1860.

Buchanan largely ignored the Southern secession issue which would explode at Fort Sumter. He believed it to be unconstitutional for a president to simply march troops into South Carolina or any Southern state to keep them from succeeding. Likewise, Congress did almost nothing and so Buchanan merely waited for his Republican successor—Abraham Lincoln—to take office. Many historians have remarked that Buchanan should have used presidential power to keep the union together. Jackson had threatened force and had refused to let South Carolina threaten Civil War in the 1830s, but Buchanan had done nothing. If anything, Buchanan gave the South exactly what they wanted to hear by proclaiming that soon an "open war by the North to abolish slavery in the South" would occur.

At the end of his presidency James Buchanan said at Lincoln's inauguration "If you are as happy in entering the White House as I shall feel on returning to Wheatland, you are a happy man."

Abraham Lincoln
(1861-1865)

"The nation, shall have a new birth of freedom, and that government of the people, by the people, for the people, shall not perish from the earth."

Introduction

Abraham Lincoln was born in Hodgenville, Kentucky on February 12, 1809. He grew up in extreme poverty in a small log cabin. He had two siblings, Sarah, who lived to twenty and Thomas who passed away as a baby.

When Lincoln was eight years old, his father moved to Indiana, taking the family with him. A year after their arrival in Indiana, Lincoln's mother died of an illness she acquired from drinking unpasteurized milk. Lincoln's father mourned, but six months later decided to marry Sarah Johnston.

In his youth Lincoln only attended less than a year of school. He became an autodidact and taught himself by reading anything he could. Poverty made obtaining books difficult, but Lincoln's family owned a bible which he read constantly. He would also travel long and far to borrow books, being most intrigued by texts on the Founding Fathers.

At sixteen Lincoln began to work. He held jobs from farm laborer to ferryboat rower. The job as a rower proved to be his most important work in his youth, as he took trips to New Orleans which exposed him to urban life and slavery. When he took his second trip to New Orleans in the early 1830s, Lincoln realized his hatred of slavery after witnessing the terror of the torture and bondage forced upon blacks.

In 1830 Lincoln's father moved again, this time to Salem, Illinois. Lincoln accompanied the family during the move, but shortly after arriving in Illinois decided to leave home and become independent. Lincoln settled down and volunteered in a local militia formed to serve in the Black Hawk War. Lincoln was elected their Captain and stayed in the militia for three months but saw no combat. After serving in the militia, Lincoln ran for the State Legislature but lost.

He decided to trade politics for business and opened a general store. The store went out of business quickly, leaving Lincoln with debt for nearly two decades. Shortly after the business debacle, Lincoln decided he wanted to learn more about law. He had to walk to Springfield to borrow law books which Salem did not have.

In 1834, Lincoln joined the new Whig party and secured a seat in the state legislature. Lincoln was drawn to the Whigs because of his disdain for slavery, but also because he thought greatly of Henry Clay, even saying of Clay that he "is my idea of a great man." It was in 1834 that Lincoln also met Ann Rutledge, a local girl whom he fell in love with. She died in 1835, leaving Lincoln heartbroken. Lincoln was used to loss throughout his life, but the loss of his mother, siblings and Ann Rutledge solidified a great melancholy that lasted throughout the rest of his life. People who knew Lincoln or met him seemed to comment that he was a sad but great man.

In 1836 Lincoln received his license to practice law and was reelected to the legislature. He voted in favor of moving the state capitol to Springfield, Illinois and decided to move there from Salem. He became law partners with John T. Stuart and became engaged to Mary Todd Lincoln in 1840. However, Lincoln had second thoughts and seemed to be nearing a mental breakdown from 1841-1842. Friends even worried that Lincoln was so depressed that he had become suicidal. Despite the bout of depression Lincoln recovered by 1842.

That year, Mary Todd wrote some political satire about James Shields, a Democrat in Springfield. Shields, believing it was Lincoln who wrote it, challenged him to a duel. Lincoln nervously and reluctantly accepted, but before the duel happened, Shields backed down. At the end of 1842, Lincoln married and purchased his home.

In 1843, Lincoln sought the Whig nomination for Congress but could not get nominated. However, he was able to secure the nomination in 1846 and won a seat in the House. He became a vocal critic of President Polk, denounced the Mexican War and called for the abolition of slavery in Washington D.C. He became unpopular because of this and lost the Whig party support. Lincoln once again drifted back into focusing on his law practice, leaving politics aside.

In 1854, Lincoln was called back to politics by his outrage against the Kansas-Nebraska act, promoted by Stephen A. Douglas. Lincoln believed that the bill, which repealed the Missouri Compromise, essentially allowed slavery back into the Northern states. Lincoln was nominated for the US Senate by the Republican Party and debated Stephen A. Douglas over the issue of slavery. The debates made Lincoln, a man who was unknown outside of Illinois, a national figure. Douglas won the Senate seat, but Lincoln won the Presidency in 1860.

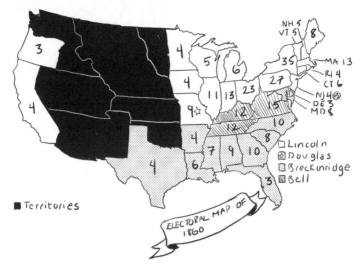

Election of 1860

The election of 1860 was a four way election between Republican Abraham Lincoln, Democrat Stephen A. Douglas, Southern Democrat John C. Breckinridge and Constitutional Party candidate John Bell. Lincoln's fight to the general election was uphill as he was not the frontrunner for the Republican nomination.

William Seward—eventually Lincoln's Secretary of State—was the Republican frontrunner all the way to the convention. In fact, Seward had won the first ballot at the convention. Lincoln's reputation was only notable for his Lincoln-Douglas debates, he had done little as a Congressmen. However, Lincoln's campaign wizards outsmarted Seward's, promising cabinet appointments to any pro-Lincoln delegates—a tactic Lincoln stressed that his managers NOT use—giving Lincoln a victory and the nomination.

Douglas, the popular sovereignty supporting Democrat—and a moderate at that—quarreled bitterly with the conservative Southern Democrats that were pro-slavery. The result was a split in the party; Douglas ran in 1860 on popular sovereignty and Breckinridge ran on supporting slavery. The fourth party which entered into the election, the Constitutional Union Party, led by John Bell, ran on compromise and leaving the Constitution intact. Breckinridge had nearly no support in the North, but carried all the Southern states. Douglas contested Lincoln in the North, but lost in the popular vote. John Bell had the majority of his support from Border States, even carrying Tennessee, Kentucky, and Virginia. However, with a split Democratic Party, Lincoln garnered up a majority popular and electoral votes, making him president.

Abraham Lincoln delivered his first inaugural address on March 4, 1861. He made it as clear as he could to Southerners that his main priority was holding the union together, whether or not this meant the continued existence of slavery or its abolishment, did not matter. Moreover, in the eyes of Lincoln, secession was not legal or constitutional.

Cabinet

Lincoln's cabinet was central to the success of the Civil War. Presidents before him had many successes and failures that revolved around the competency of their cabinet members and Lincoln was set upon choosing a top team of men. Lincoln was careful in his choice of members assembling a group of both Republicans and Democrats, varying from moderate to conservative who used their brain trust to win the war.

Secretary of State, William Seward: Abraham Lincoln's right hand man and best friend, William Seward was the closest advisor to Lincoln. Seward was the constant reminder to Lincoln that the war was over slavery. Moreover, as Lincoln felt weak in the realm of foreign policy, Seward took charge of foreign affairs. No doubt it was wise to allow Seward this control, he kept peace with Great Britain when they wanted to intervene and aid the South, forced the Tsar of Russia to back down in Mexico in 1864 and advised Lincoln on smart foreign appointments, such as Charles Francis Adams as Minister to England. Seward also took up some of the more unpleasant work of the administration, such as dealing with the stripping of Habeas Corpus in some of the Border States, which almost got Seward assassinated.

Secretary of the Treasury, Salmon P. Chase: Salmon Chase was Lincoln's great advisor on the issues of economics and fiscal solvency during the war. It was Chase who would come up with the idea of reinstating a national bank and printing greenbacks to fund the war.

Secretary of War, Edwin M. Stanton: A Democrat who served as Attorney General in the Buchanan administration, Stanton was prone to fighting with Lincoln over policy and was headstrong at the War Department. Despite his occasional stubbornness, Stanton was a capable leader of the War Department and indispensable to Lincoln. He helped hold the Border States for the Union by the implementation of a somewhat radical policy that quieted the secessionist voices. Lincoln said of Stanton, "Without him I should be destroyed."

Secretary of the Navy, Gideon Welles: A former Democrat turned Republican, Welles was brought into the Department of the Navy and cleaned up a house he found to be in "disarray." Welles clashed with other cabinet members, often challenging their policy on the war, especially Seward's.

Start of the War

By the time Lincoln came into office, the civil war had become inevitable. The majority of federal forts in rebel states had been taken by Confederate forces. However, this was not the case for Fort Sumter, located in Charleston, South Carolina. Lincoln, after notifying the South Carolina government of his intentions, supplied the Fort. Confederates fired on Fort Sumter and captured it in two days after the supplies reached there. In response the government marched 75,000 troops to take back the fort.

Thus the war began, a war that many hoped would be quick. Lincoln as well as much of the North had hoped for a fast and painless war and for the South to be overwhelmed in short time. However, that all fell apart at the Battle of Bull Run. The Union forces were beaten in a Confederate victory; the battle proved to Lincoln that the Civil War would be an uphill fight.

After Bull Run, Lincoln and his team of cabinet members and generals had to come up with a sound strategy for victory. Although the North fell short in the early stages of war due to its lack of talented generals, their overall policy was genius. In 1861, General Winfield Scott—old, but still as bright as ever—developed the Anaconda plan. The plan was to crush the South through division and attrition, blockading the South to reduce their supplies and marching troops down the Mississippi to cut the South in two.

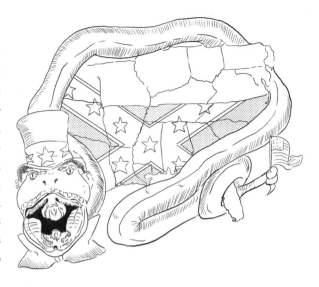

While the plan was eventually successful, in the early war years the plan was carried out poorly. Generals such as George B. McClellan—the man who eventually ran against Lincoln in 1864—were often timid in their battles against Confederates and ignored orders from the White House.

Holding the Border States and Presidential War Powers

One of Lincoln's greatest concerns at the beginning of the war was holding the four Border States of Delaware, Maryland, Kentucky and Missouri. In one of Lincoln's most controversial acts, he stretched constitutional power and suppressed many rebel sympathizers and politicians, in part by suspending habeas corpus. Lincoln, Seward and Stanton imprisoned thousands of people and stripped them of their civil liberties. Lincoln was successful in holding the Border States, however, historians still debate how ethically sound Lincoln's policy was. Lincoln believed that the "Constitution is not a death pact" and felt that his war time powers as president were sufficient for his actions in the Border States.

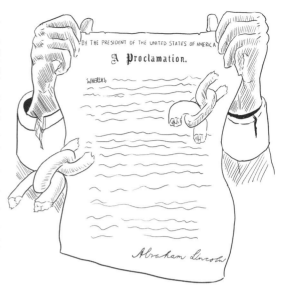

The Middle War and Emancipation

The most volatile years for the North were the middle years of the Civil War, years that marked the height of military defeat for the Union. The Second Battle of Bull Run in 1862 resulted in a Union loss, even though the Union army outnumbered the confederates 75,000 to 55,000. The only general to claim much victory during this time was the rising star Ulysses S. Grant who was still fairly unknown. His victory at the battle of Shiloh began to raise his notoriety.

By 1863, Lincoln's popularity was fading, the war seemed to be favoring the South and Lincoln needed to change something. He had been writing what became the Emancipation Proclamation, what he believed could change the face of the war. However, Lincoln knew that it would be politically impossible to announce the Proclamation without a military victory since public opinion was turning against him due to multiple defeats from the union army. The opportunity came when George B. McClellan won a pyrrhic victory at the Battle of Antietam, where although the Union army "won," the confederates had decimated the Union forces numbers. However, the victory—pyrrhic or not—ignited a new hope in the North and gave Lincoln his opening to announce the Emancipation.

On January 1, 1863, Lincoln announced the Emancipation Proclamation. The presidential proclamation freed the slaves in the states in rebellion, freeing 3,100,000 slaves in the South. As the Union army marched into rebelling states, they freed the slaves under the terms of the Emancipation. However, the Emancipation was a war measure, which meant that the future of those slaves was unsure after the war was over, leading Lincoln to pursue the ratification of the Thirteenth Amendment which abolished all slavery.

One of the major turning points in the war came in July of 1863 when General Meade fought Robert E. Lee in the bloodiest battle of the Civil War at Gettysburg. It was a victory for the North and turned around a series of defeats, it also bolstered Lincoln's standing. A few months later on November 19, 1863, after a two hour speech by Edward Everett in a dedication ceremony for the Soldier's National Cemetery, Abraham Lincoln delivered a very different kind of speech. Short but immensely powerful, Lincoln's Gettysburg address became one of the most famous in history.

Politics during the War

While the Southern states had left the Union, the House of Representatives and the Senate did not stop meeting. With Southern Democrats gone, the House and Senate became divided among three groups, radical Republicans—represented by House "dictator" Thaddeus Stevens and Senate Majority leader Charles Sumner—moderate Republicans and Northern Democrats.

Lincoln had a domestic agenda and worked closely with all three factions to get his policies passed. Lincoln signed railroad acts in 1862 which brought about the creation of the transcontinental railroad. In that same year, Lincoln signed the Morrill Land-Grant Act which established land grant colleges throughout the nation. Moreover, Lincoln signed one of the important bills ever passed, the Homestead Act, which allowed any non-rebel to settle a homestead in Western territory.

Lincoln, with his Treasurer, Salmon Chase, began reestablishing a National Bank and printing Greenbacks in 1861 and 1862. Greenbacks became the inspiration for the currency we have today and Chase's plan saved the Union from bankruptcy.

A common misconception about the domestic politics of the Civil War was that the House and Senate were overwhelmingly in favor of Lincoln and his proposals. This is largely untrue, Lincoln a difficult political climate and had to constantly face battles in the House and Senate where he cautiously dealt with radicals and conservatives. During 1862 and 1863 Lincoln became very unpopular throughout the North, being perceived as a failure and many believed he was guaranteed to lose in 1864. Without the turn around that occurred after the Emancipation, the victory in Gettysburg and the appointment of General Grant to leading the union army, Lincoln's chances were slim for reelection.

Diplomacy during the War

While the Civil War is known more for its battles, the conflicts in diplomacy were just as significant. Throughout the early and middle years of the Civil War, Lincoln feared intervention by Great Britain. Bogged down by war on the home front—which was taking place less than a state away from the White House—Lincoln turned the power of foreign policy over to two men. The first was William Seward and the second was Charles Francis Adams, son of John Quincy Adams. Adams was Lincoln's minister to England, an important position, as the transatlantic cable—which was the primary means of communication between the White House and Parliament—had broken in 1859. It was up to Adams to keep the English neutral, which was difficult since the English wanted Southern cotton, which the North blockaded and would not let them export. Adams and Seward succeeded in their quest for neutrality and without this success in diplomacy, the English could

have acted as the French did during the Revolution, giving crucial support to the South and winning the war for the confederacy.

The Final Years, March to the Sea and the Triumph of the North

Lincoln's discharge of failed generals, coupled with the Emancipation brought a new face to the Northern armies. Lincoln appointed the proven and competent generals Ulysses S. Grant and William T. Sherman to the highest positions available. Grant had not been the top of his class at West Point, but he had proven himself to be a man who could win the war—something which Lincoln recognized and caused him to make Grant General of all the Union forces. Sherman struck the heart of the South by marching into Atlanta—known as "Sherman's March to the Sea"—which broke the morale of the Confederacy but with harsh tactics, by burning down a significant portion of Georgia.

Election of 1864

With some victories behind him and confidence renewed, Lincoln ran again in 1864, this time under the National Union party. Democrats chose the former general—dismissed by Lincoln—George B. McClellan as their candidate. Lincoln's Vice President, Hannibal Hamlin, was replaced by Democrat Andrew Johnson who was a man from the South who refused to leave the Union.

The Democrats ran a less than satisfactory campaign. The Democratic platform called for an end to the war and for peace with the confederacy, yet their candidate, McClellan, was openly against that platform and wanted to continue the war. However, the Democrats ignored their

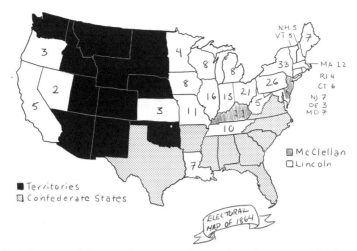

NH 5
VT 5
7
33
MA 12
RI 4
CT 6
NJ 7
DE 3
MD 7

3

4

8

8

8

26

2

16

13

21

5

5

3

11

10

7

■ McClellan
□ Lincoln

■ Territories
☒ Confederate States

ELECTORAL MAP OF 1864

own divisions and focused on attacking Lincoln, even labeling him "Abraham Africanus the 1st." New York was an especially hard fought state, as New York City had rioted for a week over the draft and was still bitter toward Lincoln.

Lincoln beat McClellan with a comfortable margin of popular and electoral votes. However, many historians have commented that had General Sherman not taken Atlanta, Lincoln's chances may have been hurt, despite the fractured Democrats.

Lincoln was inaugurated for his second term and made his famous remarks at the end of his speech:

> With malice toward none, with charity for all, with firmness in the right as God gives us to see the right, let us strive on to finish the work we are in, to bind up the nation's wounds, to care for him who shall have borne the battle and for his widow and his orphan, to do all which may achieve and cherish a just and lasting peace among ourselves and with all nations.

10% Plan, the Thirteenth Amendment and Wade-Davis

In 1863 Lincoln had outlined a plan for reinstating the states in rebellion. The plan called for 10% of the population in each rebelling state to pledge their allegiance to the union and to emancipation before reentry into the union. Radical Republicans decided this was too lenient towards the South and introduced the Wade-Davis bill, proposing much harsher rules for reentry for rebelling states. Passed by both Houses, Lincoln pocket vetoed the bill.

Finally closing the issue of slavery once and for all, Lincoln put immense pressure on Congress and oversaw passage of the Thirteenth Amendment—aided in its passage by the all-powerful Congressmen Thaddeus Stevens. The Amendment abolished slavery and solved the question of emancipation forever.

Grant and Appomattox

In early 1865, Grant launched his final offensive against Richmond, Virginia, the political capital of the confederacy. The President of the Confederacy, Jefferson Davis, fled Richmond and on April 9, 1865. After a successful push by Grant, Robert E. Lee surrendered unconditionally to Grant at the Appomattox Court House, ending the war.

Death

In Lincoln's final address to the public, he spoke in favor of voting rights for blacks. John Wilkes Booth, after hearing Lincoln's views on black voting rights, became convinced that the only way to stop President Lincoln was to kill him. Originally, Booth had planned a kidnapping, but the speech changed that. Moreover, Booth and his associates had planned to assassinate Lincoln, William Seward, Grant and Vice President Johnson.

On April 14, 1865, Lincoln attended Ford Theatre to see *Our American Cousin*—his bodyguard was not with him. John Wilkes Booth fatally shot the President and escaped from the theatre. That same night, another assassin went to William Seward's house, made his way to Seward's room where he lay sick—he had fallen off his horse and injured himself less than a month before—and attempted to kill Seward with a knife. Seward's family fought off the assassin, but not before several cuts were inflicted upon Seward's face—he lived, but with massive scars. Andrew Johnson's assassin did not go through with his plan and Ulysses S. Grant had decided not to attend the theatre, thus missing his assassin.

Lincoln was brought to a bedroom across the street from the theatre where he lay in a coma for nine hours. Surrounded by a minister and Secretary of War Edwin Stanton, Lincoln died at 7:22pm April 15. Stanton said when Lincoln passed away, "Now he belongs to the ages."

Few Presidents can match the legacy of Lincoln. He is the President who held the Union together when it seemed that war would completely disintegrate and divide the nation. Leading the Union through civil war, diplomatic turmoil with Europe and through the final resolution to the moral dilemma of slavery, Lincoln's resilience was essential during every step of the Civil War. And although Lincoln's main goal was to save the Union, he abolished slavery in the process, a system that crippled the United States in every way and degraded the image of a free nation. Lincoln freed not only slaves from bondage, but also the United States from the peril of the slavery question and allowed it become more democratic, inclusive, industrious and civil.

Andrew Johnson
(1865-1869)

"Honest conviction is my courage; the Constitution is my guide."

Introduction

Andrew Johnson—a Democrat who supported Jackson and opposed the slave power, a Southerner who stood against secession and a Governor who tailored his own suits—was born into poverty in Raleigh, North Carolina on December 29,1808. His Father, Jacob, died when Andrew was only three. Johnson's mother, Mary, took up two jobs as a laundress and seamstress to support Andrew and his brothers. There was no money for school.

At fourteen Johnson became a tailor's indentured apprentice. During his short time apprenticing he learned to read, but not how to write. He ran away to South Carolina to escape his master, only returning at seventeen to convince his mother to move West with him. Johnson settled in Greeneville, Tennessee and built a tailoring shop and married Eliza McCardle who taught Johnson how to write as well as how to improve his reading.

Johnson moved into politics by winning a seat in the village council which brought him to become mayor of Greeneville at only 21. With his new found popularity, Johnson won a seat in the state legislature in 1835. He lost re-election in 1837 but took his seat back in 1839. In 1843 he began a career in Congress where he would serve 5 terms, supporting the Compromise of 1850 and where he attempted to get a homestead act passed.

Johnson was forced out of his district by Whig redistricting, but after returning to Tennessee, he won the gubernatorial race and became a popular Governor. Johnson was a Democrat, but he had a great personal hatred for the slave power of the south. He saw himself as a man of the people and slave holders as the champions of aristocracy and privileged. Even though he supported Breckinridge in 1860, Johnson refused to secede and stayed with the North where he was regarded as a patriot for his actions. In 1864 he joined the National Union ticket with Abraham Lincoln, and in 1865, after Lincoln's tragic death, Johnson became President.

Yelling Down the House

Johnson was always a loyal Democrat, especially as president. He believed the states should hold more power than the federal government and this theme would put him at odds with Republicans and even some fellow Democrats throughout his administration. However, his deep respect for

Lincoln allowed him to embrace Lincoln's 10% plan and attempted to bring the South back into the Union by following it. However the Congress would soon learn that Johnson was not as agreeable as his predecessor.

Johnson exercised his veto power constantly. The first major veto was of a bill extending the life of the /*Freedmen's Bureau—a program setup by Lincoln to aid newly freed slaves—beyond 1867. The second bill was a civil rights act that would extend more freedoms to African Americans. Johnson vetoed them on the ground that they violated state's rights. The civil rights act and the extension of the freedman's bureau would be the first bills in history to be passed over a presidential veto, greatly embarrassing Johnson and proving the congress and senate to be the powerful agents in this era of American history. It also began the first of a series of battles with his three adversaries, radical Republicans Thaddeus Stevens, Charles Sumner and Wendell Phillips. Johnson also railed against the Fourteenth Amendment and the Reconstruction Acts which brought the equal protection clause within the Constitution on grounds that it violated states' rights.

But Johnson's political skills were not apt. When Thaddeus Stevens proposed a bill in the House of Representatives that would separate the South into five different military districts ruled by martial law and give African Americans suffrage, Johnson immediately vetoed the bill instead of waiting to pocket veto it strategically. It was no surprise when his veto was overridden by the house the next day.

Impeachment

All of this fighting led to Johnson's impeachment. The House passed a bill called Tenure of Office Act over Johnson's veto. Johnson had riled Republicans when he went on a tour of the United States giving speeches in which he threatened to fire any cabinet members that were at odds with him. The Tenure of Office Act forced the President to get approval from the Senate before firing any staff.

Johnson later attempted to fire his Secretary of War, Edwin Stanton, who he had bickered with for nearly two years. Stanton barricaded himself in his office and claimed that the Tenure of Office Act kept him immune to dismissal from office. Johnson was impeached for his actions, but the vote of conviction failed by a single vote.

Johnson's presidency was not a complete failure though. Johnson's Secretary of State, William H. Seward worked hard. While Johnson was bogged down with battles in the House and Senate, Seward attempted to take advantage of an opportunity to purchase Alaska from the Russians.

It was expensive; nearly seven million dollars in gold, and Seward had a hard sell in the Senate. Little did he or anyone know the value of its resources, but Seward was able to get Charles Sumner on his side and pass the negotiations to acquire Alaska.

Johnson also deserves a little bit of a break. Of all the vice presidents who had to succeed a President who died in office, it is fair to say that Johnson was put into the most grueling of situations. It was impossible to replace Abraham Lincoln, but Johnson was determined to see through a moderate plan of reconstruction that he believed Lincoln would have approved of. He was too headstrong, the political prowess and ability to compromise that Lincoln had did not resonate in Johnson whatsoever. Johnson was even known to give campaign speeches where if heckled by the crowd, he would simply begin screaming back at them. He made few relationships in Washington—his closest ally was Seward who had little sway in the House or Senate—and although more moderate than the radicals on Reconstruction, Johnson's Southern beliefs were apparent. He vetoed bills that Lincoln had spoken highly of before his death, causing him to stray from the path laid out by his predecessor and to go on his own path of vetoing and dismantling. However, Johnson did try and keep radicals from going too far and had some success.

Ulysses S. Grant
(1869-1877)

"It was my fortune, or misfortune, to be called to the office of Chief Executive without any previous political training."

Introduction

Ulysses S. Grant was born on the 27th of April, 1822 at Point Pleasant, Clermont County, Ohio. His family moved to Georgetown, Ohio where his father purchased a farm and became a tanner. Grant worked the farm until he was seventeen, when he went off to attend West Point.

When Grant went to West Point he received the "S" in Ulysses Grant. The school had accidentally marked him down as Ulysses Simpson Grant and he decided to keep the new name. At West Point Grant was an average to below average student graduating 21st out of 39 in his class. However, the greatest benefit Grant received from West Point was the fact that he was schooled alongside students who would become Civil War generals, giving Grant personal knowledge about men who would one day be his opponents.

After graduating from West Point, Grant joined the infantry in St.

Louis. When the Mexican War broke out, he served under Zachary Taylor and Winfield Scott and earned himself the rank of First Lieutenant. After the war, Grant took a leave of absence and married Julia Dent in 1848.

In the 1850s Grant took up an assignment in the West, leaving his family as he did not have sufficient money to support them. He began drinking heavily during his new assignment, and was forced to resign in 1854 because of it. He returned to St. Louis, moving his family to a tiny piece of land his wife had received as a gift. There he built his new home, "Hard Scrabble," a log cabin with a small amount of land to farm. Unfortunately, Grant was not a skilled farmer and his crops failed. He sold his land and attempted work as a real estate salesman—that too, failed. Desperate, he took a job with his younger siblings in Illinois.

In 1861, as the Civil War broke out, Grant quit his job and joined the Union army. He gathered up other volunteers and wrote to the governor who gave him a job organizing regiments. Grant was tested in combat soon after and had a success in battle which got him a promotion to Brigadier General. He captured Fort Henry and Fort Donaldson, both of which were in Tennessee, and captured 20,000 confederates. Later, at the battle of Shiloh, Grant repelled a surprise attack by the confederates—his reputation continued to soar.

Grant then launched a gutsy campaign to capture Vicksburg, a confederate stronghold that was geographically tough to reach. He did it, and as result he was given command of all the Western armies. He then had another impressive victory at Chattanooga which brought him to the White House where Abraham Lincoln made him a Lieutenant General—the highest rank in the army. Grant made a final push on Richmond while General Sherman focused on Atlanta. Grant drove Robert E. Lee out of Richmond successfully and Lee surrendered at the Appomattox Court House which marked the end of the war. At the court house, Grant accepted

Lee's unconditional surrender. Heroic, popular and Republican, Grant was the frontrunner in 1868 for the Presidency.

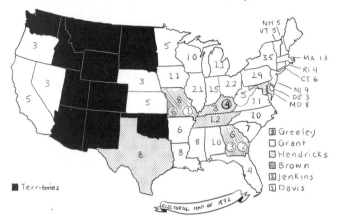

Reconstruction

When Grant became president it was no secret that he wanted to see Reconstruction through. Grant sided with radicals that the rights of African Americans was non-negotiable, and often used force to prove it. In the South, when African American legislators were run out of the halls of government, Grant used the military to bring them back into the State Legislatures, such was the case in Georgia. Grant stationed troops in Southern states at polling places to guarantee that African Americans were not intimidated when they voted. Every inch of Grant wanted protection for African Americans, but his policies were not exactly practical in the long run, troops could not always occupy the South, and eventually Jim Crowe laws would overpower what little force the North had left over from the Civil War. Grant eventually became the poster child for the argument against presidential force—a temporary solution, never solving long term affairs. Grant even passed what's called the "Force Act of 1870" for the purposes of lessening the power of the KKK in blocking African Americans from expressing their new constitutional rights.

His use of force even went so far as to Arizona and Colorado where Liberal Republicans and Republicans had such a close races for Governor that each of the parties claimed victory. Both parties' candidates swore in as governor and violence was threatened against one and the other. Grant used the army to settle the disputes, more often than not putting the Republicans into power instead of the Liberal Republicans, which led to accusations of nepotism.

Grantism and Nepotism

Senator Charles Sumner, the leader of the radicals in the Senate, coined the term "Grantism" in reference to President Grant's leadership style. Grant often used nepotism and appointed close friends and allies who were not adequately prepared for their positions to high seats of power. It also did not help that his administration was heavily corrupt and many of his cabinet members were incredibly inept. His appointment to the position of Secretary of War, John Aaron Rawlins—a millionaire businessman—who was forced out of office within a few months of taking his post was a prime example of the weakness in Grant's choices for cabinet members. His Secretary of the Navy, Adolph Edward Borie lasted just as long, not even serving a full year.

Light near the end of the Tunnel

Grant did have a few successful ventures while president. He preached that "Wars of extermination ... are demoralizing and wicked." Grant attempted to carry out this peace process by appointing Quakers in positions that dealt with Native American affairs. Moreover he signed the Treaty of Washington to finish what William Seward had begun in the Andrew Johnson administration, which was to arbitrate a fair payment for damages done by Britain to the United States during the Civil War. His representative in Britain, Charles Francis Adams, went so far as to travel to Geneva to negotiate. Adams was able to secure a Treaty that included an admission of British guilt for perpetrating damages against the United States, as well as $15,000,000 in payment for the damages. And Grant accomplished passing a civil rights act and a bill establishing Yellowstone National Park.

Grant led his administration as he did his army, by force and trust. He used force to guarantee African American's rights in the South and while this had great dividends for African Americans during his presidency, it would collapse in 1877 when southern democrats instated Jim Crowe laws. Moreover, force caused the South to feel threatened and beaten while they were down, much of the aggressive backlash that formed after Reconstruction was because of that force exerted by Grant.

Trust was equally harmful for Grant. As a military leader, Grant would delegate command and his troops would follow them—he could trust his men. Politicians on the other hand needed oversight. Grant had a hard time believing that his appointments and political allies would betray him, but they did. His military skills did not transfer over well to presidential leadership.

Rutherford B. Hayes
(1877-1881)

"He serves his party best who serves his country best."

Introduction

Rutherford Birchard Hayes was born in Delaware, Ohio, on October 4, 1822. His father—Rutherford, Jr.—passed away before he was born, but his success as a storekeeper allowed for money and land to be left for his son's education. When Hayes grew older, he attended Kenyon College and graduated at the age of twenty. He returned home after graduating to study law. After becoming proficient in it, he studied at Harvard Law School for three years.

He once again returned home and moved to Cincinnati. Hayes gained a reputation as a defender of fugitive slaves and as a man of great intelligence. He eventually became an abolitionist and helped found the Ohio Republican party. Shortly after assisting in the creation of the party, Hayes, at the age of thirty, married Lucy Ware Webb; they had three sons. A few years later, in 1858, Hayes was elected to a seat in local politics. However, his time in politics was cut short by the outbreak of the Civil War in 1861. He dropped everything and volunteered for the Union army. He was commissioned as a major and led an Ohio regiment through many battles. He experienced everything from mounted combat to hand-to-hand encounters, and his bravery earned him the rank of brevet major general in 1865. He was seriously wounded four times in the war and became popular for his strength and resilience. During the war he was even drafted and elected to Congress, however, he refused to take his seat until the war was over, and so he continued fighting. He eventually was sworn in 1866 and joined forces with the Radical Republicans.

He left Congress to run for governor of Ohio in 1868 and won the election very narrowly. He was an efficient and popular governor once in office and secured two more terms. Hayes's popularity as a brave Civil War veteran, successful governor, and loyal Republican made him the safe choice for the Republican nomination in 1876.

What you leave behind

Hayes was a President hamstrung before even entering office. The close election in 1876 between Hayes and Democrat Samuel Tilden had almost resulted in an armed rebellion due to the election results. Tilden had won the popular vote but Hayes won the Electoral College. The Compromise of 1877 settled the election and made Hayes president, but he was forced to end Reconstruction in the south. The director of the Rutherford B. Hayes Presidential Center, Thomas J. Culbertson, suggests that Hayes came into office when Reconstruction was already falling apart, and that the compromise had simply struck the final blow. "By the time that Rutherford B. Hayes assumed the presidency, the South was back in the hands of the former Confederates except for two Republican governors who were holding out in Louisiana and South Carolina…. He wrongly expected the 'good element' of southern society to protect Blacks as promised by the incoming Democratic governors of South Carolina and Louisiana."

Hayes' only real chance to display presidential power was during the rail strikes during his administration which paralyzed trade across the country. Hayes used General Winfield S. Hancock to break the workers strike and get the economy going again in one of the first federal strike breaks in American history. He was also an advocate of prison reform and issued many pardons during his time in office. Realizing that the political climate was not in his favor, Hayes did not run for reelection.

James A. Garfield
(1881)

*"A brave man is a man who dares to look the
Devil in the face and tell him he is a Devil."*

Introduction

James Garfield was one of seven presidents to be born in a log cabin.
He was born on November 19, 1831, in Orange Township, Ohio and
only a year later—in 1832—his father died from a throat infection.
Garfield's mother, Eliza Ballou Garfield, was resilient and took care of
Garfield and settled her husband's debts by selling a portion of their
farm. Garfield and his mother had very little, but they managed to eat
and to hold onto their land.

Garfield wanted to attend college for he had become a voracious
reader in school; however he first became a sailor—a job that did not
last. He then drove horses and mules on boats in the Ohio Canal, but
after numerous close encounters with death he accepted the hard-earned
$17.00 his mother offered him and attended the Geauga Seminary. The

seminary allowed him to teach and make some money and in 1851 he entered Western Reserve Eclectic Institute—now known as Hiram College—where he excelled in learning languages. He once again used his talents as a teacher and tutor to pay his way through school and more importantly met his future wife while tutoring. In 1854 he attended Williams College in Williamstown, Massachusetts, with the help of a benefactor and graduated with honors in 1856. Returning home from college with his new diploma, Garfield became a professor of Latin and Greek act Hiram. Two years later he was made the school president and married his wife—Lucretia Rudolph. They had seven children together.

Garfield decided to expand his horizons in the late 1850s and became a preacher as well as a politician. He was elected to an Ohio state senate seat as a Republican in 1859. However the Civil War brought an end to his tenure in1861, when he joined a volunteer regiment of former Hiram College students and became its leader. He became a brigadier general in 1862, when he and his regiment expelled Confederate forces out of eastern Kentucky and fought in the Battles of Shiloh and Corinth. Garfield continued to fight and received promotions for his bravery and was elected—while still fighting—to the House of Representatives. He did not go to Congress until asked to by President Lincoln, but when he finally arrived at the House he began serving the first of his many terms.

Garfield became a Radical Republican who voted for the Reconstruction Acts and President Andrew Johnson's impeachment. He continued to rise through the ranks during the years that followed. He earned important House seats during Grant's administration and was a member of the Electoral Commission during the disputed election between Rutherford B. Hayes and Samuel J. Tilden. When Hayes won, Garfield became the minority leader in the House and was soon after elected to the Senate.

Amidst a fractured Republican Party split between "Stalwarts" and "Half-Breeds," Garfield took neither side at the Republican convention in 1880. After the balloting continued to split between Stalwarts and Half-Breeds—reaching no majority after more than thirty-five ballots—Wisconsin threw their votes to Garfield and others followed leading to his victory.

Death

The problem of civil service corruption and nepotism in party patronage reached its height during Garfield's tenure. And ultimately, Garfield was shot because of it. His assassin, Charles J. Guiteau screamed out after shooting Garfield, "I am a Stalwart, and I want Arthur for President."

Garfield died on September 19, 1881, after doctors were unable to find the bullet that was lodged in his body. Many physicians say that had the doctors let him heal and not continued to search for the bullet—which infected his wounds—Garfield may have lived. He was president for only 200 days.

Chester A. Arthur
(1881-1885)

"The extravagant expenditure of public money is an evil not to be measured by the value of that money to the people who are taxed for it."

Introduction

Chester A. Arthur was born on October 5, 1829, in Fairfield, Vermont. Son of a Baptist clergyman, he lived a modest life and attended local schools. He was admitted to Union College and upon graduation decided to practice law. As his father had been an ardent abolitionist, Arthur received a reputation for defending fugitive slaves and any persecuted blacks. In 1856 Garfield attended the first Republican state convention in New York to support John C. Freemont—the first presidential antislavery Republican candidate—and devoted the rest of his life to politics.

A lifelong Republican who never won an election to public office aside from the vice presidency, Arthur's political career was one that relied on appointments in the party machinery. He married Ellen Lewis Herndon in 1859—with whom Arthur had three children—and received his first appointment as state engineer-in-chief in 1860. From then on Arthur was appointed to numerous political positions and orchestrated political campaigns that helped Republicans remain formidable in New York. He was known as a "gentleman boss," and despite his presidency—a quite honest one—he had a somewhat controversial reputation. He was fired from his important post of Collector of the Port of New York by President Hayes and became an ardent Stalwart. In 1880, with Garfield—an independent but seemingly more sympathetic to the Half-Breeds—chosen as the presidential nominee, Arthur balanced the ticket as a Stalwart.

Although the vice presidency was typically one of the least powerful positions in Washington, Arthur was vice president with a split Senate, meaning he could break tied votes—which he often did against President Garfield's wishes. After Garfield's death, Arthur became the twenty-first president.

Initiatives

Chester A. Arthur came into office because of the death of James Garfield, making him an accidental president from whom people expected very little. However, by the end of his term in office, he had proved to be an impressive president for his time. He reformed what seemed an eternally corrupt civil service by passing the Pendleton Act of 1883 (which declared merit as the basis for government jobs) and remained active in foreign affairs. Less important than civil service reform, but still relevant, Arthur also repaired and renovated the White House and dedicated the Washington monument before leaving office. Mark Twain said of Arthur, "I am but one in fifty-five million, still in the opinion of this one-fifty-five-millionth of the country's population, it would be hard to better President Arthur's administration."

Grover Cleveland
(1ˢᵗ Administration: 1885-1889)

"Officeholders are the agents of the people, not their masters."

Introduction

Grover Cleveland was the son of a Presbyterian minister and one of nine children. He was born on March 18, 1837, in Caldwell, New Jersey, and moved throughout his early life due to his father's work. He attended schools until he was fourteen, when he started to work to support the family. Two years later, his father died, and young Cleveland had to find work. He became a teacher at the New York Institution for the blind and also took on other odd jobs to support his mother and other family members.

A few years later he headed west to make some money but eventually landed in Buffalo, where a relative gave him a job. He soon started working a clerkship and was admitted to the bar in 1859. Cleveland became a supporter of the Democratic Party during the 1860s—in part because of his antiwar stance during the Civil War—and tried his hand at politics, unsuccessfully. In 1870, however, he won an election as sheriff, where his reputation as an honest and credible man began. In 1873 his role as sheriff ended, and he returned to law, making a good amount of money. In 1881 his life changed when he became the mayoral candidate for reform in Buffalo, New York. He won a narrow victory but proved his reforming capability by vetoing countless corrupt bills passed by the council. Cleveland earned himself quite the reputation, which led him to become the Democrats' nominee for New York governor in 1882. Although Cleveland had to rely on some support from the corrupt Tammany Hall Democrats, he made very few promises to the dishonest politicians of Tammany. He beat his opponent, Charles J. Folger—who was in the pocket of Jay Gould, a very corrupt millionaire—and became governor. Just as he did when he was mayor, Cleveland did not let a single bill pass his desk without his knowledge of every last sentence, for if there were any hint of corruption, he vetoed the bill and refused to placate the New York-based political machine—the Tammany Democrats. His reform-mindedness, honesty, and consistency made him a favorite in 1884 for the Democratic presidential nomination.

Cleaning up government and the power of the veto

Cleveland took a bold step when he first entered office and refused to follow the spoils system. He appointed people on merit, experience, and ability, not party favoritism. Cleveland cleaned out federal posts that had been overfilled with workers who were siphoning money from the budget and he created the Interstate

Commerce Commission, the first regulatory agency created to oversee the railroads. Cleveland also vetoed 300 bills in his first term, twice as many as the combined vetoes of all his predecessors.

While Cleveland is often known for being a supporter of the gold standard and for opposing government funding of programs such as pensions, his defining trait as president during both terms was his resurrection of presidential power. The gilded presidents before him had been the hostage of the Congress, but with his clever use of the veto against the House, the fiscally conservative Cleveland was able to assert presidential authority.

Benjamin Harrison
(1889-1893)

"I pity the man who wants a coat so cheap that the man or woman who produces the cloth will starve in the process."

Introduction

The son of John Scott Harrison and the great grandson of President William Henry Harrison, young Benjamin Harrison was seven when his grandfather was inaugurated as president. Benjamin was born in North Bend, Ohio, on August 20, 1833. He was privately tutored in his youth due to the lack of schools near the Harrison residence and went to a college prep school when he was fourteen. After preparing for college he went to Miami University in Oxford, Ohio, where he graduated at eighteen in 1852.

After college Benjamin determined to become proficient in law. He began learning the trade in a law office in Cincinnati and married Caroline Lavinia Scott shortly after. Once he finished his studies he opened his own practice in Indianapolis, Indiana, where he would live for the rest of his life. He eventually become a well-known member of the community and went into partnership with another lawyer.

His first experience in politics was his victory as a Republican running for the office of reporter to the Supreme Court of Indiana. In 1862, after the Civil War broke out, Harrison accepted the offer from Governor Oliver Morton to command a regiment of volunteers. He was an able leader and led charges against Confederate troops multiple times. He served until 1865 and was promoted to brigadier general.

He returned to his private law practice until the Republican Party insisted that he run for governor in 1876. In a very narrow election, Harrison lost to his opponent Jimmy "Blue Jeans" Williams—an avid wearer of the workman's pants even while in office.

In 1880, Harrison led the Indiana Republican delegation to the convention. He was one of the key supporters of James Garfield, which ultimately helped to give Garfield the nomination and the Republicans a victory in 1880. After the election, Harrison became a senator and served for six quiet years, causing little trouble and following party lines. Harrison eventually benefitted from placating the Republican moderates. In 1888 when the Republican convention once again divided, Harrison was chosen as a safe candidate who could beat Grover Cleveland.

Building blocks of power

Harrison's presidency is largely overlooked today but incredibly important when tracing the evolution of the presidency. Harrison's administration passed the first U.S. antitrust laws and began sliding the country towards a less isolationist global view of foreign policy when he accepted Hawaii's offer of annexation to become a state. Moreover, he signed the McKinley Tariff of 1890, which raised tariff levels but more importantly gave the president the power of reciprocity, which allowed a president to reduce or raise the tariff if another nation did the same to a U.S. product. While interventionism did not come into full swing until William McKinley's administration and antitrust legislation was not actually used until Theodore Roosevelt's administration, the success of the progressive presidents has its roots with Harrison's presidency. However, Harrison's reputation was and is heavily damaged by the Silver Purchase Act, which led to a panic in 1893. The Act forced the Treasury to purchase 4,500,000 ounces of silver every month at market price gradually depleting the Treasury coffers.

Harrison lived a moderately active life after his Presidency. He gave lectures at colleges, attended the first peace conference at The Hague, Holland, and defended the Republic of Venezuela in a border dispute claim with Britain.

Grover Cleveland
(2nd Administration: 1893-1897)

"A government for the people must depend for its success on the intelligence, the morality, the justice, and the interest of the people themselves."

Introduction

Grover Cleveland returned to the White House for a nonconsecutive second term after having lost the Electoral College vote in 1888. Grover Cleveland's record in domestic policy is as strong as his efforts in diplomacy—both of which had a lasting effect on the nation. As his second term began the economy crashed shortly after he took office, but Cleveland followed a conservative agenda and focused on cleaning up government and saving money. Nevertheless, his inability to work with his adversaries and his combative leadership style—seen clearly by his 300 vetoes—made his efforts more temporary than lasting. Once Cleveland left office, corruption returned.

Arbitration and gold

Cleveland made two important and lasting contributions to the United States and the presidency during his second administration. First was his use of arbitration in diplomacy when, in 1898, Venezuela and Britain argued over controversial border disputes. Cleveland, using the foreign policy initiative of the Monroe Doctrine, forced the British Prime Minister, Lord Salisbury into an agreement of arbitration with the United States. The conference took place in Geneva, Switzerland, and the outcome was positive for both Britain and Venezuela. Britain received a fair amount of land and was pleased with the peaceful nature of the negotiation; Venezuela was pleased to have U.S. protection from encroachment of the colonial powers.

His style of conflict resolution, his second important contribution, would be used and perfected in the future by Theodore Roosevelt in a multitude of domestic and foreign affairs and would become a staple of strong presidential leadership. Moreover, Cleveland's push for a gold standard and the repeal of the Silver Purchase Act led to prosperity and stability in future years although the economic woes during his second administration were not relieved until McKinley came into office.

Although Cleveland's reputation was tarnished when he left office due to the poor economy, it would heal later during his lifetime after people witnessed the success of the nation based on the gold standard. Cleveland was very happy to see McKinley win in 1896 as he knew his policy of the gold standard would be carried out.

William McKinley
(1897-1901)

"Isolation is no longer possible or desirable"

Introduction

Another member of the long line of Ohio presidents, William McKinley was born in Niles, Ohio, on January 29, 1843. He and his family moved to Poland, Ohio, where he attended school. His mother hoped he would become a minister, but McKinley decided to go to Allegheny College in Pennsylvania instead. He eventually left the school because of illness.

When the Civil War broke out, McKinley enlisted in the 23rd Ohio Volunteer Infantry—a division that included Rutherford B. Hayes. His starting role in the war was delivering meals to soldiers under fire, but McKinley rose through the military ranks due to his bravery, eventually becoming a major.

After the war McKinley decided to study law. He began studying by working in a law office but eventually went to law school in Albany, New York. A year after entering law school he passed the bar and moved back to Ohio to start his new life. He won a race to become prosecuting attorney of Stark County despite a strong Democratic machine and soon after married Ida Saxton.

McKinley and his wife met tragedy early in their marriage when Mrs. McKinley's mother and both their daughters died—one at the age of four and the other when only an infant.

After his wife became an invalid, McKinley took care of her for the rest of her life. His extraordinary kindness, patience, and understanding gave him the reputation of an honorable man. Of all the Presidents he was one of the most devoted to his wife. When she had seizures, McKinley—even while he was president—would lay his handkerchief over her face and help her get through her episodes without the slightest hint of embarrassment.

McKinley became a congressman when Rutherford B. Hayes ran for president. He served in the House for fifteen years and became famous for his support of a high tariff. In 1890 his name became recognizable with the "McKinley Tariff," an extremely high tariff that cost him his seat after it passed. McKinley then ran for governor and won the race narrowly. His renown for supporting the tariff and his successful tenure as governor which propelled him to become the nominee of the Republicans—as well as the 10,000-mile tour of the country orchestrated by his wealthy industrialist partner Mark Hanna.

Prosperity and gold

William McKinley was a man whom the American people seemed to genuinely respect and admire. As president, his record by 1900 was stellar, the economy had bounced back, the tariff—which he raised—had restored a surplus, and the Gold Standard Act brought stability to the economy.

In foreign affairs McKinley was much more controversial; the opposition democrats formed the anti-imperial league against his overseas expansionist policy. However, McKinley never lost the support of the majority of Americans in his foreign endeavors and moreover established a precedent for American interventionism—the merits of which are still debated today.

But McKinley was also in many ways a weak president, although this was something that was apparent only behind the scenes. Mark Hanna and the power players in the Republican Party controlled much of McKinley's agenda. Moreover, he was easily pressured into signing onto initiatives—such as the war—about which he was uncertain. Theodore Roosevelt said McKinley had the "spine of a chocolate éclair." Roosevelt's analysis is too harsh, but his point is relevant; McKinley did cave in to pressure from his party.

At the mercy of the machine: Ending age-old isolation and the Spanish-American War

Before McKinley came into office, Cuban rebels had attempted to break away from Spain. The Cuban War of Independence, as it was called, ripped Cuba apart; and many Americans sympathized with Cuban wishes to break free from the Spanish tyrants.

McKinley, while sympathizing with the Cubans, felt that a peaceful resolution to the issue of Cuban independence would be preferable to war. However, negotiations with Spain proved futile, and Americans were losing hope of a successful and peaceful end to the conflict.

The Maine

The USS Maine—stationed near Cuba to guard American property—was sunk in 1898. The cause of the destruction of the ship was determined to be an underwater sea mine. McKinley wished to wait for further investigation but Congress went ahead and declared war on Spain without his initial approval. When McKinley finally relented and supported the war, many attributed this to his inability to cope with the strength of the party bosses and wealthy business supporters of the Republican Party who had a vested interest in the war.

"Splendid little war" and the Battle of San Juan Hill

The Spanish-American War of 1898 was quick and decisive—lasting only ten weeks. The naval battles were won quickly by Americans, and the land battles were short and exceptional victories for the American troops. Theodore Roosevelt and his Rough Riders of the First Volunteer Calvary made their famous charge up San Juan Hill against the weak Spaniards and took the entire hill without much pushback. The capture of the hill marked the end of the war and made Roosevelt one of the most popular figures in the United States.

Consequences of war

The McKinley administration forced the Spaniards to grant Cuba its independence and forced Spain to cede Puerto Rico, which the U.S. took as a protectorate, and also the Philippines, the most controversial of the territories granted to the United States. Democrats and anti-imperialists such as William Jennings Bryan, ex-president Grover Cleveland, and Mark Twain thought that the U.S. should leave the Philippines alone. However, expansionists and interventionists like Theodore Roosevelt, Henry Cabot Lodge, and John Hay wanted to take the Philippines under America's protective wing. Ultimately, the United States ended up with the islands of Guam, Puerto Rico, and the Philippines.

Philippines

The Philippine's did not come to the United States easily. Many rebel groups began to form in 1900, and the U.S. Army and Navy had to suppress them. McKinley, however, did not want to hold on to the Philippines permanently. In Congress, bills were being drafted to figure out how to eventually cede control of the Philippines and allow self-rule. However, many Republicans believed the Filipino people were not ready to rule themselves. Eventually the United States would give the Philippines, its independence, in 1946.

Assassination

President McKinley was greeting well-wishers and supporters at the Exposition's Temple of Music in Buffalo, New York on September 6, 1901, when a man approached and shot him. Right after the shooting, McKinley remarked that the assassin should not be hurt. The assassin was Leon F. Czolgosz, a crazed anarchist who wanted to kill a "leader." After McKinley passed away, a funeral train traveled from Buffalo to Washington carrying him, as millions of Americans in mourning watched.

Theodore Roosevelt
(1901-1909)

"Far better it is to dare mighty things, to win glorious triumphs even though checkered by failure, than to rank with those timid spirits who neither enjoy nor suffer much because they live in the gray twilight that knows neither victory nor defeat."

Introduction

Theodore Roosevelt is usually associated with the grand accomplishments of his presidency, his charismatic and energetic attitude, his thirst for exploration, and his immense intellect. However, before Roosevelt became the legend we all know today, he was a very sickly child.

Theodore Roosevelt, the son of a wealthy banker—Theodore Roosevelt, Sr.—was born on October 27, 1858. The young Roosevelt was asthmatic and was often bedridden by his coughing. The asthma stopped him from attending public or private school, and so he was privately tutored. His years living at home allowed him to become close with his father, a man who influenced Theodore more than anyone. Asthma originally left him susceptible to bullies, and when he could not defend himself his father decided to encourage the youngster to exercise, box, and keep his body in good shape. He also began to wear glasses after his parents realized he could not hit targets with his gun because of his poor eyesight. His early life of private tutoring and traveling to Europe with his father ended when he went off to Harvard at age eighteen.

Theodore did not make many friends at Harvard, having grown accustomed to private tutors. His methods for learning involved questioning professors, challenging them when he believed something to be incorrect, and trying take advantage of every opportunity to advance. At college, he began outlining his first book on the War of 1812. His classmates had been more interested in passing and less interested in challenging the professors, so Teddy's antics were not welcome. It was also at Harvard that Theodore decided to devote his life to public service—but not because of his studies, although he graduated with excellent grades in 1880. His father died in 1878, and the young Roosevelt decided to pursue a life in politics to honor him. After graduating, he married Alice Hathaway Lee, whom he had courted in college. Then he began attending Columbia University to study law. After finding legal studies intolerably boring, Roosevelt went to Europe with his wife. He climbed the Matterhorn in the Alps and wrote more of his book, *The Naval War of 1812*.

When Roosevelt returned from Europe, his old Republican friends decided to run him for the New York State Assembly. Roosevelt won the election and became an assemblyman at the age of twenty-three. He immediately became a reformer, calling for investigations into the conduct of Jay Gould, a highly corrupt millionaire. However, his political career was interrupted by tragedy. His wife—who had just given birth to their son—died on February 14, 1884. His mother died on the same day. Roosevelt wrote in his diary after their deaths, "the light went from my life forever," and he fell into a state of depression.

Roosevelt finished his term but decided to make a change in his life. Instead of running for his seat again, Roosevelt went West to South Dakota and lived there as a cattle rancher for three years. Although he traveled back and forth to New York during those years, he gained respect among the cowboys and even became one himself. He established a reputation for his toughness in a bar fight with a cowboy who had called him "four-eyes," became a deputy sheriff, capturing criminals and thieves;, he took care of cattle until the winter of 1886, when many of them died. By 1887 Roosevelt had been healed by the American West, and he left the Badlands and rode back to New York to begin the next chapter of his life.

Roosevelt returned to New York and became the Republican candidate for mayor in the city. Although the Democrats typically won the election for mayor, Roosevelt was running in a three-way race that should have been easy for a Republican to win. However he lost the race, and many commented that his career was over. Roosevelt decided to refocus on his writing and to remarry, this time, wedding his childhood sweetheart Edith Kermit Carow.

In 1889 Roosevelt was appointed as the U.S. Civil Service Commissioner due to his campaigning for President Benjamin Harrison in 1888. He served for six years and was even reappointed by Democratic reformer Grover Cleveland. Roosevelt's most important appointment came with the election of Mayor William Strong, who made Roosevelt the commissioner of the New York City police force. The force was heavily corrupt, and Roosevelt was determined to clean it up. In one of his first steps as a reformer, he forced the police chief to resign after the chief admitted being in league with industrialist millionaire Jay Gould.

To make sure his men were performing their job honestly, Roosevelt began to walk the police beats, often going into the most dangerous parts of the city.

His reputation earned him the job of assistant secretary of the navy, where Roosevelt became a hawk on foreign affairs and helped lead the country into war with Spain. When war finally broke out, Roosevelt joined and led the "Rough Riders" in Cuba and charged up San Juan Hill, earning him an immense amount of fame. That fame carried him to the governorship of New York, where Roosevelt once again proved to be a reformer. He pushed through a tax on corporations, which showed the Republican establishment he was independent of their control, startling Republican businessmen. The business wing of the Republican Party wanted to get rid of Roosevelt by making him vice president—a weak position that typically ended political careers. Roosevelt insisted that he would not accept the nomination. However, at the Republican convention Roosevelt was made McKinley's running mate. There were two people at the convention who opposed the motion, Mark Hanna—McKinley's right-hand man, who stated, "Don't any of you realize that there's only one life between this madman and the White House"—and Theodore Roosevelt, who voted against his own nomination.

Despite his efforts, Roosevelt became vice president. And after McKinley's death Roosevelt became the president—a position more palatable to him.

Cowboy in the White House

Theodore Roosevelt had a reputation for energy and activism both before he moved into the White House and after, when he was finally president. The public, as well as the political bosses of the Republican Party, knew about his crusades for good government and progressivism in New York and all around the country. And as the Republican Party was run mostly by political operators loyal only to business interests, Roosevelt's swearing in in 1901 was not exactly welcome. Hanna stated after Roosevelt became president, "Now that damned cowboy is in the White House." And just as in his cowboy days, Roosevelt walked into the presidency with a fearlessness and a sense of exhilaration that led him to develop the presidency into a position that was more than just curatorial; he developed it into a position that guarded and championed the public good.

Senators, congressmen, and even foreign diplomats all got to experience the Theodore Roosevelt treatment. Instead of sitting on couches and sipping tea, Roosevelt took visitors horseback riding, mountain climbing, exploring, and hunting. A visit to the White House could be exhausting, but every man who met Roosevelt came to know him well through the experience and knew of his sincere ability to change America and the presidency. In Roosevelt's view, the president was like the Roman tribune; he represented the entirety of the American people.

The great mediator

One of Roosevelt's greatest talents was his ability to bring people together to solve seemingly impossible problems. Presidents in the past had rarely used the mediation technique, especially not in foreign policy, as the president traditionally acted only in tandem with the House of Representatives. However Roosevelt utilized mediation at both the domestic and foreign level throughout his presidency. His first incident involving mediation was sparked by a coal strike in Pennsylvania.

In 1902, anthracite coal miners in Pennsylvania went on strike in order to gain higher wages and a shorter workday, as the average miner worked nearly twelve hours a day for little pay. The strike seemed to go nowhere and winter was coming quickly. The strike was poorly timed, Americans soon realized that there would be no coal to heat their homes and stay warm. The effects of such a chilling winter would have been detrimental to the American economy and also put countless lives at risk to exposure. Roosevelt intervened in the situation by setting up a commission of nine people to investigate the workers claims. The commission comprised four men with backgrounds in business, four from unions, and one from a neutral party. The investigation ended in a pay raise for the miners and the continuation of mining for the companies—a major success for Roosevelt and the country.

Roosevelt used the mediation technique again at the end of his presidency in a very dramatic way to bring an end to the Russo-Japanese War. The war had ignited in 1904 when Russia and Japan engaged in combat. Nearly a year into the war Roosevelt decided that there was an opportunity for a mediator to assist in bringing peace to the Far East.

The Russians, who had initiated the war for imperialist purposes, attempted to occupy a Japanese-lease harbor in Manchuria. The Russians, too their surprise, were beaten back and their navy was almost totally decimated by Japanese forces. By 1905, the bloodshed was so great that it had overshadowed most casualty rates of any previous war, but both sides were becoming tired of fighting. Roosevelt pressured the Russian tsar, Nicholas II, to allow him to mediate the situation. The tsar eventually came to the table, and Roosevelt became the mediator between the two nations.

Through many weeks of tough debate, Roosevelt was able to get the Japanese to concede some of their harsher terms to a point where Tsar Nicholas was satisfied. Both nations signed the Treaty of Portsmouth, ending the war. Roosevelt ended what could have boiled into a world war and brought temporary peace to the Far East—an action that awarded him the 1906 Nobel Peace Prize.

Trust busting and the power of legalism

When Roosevelt gave his inaugural address he had promised the American people that he would fight the power of trusts and monopolies. But before we look at how he would eventually tackle these monsters, we should define *trust* and *monopoly*.

A *trust* is…a legal device used to consolidate power in large American corporate enterprises, a large business with significant market power.

A *monopoly* is a company that uses anticompetitive business practices to dominate markets. It is broken by an antitrust law that restores competition to the marketplace. Oil barons such as John D. Rockefeller would buy up large amounts of stock in as many oil companies as he could find and pressure every oil company into following price agreements determined by him. Rockefeller could set any price and not have to worry about any competition in the marketplace. If competition existed or began to appear, he had the power to set prices so low near the competition that any competitor would be driven out of business, and thus he could consolidate his grip on the market.

Roosevelt shared a belief held by many that monopolies were dangerous, and that businessmen would use the uncompetitive nature of monopolies to squeeze every penny out consumers. Additionally, monopolies broke the rules of the American business tradition, which was in part, based on the idea of competitive markets established by Adam Smith's *Wealth of Nations*. Those opposed to antitrust laws—usually oil tycoons or executives—believed that having the power to set prices meant that companies could give their consumers the greatest deal possible. But, more often than not, this was not the case. And by 1903, over 300 trusts controlled more than half of all manufacturing output.

A "trust," or "corporate trust" is a large business

OIL

CONSUMER

Mo·nop·o·ly
/mə' näpəlē/
noun
noun: monopoly; plural noun:
monopolies; noun: Monopoly
1.
the exclusive possession or control of the supply or trade

Once Monopolies are estabslished trusts can set whatever prices they deem fit for goods and services.

133

Roosevelt and his attorney general, Philander Knox, first filed suit against the Northern Securities Company, a railroad monopoly held by J. P. Morgan. Shocked by this, Morgan and other business leaders realized that Roosevelt was not the typical conservative Republican who wanted to allow business to run government. Roosevelt's case was successful, and although it took until 1908 to settle, the Northern Securities Company was broken up. Roosevelt continued to break up monopolies throughout his presidency, landing himself the title of "Trust Buster." It should be noted that Roosevelt did not rely on Congress to pursue his agenda. Setting a new precedent for the presidency, Roosevelt used other powers such as executive power and legal routes in order to keep markets competitive.

America's place in the sun

For all the difficulties Roosevelt had with his fellow Republicans on domestic policy, he did find common ground with them on issues of foreign policy. Roosevelt firmly believed in what we now call "American Exceptionalism." A core belief of his was that America could make a difference in the world and make it a better place through intervention. However, before Roosevelt could pave his own way in foreign affairs he had to deal with the war in the Philippines that had begun under McKinley. The war ended up being politically costly to Roosevelt, as accusations of abuse of the Philippine people quickly spread among the public. The horror stories of the war made it politically difficult to finish carrying out the ongoing battle in the Philippines, and Roosevelt—despite calling on Republican ally's to defend American action in the Philippines—put an end to the fighting in 1902.

Despite the initial setback, Roosevelt continued to shine in foreign affairs and give the office of the preside more power over foreign policy with what would eventually be called the Roosevelt Corollary. The Corollary came about due to problems in South America and redefined the Monroe Doctrine. Venezuela had incurred large debts with Germany over the years, and the German Kaiser, Wilhelm II, intended to exact payment. In 1902 the Kaiser decided that it was time for Venezuela pay up, and he set up a blockade around Venezuela.

Roosevelt, seeing that Germany threatened to take Venezuela ports if they continued to neglect paying their debts, issued the Corollary. Roosevelt said that as Germany's venture in Venezuela was imperialistic in nature—which violated the Monroe Doctrine—and that the Germans should leave South America alone. The United States would then arbitrate the repayment of debts between Venezuela and Germany. War was averted between Venezuela and Germany, and the debts were eventually repaid.

All these great achievements were peanuts in the eyes of Roosevelt, he always believed that his greatest triumph was the Panama Canal. The Colombian government—which at the time of Roosevelt's presidency controlled the Panama—had let other nations such as France attempt to build a canal with no success. Roosevelt thought that the United States could build the canal and sought to get the Panamanians on his side for the massive project.

Initially, the ruling government in the Colombian-controlled Panama would not go along with Roosevelt's plan. So, Roosevelt supported the Panamanians rebels who sought an independent Panama. Roosevelt sent the U.S. Navy near the border of Panama and the rebels were able to take over the government and break away from Columbia. The new Panamanian government was happy to work with Roosevelt and signed a treaty permitting the U.S. to build the Panama Canal creating a zone ten kilometers, later expanded to sixteen kilometers wide across Panama. The United States could use the Canal Zone for 100 years. The Panama Canal Zone was successfully constructed, what no nation was able to accomplish before. The president happily flaunted America's new international power and rejoiced in taking the important piece of land from the Germans, who might have constricted its practical use instead of allowing it to be a beacon of free trade in the world.

A brighter future

Trust busting had been a major success with Roosevelt, but he wanted to do more for the average American while he was president. Being the voracious reader that he was, Roosevelt had discovered a book called *The Jungle* by Upton Sinclair. It exposed the grotesque environment in which meat was processed and packaged. Roosevelt felt that regulation could be the proper fix for the situation and pursued the Pure Food and Drug Act, which protected consumers from adulterated products.

However Roosevelt's biggest concern about America's future was preserving the beautiful landscape he had explored throughout his life. From South Dakota to West Virginia, California to Texas, Roosevelt was passionate about the beauty of the country. Moreover, as an explorer and enthusiast of zoology, he was distraught by the numbers of species on the verge of extinction in the 1800s. He fostered the passage of the Antiquities Act, which created the first efficient forest service and protected more land than any other president in history.

The active president

Few Presidents have had more of an effect on the presidency and on the nation than Theodore Roosevelt. Roosevelt stepped into a seemingly terminally-ill presidency stymied by the power of the lobbyists and corporations that rose in power after the Civil War. In eight years Roosevelt reasserted presidential authority, convinced the American people that antitrust laws and an interventionist foreign policy were beneficial, and developed a new ideology—*progressivism*, by way of his "Square Deal"—which would become a dominate force in American politics and thought for the next century. Moreover, Roosevelt scared political parties by going straight to the people in 1904. Roosevelt also brought personality to the White House. Historians have examined this in detail, with John Milton Cooper calling Roosevelt a "warrior" in comparison to the "priest" future president Woodrow Wilson. However, Roosevelt feared that his presidency would go unrecognized because he was not president during wartime, an important merit for presidential reputation back then. But Roosevelt's legendary reputation was secured when his likeness was sculptured next to Lincoln's on Mount Rushmore in South Dakota, and when John Bloom wrote *The Republican Roosevelt* in 1952, which brought a new generation to admire and write about Roosevelt.

Roosevelt did not retire after 1908. He went back to being an adventurer and explorer, charting rivers and hunting. However, after returning from an African exhibition during William Taft's presidency, Roosevelt realized that worst mistake he ever made was promising not to run for a third term. Victory in 1908 could have been his if he wanted it, but he had believed that Taft would carry out his polices. In reality, Taft was his own man and did not endorse all that Roosevelt stood for. Roosevelt ran in 1912 and engaged Woodrow Wilson in a debate that involved both the left and right of American thought. When he lost in 1912, he explored an uncharted Brazilian river—now named Roosevelt River—and nearly died during his quest. He also began writing more and more about politics. His hatred of Wilson grew over the years, but his friendship with Taft was eventually restored. He abandoned his own Progressive party in 1916 in an effort to bring together the Republican Party to beat Wilson—which failed. He criticized Wilson for staying out of World War I and when the war worsened, and Wilson did finally intervene, Roosevelt went as far to ask to ask President Wilson to let him fight with a volunteer division but Wilson refused. However, Roosevelt became a little less war-loving after his son from his second marriage died in World War I.

Many believed Roosevelt to be the frontrunner for the Republican nomination in 1920. However, Roosevelt died in his sleep in 1919. Woodrow Wilson's vice president, Thomas R. Marshall, said of Roosevelt's death: **"Death had to take him sleeping, for if Roosevelt had been awake, there would have been a fight."**

William Howard Taft
(1909-1913)

"The President cannot make clouds to rain and cannot make the corn to grow; he cannot make business good; although when these things occur, political parties do claim some credit for the good things that have happened in this way."

Introduction

William Howard Taft had a quiet and simple upbringing. The son of Alphonso Taft, William was born on September 15, 1857, in Cincinnati, Ohio, and excelled in his studies and in sports throughout his young life. He went off to Yale in 1874 and graduated in 1878. After Yale, Taft studied law for two years, and his father, who was a politician—and had been in President Grant's cabinet—helped him obtain a position as an assistant prosecutor in 1881. A year later, Taft was made tax collector by President Chester Arthur and was eventually ambassador to Austria-Hungary.

Despite the latter appointment, Taft returned to join his father's law firm and married Helen Herron. They had three children, one being Robert Taft, who would become a very famous senator known as "Mr. Conservative" in the 1940s and 1950s.

Until 1900 Taft bounced from appointment to appointment, establishing a reputation as an able lawyer and a generally well-meaning nice man. In 1900 he received the important appointment of president of the Philippine Commission. Taft's job was to establish a government in the Philippines, which was then being torn apart by revolution. Initially stating that the Filipinos were his "little brown brothers," Taft eventually came to feel that they were not capable of running their own government. He became the civilian governor of the Philippines and was concerned with helping to stabilize the island. Taft became sick during his tenure and returned to Washington. Once back in in the capital he was asked to participate in a Senate hearing on the Philippines and met President Roosevelt, who took a liking to him. Roosevelt offered him a seat on the Supreme Court—the position which Taft had always wanted—but Taft turned him down and felt he had to finish his work in the Philippines. However, in 1904, Taft agreed to be Roosevelt's Secretary of War. Taft used his position to travel to Panama and oversee construction of the canal and to help President Roosevelt in any way possible. Roosevelt became increasingly fond of him and soon decided Taft would be his successor.

Roosevelt goes to Africa

Roosevelt's enormous popularity would have been a hindrance to Taft's ability to be seen as the new leader of the Republican Party, so Roosevelt left for a long venture, on an African safari, to allow Taft to assert his dominance over the party.

Starting on the wrong foot

Taft's first hurdle as president was dealing with the tariff, and tariff reform did not go onto a good start in 1909. The Aldrich Tariff, proposed to him by the Congress, was a protectionist tariff that favored business. While wanting to compromise but unable to bridge the gap between progressives and conservatives on the issue, Taft passed the bill. Progressives saw the bill as Taft flaunting his conservatism, while business saw Taft as favoring progressives. Unfortunately for Taft, the bill put him at odds with both factions of the Republican Party.

Progressives did have some issues to be happy about though. Taft busted over ninety monopolies during his tenure, more than his predecessor. Just as important, John D. Rockefeller's Standard Oil Company was found to be in violation of the Sherman Antitrust Act, a law initiated by Roosevelt but expanded by Taft. By the end of his term, Taft had also passed a corporate tax bill.

In foreign affairs Taft followed a new policy of "Dollar Diplomacy," which spelled out the government's role in encouraging stability in trade in foreign markets, using money to achieve power in overseas ventures. Businesses and institutions were also encouraged to make lasting relationships with Latin America and other nations.

Roosevelt returns

In 1909, Louis Glavis—an important member of the Department of the Interior—accused Richard Ballinger, Taft's secretary of the interior, of committing fraud by selling Alaskan coal fields and protected lands to private businesses. Theodore Roosevelt's good friend, Gifford Pinchot—who was appointed by Roosevelt as the head of the Forest Service—also fired attacks against Glavis and the Taft administration, causing Taft to eventually fire Pinchot. This enraged Roosevelt and created a divide between the president and the ex-president.

After the firing of Gifford Pinchot and Taft's supposed mishandling of tariff issues, Roosevelt believed that Taft was more conservative than he initially thought him to be. Roosevelt returned from his explorations and took up political arms against Taft, which split the Republican Party.

Election of 1912

The election of 1912 was more a series of lectures than it was a campaign. In the ring was President Taft, Theodore Roosevelt, and Woodrow Wilson. Throughout the election the two frontrunners, Roosevelt and Wilson, engaged in a debate which in the modern era—when most campaigns are decided by a few sound bites—would be shocking, as Roosevelt and Wilson stormed through the country debating the principles of progressivism versus classical liberalism.

Although Theodore Roosevelt attempted to take the Republican nomination at the beginning of 1912, President Taft was re-nominated by the party. Roosevelt quickly formed his own party—the Progressives—to run against Taft and the eventual Democratic nominee, Woodrow Wilson. However, Roosevelt quickly realized that Taft was not his main opponent. Taft had essentially admitted defeat before the election began. He had not enjoyed being president and stayed in the race more or less to spoil it for Roosevelt, whom Taft felt had betrayed him.

The Democrats chose Woodrow Wilson—professor of jurisprudence, president of Princeton University, and reform governor of New Jersey—as their nominee. He had just defeated Champ Clark, popular Speaker of the House, for the nomination.

Roosevelt and Wilson then laid out their two agendas, which shaped the election of 1912. Roosevelt ran on his "New Nationalism," a progressive platform that called for the regulation of big business, women's suffrage, shorter work days, higher wages, and a health service. Wilson ran on the "New Freedom," which was a legalistic take on dealing with big business and much more closely based on Jeffersonian principles than Roosevelt's Hamiltonian policies. Their platforms differed in some key respects. Roosevelt wanted a regulatory agency to deal with businesses, and Wilson preferred to simply break up monopolies and big business with antitrust laws. Roosevelt wanted a higher wage for workers, while Wilson believed that a minimum wage law would be manipulated by big business. Roosevelt felt that the only way to protect people from big business was to regulate it; Wilson believed that such regulation was akin to the government taking big business under its wing.

Both men campaigned vigorously until the fourth of October, when an assassin shot Theodore Roosevelt on his way to give a speech. The bullet penetrated Roosevelt's front pocket, where his speech and spectacle case were, keeping the bullet from striking his heart. Roosevelt, hurt and bloodied, continued to enter the hall and gave his speech with the bullet lodged in his chest. For ten days Roosevelt recovered in the hospital, and Wilson, out of respect, did not campaign.

The election ended in a victory for Wilson, he carried the South, the North, and much of the West. Roosevelt came in 2nd and was able to carry Pennsylvania, Michigan, Wisconsin, South Dakota, Washington, and California; while Taft only picked up the ever-conservative states of Vermont and Utah. To date, Roosevelt's grand campaign in 1912 is the most successful third-party campaign in American history.

Taft had both the fortune and misfortune of being sandwiched between two giants, Wilson and Roosevelt. Had it not been for Roosevelt, Taft would not have been president; and had it not been for Wilson, Taft would have been embarrassed by losing to Roosevelt in 1912.

In 1921 Taft was made Chief Justice of the U.S. Supreme Court, the only man to have served in both executive and judiciary positions.

Woodrow Wilson
(1913-1921)

*"Liberty has never come from Government.
Liberty has always come from the subjects of it.
The history of liberty is a history of limitations of
governmental power, not the increase of it."*

Introduction

Born Thomas Woodrow Wilson in Staunton, Virginia, on December 29, 1856. Wilson was able to remember the beginning of the Civil War and got to observe Reconstruction. His father was a minister, and Wilson remembered seeing wounded Confederates come to his father's church—young Wilson even saw Robert E. Lee.

Despite being the only president to earn a Ph.D. and one of the most well-read presidents, Wilson did not learn how to read until he was eleven due to the war, which had put an end to schooling temporarily. After the war his father moved the family to South Carolina. Wilson went to Davidson College in North Carolina in preparation to become a minister but was forced to return home when he became sick—so sick in fact that he withdrew from the college. Nearly two years later Wilson went to New Jersey to attend Princeton University, where he retreated from his path to becoming a minister. Instead, Wilson became a scholar of history and politics. After graduating from Princeton, Wilson began studying law at the University of Virginia. He became sick again and had to finish his studies from home, but he did graduate.

Wilson tried his hand at law but was not successful and decided to become a professor. He went to Johns Hopkins Graduate School, earning his doctoral degree in political science and began working on his book *Congressional Government*, which analyzed the incredible strength —and corruption—of the Congress, and the weakness of the presidency. The book also argues for a more British-like parliamentary system, where the president is the head of the party. The book received good reviews when it was released after Wilson completed his studies at Johns Hopkins.

Wilson began teaching at Bryn Mawr College in Pennsylvania and married Ellen Louise Axson. He eventually worked his way up to professor of jurisprudence and history at Princeton. He was very popular among the students, known for his interesting lectures, devotion to research, and scholarship. He was elected president of Princeton in 1902 and reformed the standards of scholarship, surprising many by proposing to abolish the private eating groups and to make the campus more democratic instead of being one of a series of fraternities and exclusive clubs.

1910 was also a year that Wilson showed his political ability. New Jersey was a state controlled by progressive Republicans, and Wilson was determined to become governor as a Democrat. He made a deal with some of the party bosses, and at the convention, the Democrats proposed Wilson. He won the people over and took the election with a safe margin of victory. Once he became governor, Wilson turned his back on the bosses. He instituted countless reforms—from electoral reform, breaking the bosses' control of state politics, to progressive reform like workman's compensation. His impressive tenure as governor gave him the confidence to put his name up for a presidential run in 1912.

Wilson's philosophy—words vs. action

Woodrow Wilson preached that small is better. For Wilson, regulation was a terrible way of safe guarding people from the exploitation of big business, as it brought big business under the wing of the government. Therefore, to keep things small, antitrust laws as well as policies alleviating the problems of debt and currency restriction for farmers and small merchants were the best in Wilson's view. Thus, in the 1912 campaign, Wilson continually attacked what he referred to as "The Triple Wall of Privilege—the trusts, the tariff and the banks." As president, Wilson added government reforms to deal with the previous three. But herein lies the difficulty: Although a preacher of all things small, his triple wall of reforms led to increased government—for better or worse.

Reforms

The first reform in curbing the wall of privilege was the Clayton Act of 1914. Since Wilson rejected regulation, he wanted to break up the power monopolies directly. The Clayton Antitrust Law strengthened many provisions laid out in the Sherman Antitrust Act of 1890 and made it easier for the government to break monopolies.

As a believer in free trade, his second reform was to lower the tariff—a major change in policy, since all the presidents before him had kept it high.

The third reform was targeted at the banks, but the idea behind the reform—a central bank—was a polarizing proposition, especially within the Democratic Party. The populist wing of the party, represented by William Jennings Bryan, believed that central banking benefited only the North, and that the western farmers would be hurt by the establishment of a central bank. Northern Democrats and pro-business Democrats liked the idea of a central bank because there would be more opportunity for businesses to receive loans and for capital to be created and expanded. Southern Democrats were largely in opposition to any centralization of banks for ideological reasons.

Wilson was able to bridge the gap of separatism on behalf of a central bank through meetings with William Jennings Bryan. Bryan and his populist wing would support creation of a central bank if there were multiple banks scattered throughout the nation, giving all the people easy access to the banks. Wilson agreed, and the Federal Reserve System spread throughout the North, Mid-Atlantic, and Mountain States; throughout the West, and some of the South.

The Federal Reserve Act passed the House in 1913 with some opposition from Southern Democrats and a few Republicans; but Wilson's ability to bridge party division and gaps secured passage.

The Federal Reserve, known as the FED, allowed farmers and small businessmen to take out loans and gain security in finance; however it also led to increase debt. The institution served as a catalyst for good and bad, contributing to the expansion of economic security and a more elastic currency but also having a hand in many economic crises that followed.

After the FED was created Wilson was determined to continue reforming. He signed the Keating-Owen Act in 1916. The intended goal of the act was to ban child labor, but in 1917 the Supreme Court ruled that the federal government did not have the power to void a contract between a child and its contractor, and therefore the Keating-Owen law was found unconstitutional. After the ruling, Wilson, Vice President Thomas R. Marshall, and other state leaders began to emphasize other ways to curb child labor, such as compulsory education.

Wilson also continued the fight for land conservation and created the National Parks Service in 1916.

Trouble in Mexico

In 1914, Mexican authorities in Tampico detained U.S. Marines who unknowingly went to an off-limits part of Mexico to resupply. The commanding officer who detained the marines eventually apologized, but U.S. Commander Henry T. Mayo demanded that the Mexican troops salute the American flag as part of the apology, which the Mexicans refused to do. What ensued was a conflict between the U.S. Marines and the Mexican officials. Wilson had to send a fleet to the port city of Veracruz to settle the dispute. American troops eventually seized the Mexican Customs House at Veracruz and occupied the city for six months. The Mexican President refused to apologize for the incident, but the Mexican Revolution—taking place during this time—eventually led to his ousting, which brought an end to the dispute.

Turmoil in Europe and the death of Ellen

In 1914, Austrian Archduke Franz Ferdinand was assassinated by a member of a Serbian nationalist group called the Black Hand. Killed by the "shot heard around the world," the archduke's death plunged Europe into political chaos. Accusations quickly arose that the duke's assassin was from Serbia, a country that had a complicated history with Austria. Tsar Nicholas II of Russia and Kaiser Wilhelm II of Germany held correspondence with each other to work out the conflicts in Europe, as Germany was allied with Austria and Russia was part of an alliance with Serbia. Tsar Nicholas made the mistake of mobilizing his troops, which triggered a declaration of war against Serbia by Austria-Hungary, resulting in Germany backing Austria-Hungary's war declaration. Russia declared war on Germany, and since Russia was a member of a triple entente with France and England, France joined the war with Russia. Germany's invasion of Belgium brought England to Russia's side, evidence that Germany was breaking international law by attacking a neutral nation.

Thus, the formation of the Allies—England, France, and Russia–and the Central Powers: Germany, Austria-Hungary, and Turkey—was created. In that same year, Wilson's wife Ellen died. Her death put Wilson in a state of bereavement and made him question whether he even wanted another term as president. However, in 1915 Wilson met Edith Boeing Galt and fell in love, remarrying in 1916.

Election of 1916 and the sinking of the Lusitania

In 1915, the British ship RMS *Lusitania* was sunk by a German submarine, and 128 Americans on board died, provoking an uproar in the United States. Wilson called for an end to unrestricted submarine warfare, which would be absolute and unconditional. Germany complied for the rest of 1915 and 1916, just in time for the presidential election.

Zimmerman telegram and entry into World War I

In 1916 a telegram sent from Germany to Mexico was intercepted. The telegram revealed that Germany wanted to recruit Mexico as an ally in case of a war with the United States. Germany hoped that if war with the United States was declared, Mexico would fight the United States at its southern border and join the Central Powers.

By 1917, Wilson felt that the United States had to enter the war. Germany's unrestricted submarine warfare was resurfacing. Wilson had taken a firm stance against such action and needed to respond in some manner. The Zimmerman Telegram pushed Wilson to the side of intervention, as Germany was taking incredibly hostile stances towards the United States. In 1917, Wilson called on Congress to vote for a declaration of war; the United States was at war with Germany.

Stretching the limits of the presidency

Soon after war was declared, Wilson and his administration abandoned their efforts of progressivism to focus solely on winning the war at hand. The government took control of many private manufacturing lines, kept unions from striking, and refrained from raising wages for the sake of the wartime economy. Wilson urged Americans to buy war bonds, using incredibly effective propaganda, and he pushed the United States into a fast military buildup. Much of this was unconstitutional but seen as legitimate because of the war. The stretching of presidential power didn't stop there, as Wilson passed the Espionage Act in 1917, a bill that targeted radicals and anyone interfering with the war effort. The bill was an outright violation of the First Amendment, but political violence was common throughout the world at this point, so Wilson's fears were well- founded. However, the Espionage Act was often used inappropriately, as when socialist presidential candidate Eugene Debs was imprisoned for his opposition to war and was only freed two years after the fighting was over.

Fourteen Points and breaking with Jefferson's tradition

Wilson broke the hundred-year-old State of the Union tradition established by Thomas Jefferson. Instead of writing a report and having a congressman read it in Congress, Wilson came directly to the House— something Jefferson believed to be too monarchial.

In 1918 Wilson laid out his Fourteen Points-- his direction for American aims in the war. His Fourteen Points illustrated his wishes for post-war reconstruction: open alliances and agreements between nations, freedom of navigation and trade, independence for the Balkan states as well as for Poland, and the creation of a League of Nations.

Treaty of Versailles

With the war coming to a close, Wilson and other world leaders attended the 1919 peace conference at the Palace of Versailles in France. Accompanied by English Prime Minister David Lloyd George and French Prime Minister George Clemenceau, Wilson led much of the discussion over the Treaty of Versailles.

The terms of the Versailles Treaty were very punitive towards Germany. Wilson had pleaded for softer punishment for the German states, but Clemenceau and Lloyd George were less willing to concede on the economic reparations they felt entitled to. Wilson, eager to assemble the League of Nations, which he believed could help the world avoid another war, compromised with the stubborn Lloyd George and Clemenceau. The final terms, though ruthless towards Germany, established the League.

League of Nations and the battle in the Senate

Wilson's League of Nations was put into effect after the Paris Peace Conference of 1919. The institution's main goals were to keep world peace through collective security, disarming, and giving all nations a place to arbitrate issues—an eventual framework for the United Nations in years to come. Wilson was able to get the League of Nations settled with his international colleagues, but getting the Senate to ratify the League treaty was another thing. Republican senator Henry Cabot Lodge was Wilson's foremost political enemy in the postwar years. Lodge blocked Wilson's treaty vigorously, claiming that it would hurt United States sovereignty as well as grant unfair power to the international community over the United States. Wilson was unsuccessful in passing the treaty, but much of the defeat was brought on by his own actions. Wilson would not court Republicans at all in the process of negotiation and typically was stubborn about making any changes to the treaty. In addition, Theodore Roosevelt's death during the treaty negotiation only made things worse for Wilson, as Roosevelt's more moderate stance on party policy was no longer present to counterbalance Lodge's rabid opposition.

Failing health and the collapse of Wilson's presidency

On a whistle-stop tour around the country to gather support for the League, Wilson suffered from a stroke on a hot afternoon. The stroke left him bedridden for nearly half a year, during which time his wife Edith essentially acted as president. Wilson never fully recovered from the stroke, but for the remaining part of his presidency he became more

rigid and unwilling to compromise. He spoke less and less to senators and became more secluded.

Red Scare

In the final years of Wilson's presidency, the Red Scare took over the United States. In the wake of the Russian Revolution, Americans reacted with immense hostility due to the influence of patriotic propaganda regarding the First World War and in response to the rise of radical anarchist and Communist groups. Americans became increasingly fearful of a Communist or anarchist revolution occurring in the United States. Wilson fed the Red Scare by consistently calling for anti-immigrant legislation as well as restrictions on free speech.

However, the Red Scare was not totally baseless. Although influenced heavily by propaganda, Communists and anarchists were violent throughout 1919-1921. In 1919 the police foiled a plot that intended to mail bombs to important Americans ranging from John. D. Rockefeller to Justice Oliver Wendell Holmes. In June of the same year, eight bombs exploded in eight separate cities. The culprit was an Italian-American radical. During these years the Wilson administration deported a countless number of immigrants, many guilty of crimes and many innocent.

Legacy

Woodrow Wilson's ideology and presidency leave a strong legacy. John Milton Cooper, an authority on the twenty-eighth president, has noted one of Wilson's major accomplishments; he was "one of the three great legislator Presidents, the others being FDR and LBJ... and he didn't have the intricate advantages that FDR or LBJ had." Wilson's decision to enter into World War I brought with it a change in American life and society, and his creation of the Federal Reserve was one of the largest institutional changes in American government. Both of Wilson's decisions have been hailed and criticized, some saying Wilson rescued Europe and created the groundwork for the United Nations, which has served as a power of international good; and others say that intervention permanently altered the culture of America, and that Wilson's League of Nations and Federal Reserve sanctioned governments to obtain more power over people. John Milton Cooper argues that Wilson's intervention is what eventually allowed the United States to become the superpower that it is today, ending years of isolationism.

Oddly, Wilson's ideology has faded over the years. Although his classically liberal ideology triumphed over Roosevelt's progressivism in 1912, Wilson's call for small government and small business fell apart while the government soon adopted Theodore Roosevelt's more pragmatic approach. While Wilson adhered to a more Jeffersonian type of government, Roosevelt, who believed big business to simply be inevitable, advocated for regulation instead of constantly breaking up business. As the nineteenth century developed, Roosevelt's ideology won the day. However, much of the right-wing today owes some of its rhetorical roots to Wilson, who attacked both big business and big government while opposing such things as the minimum wage.

The modern presidential image owes it roots to Wilson, who decided to make the office more public and visible, allowing Franklin Roosevelt to harness the power and celebrity of the radio and succeeding presidents to profit from the immediacy of television. However, a stroke in 1919, left him incapacitated and along with him went the progressive era. His own rigidness and failure to compromise drove the Senate to refuse to join the League of Nations—about which Cabot Lodge had legitimate concerns. For his efforts in creating the League of Nations, although the United States never joined, Wilson was awarded the 1919 Nobel Peace Prize.

Warren G. Harding
(1921-1923)

"America's present need is not heroics but healing; not nostrums but normalcy; not revolution but restoration."

Introduction

Warren Harding was born on November 2, 1865, in Corsica (now Blooming Grove), Ohio. He grew up in a rural farming area. He went to Ohio Central College, graduated in 1882 and tried teaching for a short period of time. When his father moved to Marion, Ohio, Warren followed him. He spent most of his time playing pool until he turned nineteen and got his first taste of the newspaper business. He became a reporter for a month but was fired for his political leanings.

Harding decided to publish his own newspaper with the help of two friends, John Sickle and Jack Warwick, who co-invested with Harding to establish The *Marion Star*. After some success with the paper, he created The *Weekly Star*, a Republican newspaper that became important for the Ohio Republican party.

Harding married Florence Kling De Wolfe when he was twenty-five, around the time when he decided to become active in politics. His reputation as a newspaperman and owner secured him the Republican nomination for the state senate. He won the race, and became a Republican state senator. His loyalty brought him the lieutenant governorship for two years. After his service in state office, Harding tried his hand at becoming governor. He lost the race and spent the next six years focused on his newspaper, although still being mildly active in Republican politics. His friend and political ally, Harry Daugherty convinced Harding to return to politics and to run for the open Ohio Senate seat that was vacant in 1915. Harding reluctantly agreed, believing he could not win, but was ultimately able to defeat his opponent. Harding spent 1915-1920 being a largely inconsequential senator. Additionally, Harding had an extramarital affair with Nan Britton, who would eventually write a book about it in 1927 titled *The President's Daughter,* causing a significant amount of controversy.

Harding's friend, Daugherty, once again convinced Harding to pursue higher office. In 1920 Harding entered the race for the Republican nomination. He was up against General Leonard Wood and Governor Frank Lowden. Harding won his home state of Ohio by a few votes but lost the other primaries. When the Republican convention met, Wood and Lowden were deadlocked, leaving Harding as a possible compromise. Republican heavyweights asked Harding if he had any skeletons in his closet before the final day of voting. "None," Harding said. After the next vote, Wood and Lowden were deadlocked again, and voters switched to Harding.

Frenemies and the forgotten depression

Harding summed up his own presidency well enough when he stated, "I have no trouble with my enemies….But my damn friends… they're the ones that keep me walking the floor nights." Harding came to office unprepared, with friends who did not care about his success but their own, and he was paralyzed by their scandalous natures. For example, when a large railway strike disrupted the economy during his presidency, Harding worked hard to come up with a solution. However, his brilliant compromise was sabotaged by a member of Harding's own cabinet, and the administration ended the strike with force, injuring many of the workers.

Harding does deserve some praise for his ability to work with Congress in bringing normalcy back to the American economy after the war was over. Wartime measures put in place over the economy during World War I caused some mayhem. A high wartime tax, price controls, rationing, and crippled European markets caused high inflation and economic panic at home.

Harding, along with Democrats and Republicans in the House, reduced taxes and got rid of many of the wartime regulations. By 1921, normalcy was restored to the economy, taxes were at a fair level, and business was allowed to operate as it had before the war, thus ending the mini-depression.

Furthermore, Harding did create some important programs despite their initial abuses and exploitation such as the Veterans Bureau. Even more importantly he argued for disarmament at a worldwide conference in Washington, in order to avert another world war. But often Harding was not really in charge of things. His friends and the Republican Party controlled him, which led to the loss of his reputation. Harding's biographer, John W. Dean—yes, the John Dean from the Nixon administration—has somewhat restored Harding's reputation from being worst president to being only a failed president with a good heart. Although Harding was popular even up to his death, behind the scenes his presidency was unstable and ready to crack any day. It so happened that the scandals would not unfold until 1925 and onwards, after Harding's death.

Teapot Dome Scandal

In Wyoming, a rock formation that looked like a teapot was found to be filled with oil. Harding's secretary of the interior, Albert Fall, accepted bribes from a California oil company, allowing it to lease the Teapot Dome. He did so at incredibly low rates and without allowing competitive bids.

The scandal was only revealed after Harding's death, and until the Watergate scandal of the 1970s was regarded as one of the most sensational in presidential history. Secretary Fall was imprisoned later in the 1920s, and Harding's administration was seen as untrustworthy and corrupt. Despite Harding having no involvement in scandal, he was criticized for not having enough oversight over his cabinet to keep them in line.

Death

After serving only two years, Harding died in 1923 in San Francisco, on a whistle-stop tour around the United States. As Harding's wife would not allow an autopsy, doctors were uncertain about his cause of death. He'd been known to have a weak heart and the whistle-stop tour had been strenuous.

Calvin Coolidge
(1923-1929)

"The chief business of the American people is business."

Introduction

John Calvin Coolidge was born on July 4, 1872 (the only president born on Independence Day) in Plymouth Notch, Vermont. Coolidge's father owned a general store attached to their house but young Calvin did not follow in his father's footsteps with business. Instead, at six—when his grandfather gave him a farm—he learned how to cultivate the land. His mother died when he was twelve and Coolidge was greatly affected by that tragedy. Calvin left home for school at thirteen. His school was far from home and his father, who was alone without his wife, traveled to see Coolidge every week.

Coolidge attended Amherst College in 1890 and graduated cum laude. After college, Coolidge moved to Northampton, Massachusetts, and studied law while working as a clerk. He was admitted to the bar in 1897 and setup his own law office. He also became a Republican and jumped into politics, winning election to the city council.

In 1905 Coolidge married Grace Anna Goodhue, a teacher at a school for the deaf. From 1905 to 1912 Coolidge won and held an array of positions in Massachusetts. He won a seat in the state senate, where he made many friends and became senate president in 1914. He was elected lieutenant governor of Massachusetts in 1915 and was reelected for two subsequent 1-year terms. He then ran for governor and won.

Coolidge made his name as governor of Massachusetts. During his tenure the police setup a strike to protest a ban on forming a union. When police officers did not appear for work, and crime began to rise throughout the state Coolidge brought in the militia and ended the strike, affirming his belief that no one had a right to "strike against the public safety." While Coolidge became known for his conservatism, he was a progressive governor. He passed a law requiring landlords to give 30 days' notice before evicting tenants. He prevented huge rent increases, gave a bonus to veterans, and shortened the work week for women and children, stating: "We must humanize the industry, or the system will break down." His successful tenure as governor made him a safe choice for the vice presidency in 1920. With Harding's sudden death in 1923, Coolidge became president.

Restoring confidence

Called the "Puritan in Babylon" by historian William Allen White, Calvin Coolidge had incorruptible integrity. Coolidge entered the White House amidst a series of exploding scandals relating to the Harding administration. However, the scandals did not seem to effect Coolidge's reputation or approval. In fact, Coolidge quickly put an end to much of the cabinet corruption that Harding had presided over and effectively cleaned up the White House. During 1924, when Democrats accused him of being part of the Harding scandals, Coolidge turned their accusations to his advantage and quickly cleared his name, making him even more popular.

Rocking chair and Laissez-faire

Coolidge presided over a time of incredible economic growth. Despite the slow-paced White House of the man the people referred to as "Silent Cal," the world around him was changing quickly. Urbanization spread across the United States as Americans moved into cities, and technological advances allowed for easier living for Americans. During

this immense explosion of economic growth Coolidge was not an active president. His view of government was that it should be small and not hinder business in any way. "The business of America is business," said Coolidge in an address to the American people. And so Coolidge— who happily spent his time in White House looking at D.C. from his rocking chair on the porch— followed an economic policy of laissez-faire capitalism while the economy boomed.

Many historians and economists continue to debate whether Coolidge's endorsement of laissez-faire economics contributed to the coming of the Great Depression. Coolidge typically appointed do-nothing regulators to regulatory positions. Moreover, Coolidge would often address Wall Street and report strong economic news—even when the economic news was all but catastrophic—which helped spur the Wall Street bubble. When brokers' loans reached four billion dollars in 1928, Coolidge reported that the loans were not too high and were, in fact, healthy. Even in 1928, there were plenty of people, including business editor H. Parker Willis, who knew that four billion in brokers' loans was not healthy and was, in fact, excessive. Some historians and economists have even suggested that when Coolidge declined to run for his own full term in 1928, it was because he felt a depression was coming due to the unhealthy state of the stock market. However, this has never been proven conclusively.

Foreign affairs, isolationism, and immigration

Coolidge's presidency is most remembered for its isolationism in comparison with the interventionist progressive administrations that preceded him. However, Coolidge did have two talented men in charge of the diplomacy of his administration, Charles G. Dawes and Frank B. Kellogg—both winners of the Nobel Peace Prize. Dawes was responsible for the Dawes Act of 1924, which sought to bring stability to Germany by fixing the hyperinflation that existed there. The massive inflation occurred because Germany was forced to pay war debts after World War I. While the Dawes plan still required Germany to repay their debts, the payments were staggered and tied to the American economy. But while temporary stability was brought to Germany, their economy became more entangled with the American and British economies. So, when the U.S. economy crashed in 1929, the German economy crashed as well. Dawes' efforts were commendable though, and his plan won him the Nobel Prize in 1925. Secretary of State Kellogg received his Nobel Prize for the 1928 Kellogg-Briand Pact, calling on multiple nations to sign an agreement to refrain from using war to resolve disputes. Coolidge also gave Japan dominance over the Pacific—an action that would be problematic at the onset of the Second World War—and rejected the progressive interventionism of past administrations.

There was one exception: Coolidge did intervene when a revolution broke out in Nicaragua in 1926. The government of Nicaragua called for assistance from the United States to fight off rebels and hold onto their government. The United States sent thousands of Marines to occupy Nicaragua, where they stayed until 1933.

Herbert Hoover
(1929-1933)

"Peace is not made at the council table or by treaties, but in the hearts of men."

Introduction

Herbert Hoover was born in Iowa on August 10, 1874. He had a difficult early childhood, losing both of his parents by the time he turned eight. Orphaned, Hoover had to move in with some of his Quaker family members in Oregon. He received his education at Newberg College, founded by his Quaker uncle. He received an exemplary education and decided to start working by fifteen.

He joined his uncle's real-estate business in Salem, Oregon, and took classes at a business college to learn more mathematics. During this time Hoover became acquainted with engineers and realized his calling in life. He took the entrance exams to attend Stanford —a leading school in engineering—and was allowed entry.

Hoover worked his way through college and became active in college politics, but he stayed independent of fraternities. He graduated in 1895; his diploma at the time was one of his only real possessions. Leaving school, Hoover was broke and couldn't find a job in engineering. However, he took a non-engineering job in Nevada City, saved some money, and moved to San Francisco, where his brother was working and supporting their sister. In San Francisco, Hoover began working his way up the job ladder, initially taking a position as a typist at an engineering company and eventually getting to the engineering level.

Over the next five years Hoover became a very wealthy and reputable engineer. He became a part-owner in a British engineering company that mined for gold, and he then took a job with the Chinese government. He had married his fellow Stanford student Lou Henry before he left the U.S. in 1899 and took her with him. During the Boxer Rebellion, Hoover built barricades and food supplies. After working in China, Hoover traveled the world, working wherever his skills were needed. He went to almost every continent and began writing a textbook on mining.

When World War I broke out, Hoover turned his engineering talents and knowledge to the humanitarian side of life. He was the chairman of the Commission for Relief in Belgium and helped feed the Dutch when Holland was occupied by Germany. Additionally, Hoover was in charge of a committee in London that helped 100,000 stranded Americans get back into the United States after the war. In 1917, when President Wilson declared war on Germany, Hoover was appointed by Wilson as the United States Food Administrator. Hoover stated that "Food will win the war," and he began to stabilize food prices, instate an excess-profits tax, and organize rationing.

In 1918, just as the war was coming to an end, Hoover became chairman of the Allied Food Council and dealt with the distribution of millions of tons of food in Europe. Hoover was responsible for helping to feed countless starving Europeans and rebuilding parts of war-torn Europe. Hoover was also indifferent to the politics of the time. He gave relief to starving Germans and Russians and stated to those who opposed him: "Twenty million people are starving. Whatever their politics they shall be fed!" He was a national hero when he returned to the United States and became known as one of the greatest humanitarians in history.

Even though Hoover was a Republican who had supported the progressive Theodore Roosevelt in 1912, he also supported Warren Harding in 1920 despite being in favor of the League of Nations which Harding opposed. After Harding's victory, Hoover became his Secretary of Commerce. He was extremely successful in that role and helped put an end to child labor, reduce the workday from twelve hours to eight, and consistently supported programs to develop dams. All in all, he made the Commerce department more efficient. In 1928, when

Coolidge decided not run for another term, Hoover asked him if he could seek the nomination. Coolidge responded by saying, "Why not?" Thus Hoover entered the arena of presidential politics.

Only following tradition

Misfortune haunted Hoover early. Before his first year as president was over the stock market crashed, marking the beginning of the Great Depression. Most people already familiar with Hoover have probably read that he was an abject failure. However we must remember that he stepped into the presidency only months before the depression began. Moreover, the idea that he was a "do-nothing" is not quite accurate. He did attempt to alleviate the economic tragedy of his time. However he was not comfortable with changing the traditional role of the president which Franklin Roosevelt would radically change in the following years.

Most historians criticize Hoover for not doing enough while president; that he was too conservative despite enacting early New Deal programs. There is also the complaint that Hoover did not lead the country in its time of crisis, while Franklin Roosevelt provided the necessary guidance and support that suffering Americans required. The early Hoover new deal programs such as homeless relief initiatives were created to combat the loss of housing caused by the depression. However the horrid conditions of the housing led to them being dubbed as "Hoovervilles," solidifying the belief that Hoover's policies were ineffective at combating the big problem of the depression.

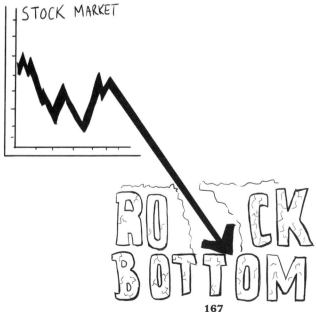

The final nail in the Hoover presidency's coffin was the Bonus Army march. Hoover vetoed a bonus bill and denied veterans of the world war any benefits. In response, the veterans camped outside the White House in protest.

Hoover called on General Douglas MacArthur to resolve the situation. MacArthur marched tanks onto the White House lawn and burned the tents of the veterans while driving them away, screaming. Hoover was outraged by MacArthur's behavior, and the veterans never forgave Hoover for MacArthur's foolhardy mistake.

Tragic mistake

Before leaving office, Hoover signed the Smoot-Hawley Tariff designed to protect industry from the Great Depression; but it was not well thought out. The tariff raised rates on more than 20,000 imports to the highest in American history and effectively shipped the depression overseas while managing to make the situation even direr inside the United States. Ultimately Herbert Hoover was badly beaten by Franklin Roosevelt in the 1932 election.

Franklin Delano Roosevelt
(1933-1945)

"The only thing we have to fear is fear itself."

Franklin Delano Roosevelt was born in Hyde Park, New York on January 30, 1882, the only child of James Roosevelt and Sara Delano Roosevelt. His early childhood education was furnished by his parents, governesses and tutors. He attended Groton, an Episcopalian preparatory school in Massachusetts from 1896 to 1900. He entered Harvard University in 1900.

Like his cousin Theodore, Roosevelt majored in history and graduated in three years, spending an extra year attending a graduate program. During his time at Harvard, Roosevelt courted a distant cousin, Eleanor Roosevelt, whom he married in 1905. During his presidency she would permanently alter the role of first lady, making speeches and public appearances in his stead and actively participating in politics. Once again, following in Theodore's footsteps, Franklin attended Columbia Law School and left after affirming his disinterest with legal studies. However he learned what was necessary to pass the bar and did so in 1907.

Franklin attempted to follow Theodore's political path but diverged from his cousin when, at twenty-eight years old, he became an active member of the Democratic Party instead of the Republican Party. However, Roosevelt became the same reformer reminded politician as Theodore. He also became a crusader for good government in New York, where corruption was rampant among Tammany Hall politicians. After battling Tammany Hall and having made a name for himself, President Woodrow Wilson appointed him assistant secretary of the navy. He served in that position throughout the First World War, becoming a loyal Wilsonian, and then received the vice presidential nomination at the Democratic convention in 1920. He defended the League of Nations— a position that guaranteed him defeat.

In 1921, on vacation in Canada, Roosevelt contracted polio, which permanently paralyzed his legs. Although he would never walk again without support, Roosevelt began using crutches and learning other techniques to lift himself from his wheelchair and was determined to continue his life and his career in politics. In 1924 Roosevelt went to the Democratic convention, where he showcased his ability and strength, lifting himself from his wheelchair to nominate Al Smith. Smith did not get the nomination in 1924, but did receive it in 1928; and Roosevelt supported him. It was also in 1928 that Roosevelt became governor of New York, where he passed a series of social reforms that resembled parts of the New Deal, e. g., farm relief and a program that worked somewhat like social security. His popularity as governor, his history of fighting against corruption, and his ability to bridge the gap between North and South in the Democratic Party secured him nomination in 1932, when he went on to win the presidency.

New Deal and a new presidency

Relief, Recovery, and Reform. Those were the "three Rs" that were the foundation for the New Deal, a domestic program enacted by Franklin Roosevelt to alleviate the Great Depression: Relief for starving farmers and the hungry in cities, recovery for closed businesses and industry, and reform for the toxic stock market, banking system, and unhealthy farming techniques that plunged the nation into the depression.

The New Deal was a massive program and required a change in the philosophy of American government. Until Roosevelt, the presidency had limited power, the president often being subservient to the House. What FDR accomplished with the New Deal would change the way the United States government would operate. In healthcare this is called a scope of practice, and Roosevelt was rewriting it. He used the radio to appeal straight to his voters with fireside chats, where he explained policy and projected a sense of strong leadership. He harnessed executive power when the House was unconvinced and took to a more liberal interpretation of the powers and limits of government. Roosevelt was so effective however that the majority of Americans went along with the new system. The greatest achievements of the New Deal reached all types of people and diverse economic sectors in the United States:

AAA

Farmers all over the country had been overproducing crops and keeping too much livestock. The old idea of "grow more and make more money" had proven to be the cause of chaos in food pricing, and so the Roosevelt administration passed the Agricultural Readjustment Act. The act gave subsidies to farmers if they reduced their crop surplus and slaughtered extra livestock.

Rural Electrification

In 1935 Roosevelt passed another bill, the Rural Electrification Act, which attempted to put people back to work and also expand infrastructure and development in the country. The act electrified huge sectors of the country—especially the South, where public works projects had been neglected since the end of Reconstruction— by constructing telephone poles, power lines, and more.

CCC

The Civilian Conservation Core was another work program of the New Deal. The goal was to bring young men back into the work force through outdoor labor. The CCC planted 3 billion trees, hundreds of parks, and provided for thousands of jobs. It was one of the most popular of the New Deal programs.

Social Security

The Social Security Act provided assistance to retirees, the disabled, and dependent mothers. It was enacted in 1935 and is one of the most significant and enduring government programs.

WPA

The Works Progress Administration was the largest of the New Deal programs to deal with employment. The project employed over 8 million Americans from 1935 to 1943 and often had over 3 million workers at once.

Blue Eagle, the PWA, and the Wagner Act

The Blue Eagle was the symbol of the National Recovery Administration (NRA) which was created in June of 1933 to reform labor in order to stimulate the economy and combat the Depression... The NRA was to develop codes for each industry by which that industry would pledge to shorter hours, higher wages, better trade practices and better labor relations.

The Public Works Administration—a part of the National Industrial Recovery Act (NIRA)—was setup in 1933 and aimed to get the country back to work. The PWA built enormous public works projects and dams, such as the Grand Coulee Dam, which helped make the Northwest more habitable by giving the region access to electricity. It was a powerhouse in building airplanes for the war effort later in Roosevelt's presidency.

However the program, along with the NRA, was ruled unconstitutional in 1935. The NRA had essentially given Roosevelt the power to regulate industry and set guidelines at will and this was seen as an overreach in federal power.

In 1935, the same year the NRA was ruled unconstitutional, Roosevelt passed the Wagner Act, which guaranteed workers the right to collectively bargain and form trade unions. Along with the Wagner Act were also a series of labor laws that provided for a safer work place and shorter work day.

Banking and Gold

A large part of the Great Depression was caused by runs on banks. When the economy collapsed, everyone seemed to run to their banks and demand their money. However, with so many going to the banks at once to withdraw their savings, the money dried up, as the banks had heavily invested it in the stock market, where it was lost in the crash of 1929. People who had worked their entire lives and saved their money conservatively now found themselves in poverty, as the banks had recklessly spent their money. Americans were also not happy with the fact that the banks also had been attempting to repossess farms when farmers couldn't pay their mortgages. Groups of farmers with weapons quickly began to defend themselves against repossession. Roosevelt realized the seriousness of the banking crisis and its effect on the economy. The first reform established was the FDIC (Federal

Deposit Insurance Corporation), which guaranteed a person's savings up to $2,500. That limit has increased over the years to a present day cap of $250,000. The second was the passage of the Glass-Steagall Act, which separated investment and commercial banking in order to keep banks from spending all their clients' deposits and from falling into a credit crunch.

In a display of the power of executive action, FDR changed the way our economy functioned via modifying the gold standard. The depression caused people to hoard gold, and as the United States was still on the gold standard, this slowed down economic growth considerably. Roosevelt signed an executive order that required people to sell the bulk of their gold back to the government—save for a small amount and exempting jewelers and collectors—which stabilized gold pricing. It was one of Roosevelt's more controversial and less popular acts, however it coincided in the same year, 1933, with his repeal of prohibition, which allowed the sale of alcohol once again, an overwhelmingly popular piece of legislation.

Court packing and the dip back into recession

In 1937 Roosevelt's second term began with turmoil. Roosevelt was tired of dealing with a Court that was ruling his legislation unconstitutional. In his biggest political misstep, Roosevelt attempted to pack the Supreme Court by adding more members —his appointees, of course. In theory this would have given the Court an edge in Roosevelt's favor. The public, however, did not support his court packing; it was seen as an unacceptable overreach of power.

Roosevelt had decided to focus on balancing the budget and paying for his New Deal programs. He stopped creating programs and spending at the rate of his first term; and to make matters worse, a dip in recession followed that did not end until 1938.

War brewing in Europe and Roosevelt's neutrality

The curse of all Democratic presidencies seems to be that of foreign affairs. Wilson had World War I, Truman would have to deal with Korea, Johnson with Vietnam, and so on. FDR would have to face the Second World War, one of the single most devastating events in human history.

During Roosevelt's second term he was publically in favor of neutrality during the early stages of the spread of Nazism and the upsurge of European tensions. However, by 1938 Roosevelt was pushing for armament support. The majority of the country was isolationist, including notable people such as Charles Lindbergh—who held immense influence on public opinion. Roosevelt himself was concerned about the growing troubles in Europe, but given the political climate, found it impossible to voice them. He began a slow attempt at changing public opinion.

Roosevelt first began what would become his legendary relationship with British Prime Minister Winston Churchill in 1940, when they met onboard ship. Roosevelt and Churchill had met before but had not gotten along so well. However their new relationship, between president and prime minister, was warm and friendly. Churchill profoundly influenced Roosevelt's eagerness to assist the Allies in wartime.

Roosevelt took his first steps toward intervention in 1941, supplying the Allies with weapons and materials under the Lend-Lease Act. While Roosevelt was trying to turn public opinion to his side, the Japanese attacked Pearl Harbor on December 7, 1941, during his third term. The sneak attack caused Americans to rally behind the president as he asked the Congress to declare war on Japan the following day. Three days later Germany declared war against the United States on December 11, guarantying the silence of isolationists and propelling the United States into World War II, ending the Great Depression but beginning the largest war effort in history. Moreover, Pearl Harbor resulted in the internment of American Japanese citizens on the West Coast. To this day, the action taken by the government has been seen as an abuse of human rights and as the dark side of the war effort. However, many suggest that had the Japanese not been secretly interned violent race riots might have broken out and resulted in the deaths of many Japanese.

World War II, Roosevelt and the generals

With America's entry into World War II, Roosevelt began assembling a strategy to beat Nazi Germany and Imperial Japan. Roosevelt wisely chose such first-rate generals as Dwight D. Eisenhower, George Patton, and Omar Bradley for the European front, and Douglas A. MacArthur for the pacific. Roosevelt's Herculean task in presiding over the war was aided by the combined efforts of U.S., Canadian, and Allied forces, who implemented the Normandy invasion in France, known as D-Day, on June 6, 1944. The Allied forces recaptured Nazi-controlled Europe, seized Berlin in April 1945, and eventually won the war.

The Big Three—Tehran and Yalta

President Roosevelt, Prime Minister Churchill, and Soviet Premier Joseph Stalin—known collectively as "The Big Three"—met at numerous conferences, the most famous being Tehran (1943) and Yalta (1945). The politics of these conferences were personal, as Roosevelt played mediator between Churchill and Stalin, who were often at odds. Roosevelt was also able to maintain a pragmatic relationship with Joseph Stalin, who seemed, when it came to Americans, only to trust Roosevelt and his closest advisor, Harry Hopkins. The Tehran conference resulted in agreements pertaining to the future of Turkey. Yalta was the more important conference though and was a discussion of what to do about the postwar world. Roosevelt attended a good deal of the conference but returned to the United States in poor condition. By 1945 his health had deteriorated immensely and during an address to Congress, Roosevelt was unable to stand for the first time—he usually had leg supports help him to do so—and said, "I hope that you will pardon me for this unusual posture of sitting down during the presentation of what I want to say, but... it makes it a lot easier for me not to have to carry about ten pounds of steel around on the bottom of my legs."

Death

Roosevelt went to Warm Springs, Georgia, for his health. While there, as his portrait was being painted, Roosevelt suffered a massive stroke and died on April 12, 1945, the first year of his fourth term—the only president to ever serve more than two terms. His body was returned to Washington in a funeral train car that was greeted by millions of Americans, a reception of mourning and respect unparalleled since Lincoln's death. While there was more work to accomplish in the world, the depression was over, and World War II was nearing its end.

Historians and the public alike continue to rank Roosevelt with Washington and Lincoln as one of the great presidents. Roosevelt's Social Security programs and handling of the war effort have secured his legacy as one of the most significant leaders of the twentieth century. While many far right-wing institutions criticize Roosevelt's New Deal policy for prolonging - the Great Depression, many see Roosevelt's policy and leadership skills as being a force that saved capitalism by restoring the American people's faith in a system that had seemed to fail in the Panic of 1929. He did not give in to the more socialist voices of the time and believed in the American system and the capitalism that had built the American empire.

Harry S. Truman
(1945-1953)

"I never did give anybody hell. I just told the truth and they thought it was hell."

Introduction

Harry S. Truman was born in Lamar, Missouri, on May 8, 1884. By age six, Truman moved with his family to Independence, Missouri, which became his lifelong home. Truman's father was a mule-trader, and the Truman's lived modestly. Harry went to a tiny school at the age of eight, receiving the bulk of his learning independently. He was truly an autodidact and taught himself a vast array of things through reading history, biography, the Bible, and anything else he could get his hands on. His poor eyesight and his thick eyeglass lenses didn't help him make many friends at the small school.

After graduating from the local high school, Truman became a page at the Democratic convention in 1900, where he witnessed the oratory of William Jennings Bryan. From 1902 to 1905 Truman supported his family, working a series of jobs; the best and most profitable being that of a bank clerk. Truman enjoyed clerking—it made very good money—but he decided to obey his father when asked to come work on the family farm.

From 1906 until his father's death in 1914, Harry worked diligently on the farm and made it quite profitable. Despite some broken bones and bruises, he proved himself an able farmer. After his father died, Truman took over his job as overseer in Jackson County, which exposed him to the world of machine politics. Independence was run by Tom Pendergast, a machine Democrat who ruled all things political, and Truman remained loyal to him. However, Truman was always an honest man, and no one ever accused him of corruption or of lying for Pendergast. His small-town political career was interrupted by the First World War. Before leaving for France in 1918, he proposed to Elizabeth "Bess" Wallace, whom he had known since childhood. In France, Truman led a battalion and saw a great deal of combat. He proudly stated that he never lost a single man in the First World War.

In 1922, after he returned home and moved into his mother-in-law's house, Pendergast supported Truman to becoming a judge for the county that held Independence. Truman lost his reelection bid in 1924 due to opposition from the KKK, as he was suspected of being Jewish—having a relative named Solomon—despite not being Jewish at all. In 1926 he was able, with Pendergast's help, to claim a political seat and became the judge of Jackson County.

In 1934, as Pendergast was having a tough time dealing with unifying his Democrats to fill a Missouri Senate seat, he chose Truman as a compromise candidate. Truman won the election and went from a state politician to a U.S. Senator. Truman supported all of Franklin Roosevelt's programs, proving himself to be savvy enough for Washington politics despite some initial doubts. Before Truman's reelection in 1940, Pendergast was brought down. Everyone believed that Truman and the rest of the Missouri Democrats would fall with him, but Truman took to the streets in his home state, winning the people to his side and winning reelection without Pendergast.

Truman made his name during his second Senate term. When the United States entered World War II, Truman shined light on the massive amount of corruption in the armaments industry. He was chairman on the Military Affairs Committee—which people soon began to refer to as the Truman Committee—and saved the taxpayers over $15 billion by investigating cases of fraud and corruption. His diligence made him a well-known figure and sparked Roosevelt's interest in having him as vice president. Truman initially wanted to turn the president down but realized very quickly that FDR usually got what he wanted. Truman became vice president in 1944, after FDR won his fourth term; and in 1945, after Roosevelt passed away, Truman became president. Roosevelt had not prepared him to take over the presidency, but FDR's death put Truman in charge of the largest war the world had ever seen. When Truman asked Eleanor Roosevelt if there was anything he could do for her when Franklin died, she said, "Is there anything we can do to help you? You're the one in trouble now."

Big shoes to fill

Franklin Roosevelt, one of the titans among American presidents, cast a massive shadow with his immense achievements during his time in office. Harry Truman, the small straight-talking Missourian, was thrown straight into the deep pool of foreign and domestic policy. 1945 was going to be sink or swim for the new president and, boy, did Truman swim.

The Potsdam conference of July 1945, held in a German suburb, would be Truman's first true international experience as president. The three nations in attendance were the United States, Great Britain, and the Soviet Union. The heads of state representing those nations were: Harry Truman for the United States, Winston Churchill and later Clement Atlee (after the Conservative party lost to Labor in the 1945 election) for Great Britain; and Joseph Stalin for Soviet Russia.

Truman gives them hell for the first time

Stalin's relationship with Roosevelt had become cordial. However, the new president had little patience with Stalin and did not give him much leeway due to Truman's high skepticism and distaste of communism. As an admirer of Jefferson and even Andrew Jackson, the mere thought of working with a tyrant was distasteful to Truman. His hostility towards communism would define his foreign policy in years to come. Despite the coldness between Truman and Stalin the conference was still a success. It reaffirmed many of the agreements made during the prior Yalta conference and set the stage for the next fifty years of foreign policy—mostly because of the division of territory that was to be agreed upon.

Main agreements of the Potsdam Conference

- Germany was to be split into four zones, represented by the U.S., England, France, and Soviet Russia
- Germany would be demilitarized in each zone
- Germany's borders would be reduced
- Germany could not maintain a military
- The Allies would lay out the terms for Japanese surrender

Decision of an era

Although soon after Roosevelt's death there was peace in Europe, the war continued in the Pacific. Truman was faced with a one of history's most difficult decisions. Although he had just called for celebration of Victory in Europe, the Allies had laid out the terms for a Japanese surrender during the Potsdam conference, Truman was faced with either sending American soldiers to certain death in a Japanese invasion or use nuclear weapons to save Americans and force a quick end to the war. Moreover, a quick end to the war in the Pacific would keep Stalin from intervening in the fighting.

Ultimately, Truman decided to use an atomic bomb on August 6, 1945. After the first bomb, "Little Boy," was dropped on Hiroshima despite the Japanese emperor's wish to surrender; but his generals objected. Truman warned the use of another atomic bomb and again called for Japanese surrender—they refused.

On August 9, 1945, the "Fat Man" was dropped on Nagasaki. At this point, nearly 90,000 Japanese had been killed by the bombs, but it took six days for the Japanese to surrender. The United States continued to threaten more bombs, even though there were no others, scaring the Japanese into surrender on August 15, 1945. On September 2, the official Instrument of Surrender was signed, officially ending World War II.

Starting over in America

After the war was over, Truman hoped to evade the economic woes that Wilson had to deal with during the Panic of 1919 after The First World War with postwar hyperinflation. So he began the demilitarization of the economy and the deregulation of economic controls.

The pressing issue would become inflation. The government had set wages and controlled industry during World War II, and with the end of the war and the return of the armed forces, the economy went into serious decline. Massive strikes by coal and railroad workers took place in 1946. Over 600,000 workers demanding wage increases and the right to strike were rallying against the effort in the House to rid them of their right to strike. Truman decided that he had to act, not wanting to risk the economy falling into even further economic chaos.

Truman threatened to draft the strikers into the army and even to march soldiers to mine the coal if the workers wouldn't. Truman—although sympathizing with the workers—could see that a wage increase would not be effective against combating inflation, Ultimately he did seize the mines and put them under the Department of the Interior until it was declared unconstitutional. His threat of drafting the workers brought them back to work, ending the strike.

However every action has an effect. With workers largely against the administration, Republicans obtained a landslide victory in the House of Representatives in the 1948 midterms. Politicians like Richard Nixon and Joseph McCarthy won elections on the basis of anti-Communist and anti-Truman stances. The Republican House went on to pass the 1947 Taft-Hartley Act over Truman's veto which enraged him. However, Truman used the act numerous times as President.

Marshall Plan

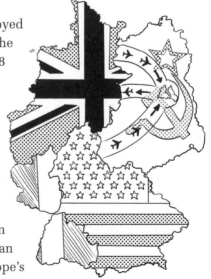

The Second World War had destroyed much of Europe, more so than the Frist World War; and in 1948 Truman's Secretary of State George Marshall, alongside George F. Kennan, the architect of much of the cold war policy, devised a plan to help rebuild Europe.

The Marshall Plan was a series of large loans given to European states that would help them rebuild. The focus was on stimulating and rebuilding European industry and improving Europe's economy. The United States loaned over $25 billion and the positive effects of the Marshall Plan could be seen within a few years, and between 1948 and1952 Europe saw its highest period of growth in history. Additionally, alliances between the United States and Europe were strengthened. The North Atlantic Treaty Organization (NATO) was formed on April 11, 1949, the treaty signed whereby member states across the North Atlantic and Europe "agree to mutual defense in response to an attack by any external party." This alliance made many nations more reluctant to succumb to communism.

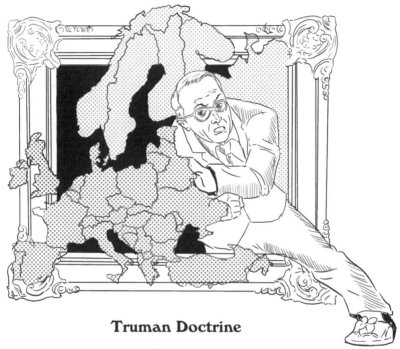

Truman Doctrine

Marking a clear beginning to the cold war, the Truman Doctrine was a declaration that the United States would support any other free nation to resist communism. George F. Kennan, devised the plan of containment that intended to keep all existing democracies free, thus isolating communism to those nations already under Communist rule.

Truman was able to get the House of Representatives to go along with his doctrine, and $400 million in aid was sent to Greece and Turkey. In addition, Greece and Turkey eventually joined NATO—a newly formed alliance of western nations that formed after the war— and were able to suppress the communists in their civil wars saving them from communist rule. The new realities of cold war politics also meant that some government organizations had to be restructured. Truman passed the National Security Reorganization Act of 1949, merging the Departments of the Navy and War into the single Department of Defense. The act also created the Central Intelligence Agency (CIA).

Truman gained a significant amount of fame and respect from the Marshall Plan, but certainly not from Stalin, who was outraged that the Allies were going to forgive Germany's war reparation payment. Stalin— believing that the Americans were being too lenient and thus allowing for the possibility of a Fourth Reich to rise—decided to seize Berlin so the Allies would not gain a stronghold in Germany. Berlin, at this point centered in East Soviet Germany, was divided between the free West and the Soviet-controlled East. The Soviet blockade cut off all railway connection to West Berlin, as Stalin planned to starve out West Berlin and take over when it weakened.

Truman had to act quickly. His advisors proposed the idea of airdropping supplies. The chance of success was slim, but Truman decided that the fall of Berlin would shift the entire balance between the free West and the Communist East.

The risky airlift began in 1948, as 1,500 planes flew over Berlin a day, dropping 4,500 tons of supplies. What the Russians had believed would be a useless gesture by the United States turned out to be one of the most successful foreign policy operations in American history. Within a year ground access was returned for the Allies, and the airlift ended—not one airplane lost in the operation. After the airlift, the Soviets formed the German Communist state that would rule of the East side of Germany until the end of the cold war. While the Allies still held onto Wes Berlin, East Germany was a full-fledged Communist state.

Truman's foreign policy grew even more complicated when the Middle East came into play. Truman had the opportunity to recognize the state of Israel. Secretary of State George Marshall was opposed, telling Truman, "I will not vote for you if you do this"; and Secretary of Defense James Forrestal told Truman that upsetting the Arabs by recognizing Israel might give the United States a problem obtaining oil from the Middle East. Truman made it clear that he was not concerned about oil, but with doing the right thing.

A fair deal for all Americans

Truman fought for a 'Fair Deal,' which became a theme throughout his presidency. The Fair Deal, harking back to Theodore Roosevelt's Square Deal and FDR's New Deal, called for a creation of a single-payer healthcare system, expansion of Social Security, wage increases, strengthening of workers' rights, and to the surprise of some, desegregation of the military.

Truman was able to expand Social Security programs, wage increases, and more investment in public housing; but was unable to get the single-payer healthcare system passed. Nevertheless, desegregation is one of the biggest accomplishments of his quest for fairness. In 1948, Truman issued an executive order that desegregated the military. Shortly after, in front of the Lincoln Memorial, Truman gave a speech in favor of civil rights for African Americans.

Election of 1948

No one in the United States could have predicted that Harry Truman would win in 1948. The idea that he could even get 30% of the vote seemed preposterous. Very few presidents up for reelection have ever faced political challenges that Truman dealt with in 1948. Two members of his party defected and ran campaigns against him. Henry Wallace—

FDR's vice president—left the Democratic Party, calling Truman too conservative. Wallace, ran as a progressive. Strom Thurmond left the Democratic Party and ran as a Dixiecrat because he found Truman too sympathetic to civil rights. To make matters worse, popular Republican Tom Dewey—a man who had made a strong showing against Roosevelt in 1944—was running against Truman.

What exactly happened at the Democratic convention of 1948 was uncontrolled splintering. Desegregation was wildly unpopular with southerners, and Minnesota Democrat Hubert Humphrey's convention speech comparing Truman's desegregation of the military to a "Second Emancipation Proclamation"only provoked Thurmond to walk out.

Truman was determined to win in 1948, despite the odds, and he took his fight right to the people. He launched a whistle-stop tour around the country, traveling to every state in the Union, delivering over seventy-one off-the-cuff speeches. Thousands of Americans gathered at every train stop in the country to see the president "Give 'em Hell." Truman became fearless in the crowds as well, often listening to people shout at him and giving every individual a response. He not only laid out a plan for the future, but defended his first-term policies to the people.

So even with Truman winning over the hearts of the public, why did pollsters guarantee his defeat? The reason is that pollsters were using telephones to sample their information and numbers, and as telephones were still quite expensive and owned by predominantly wealthier Republicans, they called more Republicans than Democrats. Despite the *Chicago Daily Tribune* report "Dewey Defeats Truman," Harry Truman won the 1948 election.

Korean War

Korea had been divided along the 38th parallel across the three-mile-wide Demilitarized Zone (DMZ) after the war in the Pacific had ended. NATO and the west controlled the Republic of South Korea, and North Korea was controlled by China and backed by the Soviet Union.

Kim Il Sung, the leader of Communist North Korea, marched his army into South Korea in June 1950, using force to take over the South and reunite the peninsula. By September, he controlled almost all of South Korea.

Truman took swift action to intervene. North Korea was spreading its influence over South Korea, in direct violation of Truman's doctrine

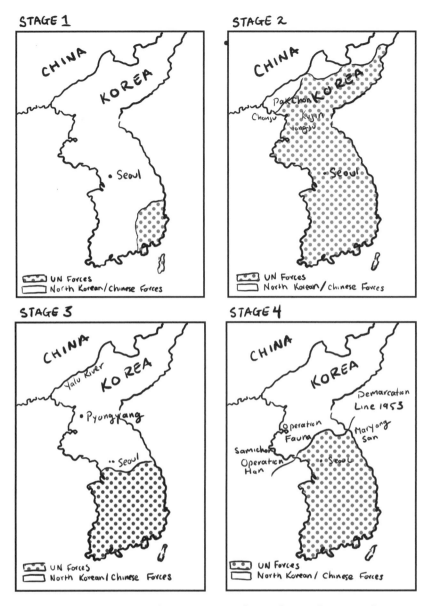

STAGE 1

CHINA
KOREA
• Seoul

UN Forces
North Korean/Chinese Forces

STAGE 2

CHINA
KOREA
Pakchon
Chonju
Kujin
Yongju
• Seoul

UN Forces
North Korean/Chinese Forces

STAGE 3

CHINA
Yalu River
KOREA
• Pyongyang
•• Seoul

UN Forces
North Korean/Chinese Forces

STAGE 4

CHINA
KOREA
Demarcation
Line 1953
Operation
Fauna
Maryang
San
Samichon
Operation
Han
• Seoul

UN Forces
North Korean/Chinese Forces

of containment. In 1950, the Russian ambassador to the United Nations returned home for a short conference. Truman took this opportunity for the Security Council to pass a resolution without a possible Soviet veto that enabled the United States—along with other NATO countries — to intervene in the conflict.

General Douglas MacArthur, commander of the UN forces defending Korea, managed to make up extraordinary ground during the early days of battle. By October of 1950 MacArthur had retaken all of South Korea and held the fighting at the 38th parallel.

Truman as commander in chief

The question remained of what to do about North Korea. Truman asked General MacArthur if the United States should simply hold South Korea or push into the North.

Meeting on Wake Island in the Pacific, Truman and MacArthur discussed the future of the war. MacArthur said that it would be best to invade North Korea, and that pushing over the 38th parallel into North Korea would not draw the Chinese into the war. With a stenographer in the room, MacArthur signed his name and gave his word to Truman not to invade, but he did.

In the following weeks the UN offensive began, and troops pushed over the 38th parallel. With some initial victories, the forces were stopped on the Yalu River. The Chinese entered the war, coming to aid the North Koreans with over a million troops. Thousands of American and UN forces were massacred on a retreat back to the parallel boundary. For the rest of the war, trench warfare set in, as the American and UN forces attempted to hold the line. MacArthur made public statements attacking Truman after the Yalu River conflict and refused to acknowledge his mistake in pushing over the 38th parallel, continuing to assail the president.

On April 11, 1951, Truman dismissed MacArthur for his disrespect. MacArthur's actions made him unfit for leadership, and his mistake in tactics during the Yalu River conflict was so great that he could no longer be trusted. Truman importantly reasserted his position as commander in chief, punishing the general for breaking the rules.

The public at large sympathized with MacArthur and had an especially positive response to his "Old Soldiers Never Die" speech which he presented during a joint session of Congress. Historians, like Robert Schlesinger, credit Truman with having the courage to relieve MacArthur, averting a war with China.

Back to Missouri

Harry S. Truman—frequently regarded by modern historians as one of our greatest presidents—left office with the lowest presidential approval ratings in polling history until 2008 when George W. Bush left office. He is undoubtedly one of the best examples of what's popular is not always best. By 1952 Truman had alienated everyone from labor and veterans to academics and strategists. He advocated for American workers but used the 1947 Taft-Hartley Act to break up strikes when they threatened national security. He stayed hawkish on foreign policy, defended South Korea—now a free constitutional republic—from communism, fired MacArthur, and reasserted presidential control of the military; and never passed the buck. When Truman took action, he did so because he felt it was the right thing to do, which often made him more enemies than friends.

The Truman administration had many obvious successes, but the most important by far is that it set the stage for American foreign policy in the cold war. Moreover, the Marshall Plan's rebuilding of Europe— which brought a stricken continent back to growth and stability—and the spectacular achievement of the Berlin airlift speaks for the success of Truman foreign policy. If any administration in American history proved that interventionism can have a positive effect and better a situation overseas, it was Truman's. However, Truman made two controversial decisions that are still heavily debated. The first was his recognition of Israel, which, for obvious reasons, was both praised and decried within the administration. The other controversial decision was the bombing of Japan with atomic weapons at the end of the Second World War—an action much more accepted by the generation that fought in the war and had their lives at stake in the Pacific than by subsequent generations.

Truman also became a legend as one of the last statesmen to really "fight" in an election, best illustrated by his 1948 whistle-stop tour, which would inspire future generations of Democrats. He always insisted throughout his retired life that his presidency was nothing special, and that modesty was truly the best policy. Perhaps the most important characteristic of Truman was represented by the sign on his oval office desk that said "The Buck Stops Here."

Dwight D. Eisenhower
(1953-1961)

"Every gun that is made, every warship launched, every rocket fired, signifies in the final sense a theft from those who hunger and are not fed, those who are cold and are not clothed."

Introduction

Dwight D. Eisenhower was born on October 14, 1890, in Denison, Texas; but by the time he was two his father had moved the family to Abilene, Kansas. Life was difficult for the Eisenhower's as there were many children but little money to go around so all of the Eisenhower's worked. Dwight juggled school and work, and in 1909 he graduated from high school where he became a great fan of military history.

He took a job working with his father for a year and decided that laboring for the rest of his life was not enough for him. He took entrance exams for the U.S. Naval Academy but performed so well he was accepted at the U.S. Military Academy at West Point. He was an average student there, graduated in 1915 and was then posted to Texas. There, Eisenhower met his wife Mamie Geneva Doud and married her in 1916.

When President Wilson brought the United States into the war in 1917, Eisenhower was kept in the United States to teach at military camps and to instruct soldiers how to use tanks. During the years following the war Eisenhower served in the military until he went off to the Army General Staff College in 1926. He graduated at the top of his class and hoped to rise through the ranks. When the depression hit, Eisenhower was sent to the Philippines as an assistant to General MacArthur.

After Pearl Harbor, George C. Marshall—former general and credited with the Marshall Plan—called Eisenhower to Washington to help devise strategies for World War II. He wanted Eisenhower's perspective since he had been in the Philippines operation. Eisenhower developed a strategy for the invasion of German-occupied France. The proposal impressed Marshall and caught the attention of President Franklin Roosevelt. When the time came, Roosevelt and Marshall agreed that Eisenhower would be the best choice for Supreme Allied Commander. Eisenhower had the political knowledge that many other generals lacked plus his great knowledge of military affairs. While Omar Bradley ran the day-to-day operations of the war, Eisenhower used his considerable political skills to set everything in motion, the planning of D-Day, for example. He also dealt with the massive egos of generals such as George Patton and Britain's Bernard Montgomery.

After World War II, Eisenhower was in charge of demobilization and became army chief of staff. And in 1950, President Truman put Eisenhower in charge of NATO, believing him the only man for the job. Despite previously rejecting the idea of running for president or even of declaring party affiliation, 1952 became the year that Eisenhower decided to run for the office that was simply waiting for him. Eisenhower had never voted until 1952 when he voted for himself.

Going his own way

Eisenhower placated the conservative Republicans in the 1952 election. But once he stepped into the White House, the tactical general pretty much continued Roosevelt's New Deal policies. In fact, during Eisenhower's presidency, Social Security was expanded, and top-bracket tax rates rose to the highest peacetime level in history. Moreover, Eisenhower largely supported public works projects including the interstate highway system and—after Russia launched Sputnik (the artificial Earth satellite—invested heavily in space technology and education. Eisenhower appointed Earl Warren—the vice presidential nominee who ran with Thomas Dewey in 1948 and the three-time governor of California—as chief justice to the Supreme Court. He thought that Warren would be a fairly moderate justice, but Warren quickly showed his true colors and sided with the liberals on most court decisions. The most famous decision was that of *Brown v. Board of Education* in 1954, where the Warren court banned public school segregation. This led to the infamous Little Rock incident in Arkansas, in 1957, where a group of African American children were barred from entering the public school. Eisenhower eventually had to send federal troops to quell the situation.

Eisenhower was able to accomplish this entire moderate and even borderline liberal agenda due to his high popularity with the voters, the progressive attitude in large parts of the country, and with his charm. Ike possessed a natural mastery of language with the media in terms of realpolitik. Where Truman had been a straight talker who exposed his entire thinking on any and every subject, Eisenhower harnessed the power of confusion and doublespeak to handle opposing political factions. When asked by advisers how he would deal with questions about China in 1955, he responded: "Don't worry I'll just confuse them." This tactic, although a little devious, often worked.

Ike's heavy hand in foreign affairs

Eisenhower is well known for his success with domestic policy but he was also quite active in the realm of foreign policy. Early on in his administration an Iranian nationalist movement grew that was determined to depose the existing Shah of Iran, the country's monarch. The movement was led by Mohammad Mosaddegh, who then became the prime minister after the Shah was successfully dethroned. Mosaddegh nationalized Iran's oil and cut off trade with the West.

The Truman administration had refused to take part in the CIA's proposed coup, but the Churchill Conservative government in England recruited the Eisenhower administration to overthrow the new Iranian government in 1953. Under the aegis of the CIA and the SIS (the British Intelligence Service), using bribery, assassination, and economic warfare, the Shah was returned to power with near absolute rule.

American relations with Iran soured and created Iran's long-lasting distrust of the United States with the Iranian people. (Even in 1979, they still believed the United States was actively working against them, fueling the environment that led to the eventual hostage crises of 1979.)

In 1955 the foreign policy focus shifted to Vietnam. Eisenhower recognized South Vietnam and began to give it military and economic aid. The first military advisors were sent to aid Ngo Dinh Diem, the leader of South Vietnam and his army. Then in 1959, in Cuba, revolutionary Fidel Castro seized power and overthrew Dictator Fulgenicio Batista. Castro had sought U.S. aid, but Eisenhower refused. Castro then turned to the Soviet Union for support, and Eisenhower responded by ending all trade with Cuba.

In Hungary a revolution broke out in 1956. The revolutionaries wanted to overthrow the Communist occupation. The Eisenhower administration decided not to intervene in the conflict, which drew criticism from some interventionists. However, Eisenhower's decision was largely accepted by a war-weary populace that had just gone through World War II and Korea. Ultimately the Soviets crushed the rebellion and held onto power in Hungary.

One of Eisenhower's more questionable foreign policy decisions was probably one of his last. After Egypt nationalized the Suez Canal, England and France invaded the country in 1956 to regain control of the canal. Eisenhower rejected the Europeans' request for aid and left them to struggle. This resulted in the Egyptian nationalists holding onto the canal, destroying the conservative administration of Anthony Eden in Britain, and severely diminishing Western influence on Egypt. Consequently, England refused to assist us in our struggle in Vietnam a decade later.

Second term blues

The United States was conducting covert operations during the 1950s, and one of its more common actions was the use of U-2 spy planes to gather information on the Soviets.

On May 1, 1960, a U-2 spy plane was shot down by the Soviet Union. Initially, Eisenhower claimed that a weather plane's pilot had possibly been suffering from lack of oxygen, and that the planes autopilot brought it over the Soviet Union. Nikita Khrushchev, the president, announced that the Soviets had the plane, but neglected to mention that they had the pilot—Gary Powers—alive. Eisenhower continued the weather-plane tale, but Khrushchev eventually revealed that Powers had been captured, exposing the administration's lie about the plane.

Eisenhower's foreign policy also got him and succeeding administrations into trouble. Although cautious of dealing with the European nations in what seemed like colonial ventures—such as the recapture of the Suez Canal—Eisenhower's actions in Iran and Cuba and with the U-2 incident had problematic long-term consequences. The Iranian intervention eventually led to the Hostage Crisis in 1979 during the Carter administration, Cuban foreign policy led to the Missile Crisis under Kennedy, and the U-2 incident set a terrible precedent in truth telling. Lincoln, Wilson, and Franklin Roosevelt had all misled but when the Kremlin exposed Ike's deception about the U-2 spy operation Eisenhower became the first president in a long time to be caught in an obvious lie and cover up. Eisenhower said that this was his greatest regret: "If I had to do it all over again, we would have kept our mouths shut."

John F. Kennedy
(1961-1963)

"Let us never negotiate out of fear. But let us never fear to negotiate."

Introduction

John F. Kennedy was born on May 29, 1917, in Brookline, Massachusetts. His father, Joseph P. Kennedy, Sr., was one of the wealthiest Americans alive and had served as the ambassador to London. Joseph moved his family to Bronxville—one of the most expensive parts of New York— and eventually sent John to private schools in Connecticut. Kennedy was an average student but was able to attend the London School of Economics in the summer of 1935 and study under Professor Harold Laski. However, his studies were cut short, as Kennedy became too ill to stay in London. Throughout his life he was sickly, and after World War II, suffered from major spinal problems. Kennedy tried going to Princeton in 1935 but left because of illness.

In 1936, Kennedy entered Harvard, where his father had gone to school; he was an average student for the majority of his time there.

During his last year, however, he impressed the college staff by writing an interesting thesis on Hitler and appeasement, which he eventually turned into a book called *Why England Slept.*

Kennedy then went off to Stanford Graduate School for Business. That venture too was cut short, as Kennedy signed up to become a seaman during World War II but was bound to desk duty. His father used his influence to get Kennedy command of a PT boat in the Pacific, where Kennedy became a war hero when his boat, PT-109, was destroyed by the Japanese and he led his men to safety. He led them through shark-infested waters for four hours and swam to a nearby island— using a life jacket strap clenched between his teeth to tow one of his wounded mates the entire way. Once his men were safe on the island, Kennedy swam to two other islands to find food and water as well as a way to make contact with American forces. After carving a message into a coconut shell and giving it to the island natives, Kennedy and his men were rescued. Kennedy spent some time in the hospital after being stricken by malaria and spinal problems, then returned to Massachusetts. He ran for Congress in 1943, and with the support of powerful family members and associates He won the seat served three terms in the House of Representatives.

Kennedy decided that he would go after the Senate seat held by Henry Cabot Lodge, Jr.—who would eventually run with Nixon against Kennedy in 1960—and once again got the Kennedy family power players, including his younger brother Bobby, to work on his campaign. Kennedy safely defeated Lodge and became a senator. The next year, he married Jacqueline Bouvier.

In 1956, after distinguishing himself by writing *Profiles in Courage*, Kennedy sought the vice presidential nomination when Adlai Stevenson was the democrats presidential candidate. He lost the nomination but did have an important role at the convention. JFK, as he came to be called, became better known throughout the 50s by suggesting there was a "missile-gap." between the US and the Soviets due to the previous Eisenhower administrations weakness on defense, however Kennedy was eventually proven wrong on that notion. Kennedy hid his health problems from the public, but he was chronically ill during his Senate tenure. Majority leader Lyndon Johnson even remarked, "The boy barely attends votes in the Senate." Despite all of that, Kennedy was popular. He was a war hero, had good looks, was wealthy, and he badly wanted to be president.

Great heights and rocky starts

For many people President Kennedy was an inspiration and a hero. He boldly proclaimed that the "denial of constitutional rights to some of our fellow Americans on account of race—at the ballot box and elsewhere—disturbs the national conscience." It had been a long time since a president had raised the issue of civil rights. However there was also another side to Kennedy, one that struggled with foreign policy and getting legislation passed with the House. Although he remained popular during his short time in the White House, Kennedy faced many challenges, the first major one being Cuba, followed by a long struggle with southern Democrats and civil rights bills.

To Cuba with subterfuge

In 1960, under Eisenhower, the CIA began a program to train Cuban exiles in preparation for an invasion of their homeland. The intended goal was to overthrow Fidel Castro's left-wing government and establish a democratic-republic on the island.

Kennedy, in 1961, gave the CIA the green light for the operation, known as the Bay of Pigs Invasion; but pro-Castro Cuban nationalists fought off the invaders. With this stunning victory Castro solidified his leadership of Cuba and embarrassed the United States. Moreover, Castro was permanently alienated from seeking further relations with the United States and began dealing with the Soviet Union instead, which would lead to problems later.

In 1963, Castro and Soviet Premier Nikita Khrushchev decided to join forces after U.S. provocations became overbearing. In response to the United States invasion attempt—and the U.S. Nuclear missile sites in Italy and Turkey— Khrushchev determined that the Soviet Union should build missile silos in Cuba.

After the construction of the Soviet silos was completed, an American U-2 spy plane captured photos of the missile sites. The Kennedy administration responded to these new developments by blockading Cuba and demanding that the nuclear missiles be returned to the Soviet Union and the silos dismantled.

Khrushchev responded that Kennedy's actions implied "an act of aggression propelling humankind into the abyss of a world nuclear-missile war." The two superpowers continued escalating the dispute, bringing the world close to Mutually Assured Destruction (MAD), a situation where the United States and Soviet Union would decimate each other with nuclear missiles. To make matters worse, American and Soviet ships fought each other, the former attacking and the latter defending the blockade; and the Soviets even shot down a U-2 spy plane.

Kennedy and Khrushchev were able to come to an agreement about the nuclear weapons through United Nations mediation. The Soviets would withdraw their weaponry from Cuba, and in turn the United States had to withdraw from Italy and Turkey. Additionally, the United States could never enter Cuba again unless provoked. Finally, to keep things from ever becoming that tense again, a nuclear hotline was setup between the United States and the Soviet Union.

To the Moon! ...and Vietnam

Kennedy continued to send military advisors to Vietnam. This allowed the CIA to finish their operations there, which were initially green lighted by Eisenhower but led to the assassination of Diem, the leader of the South Vietnam, causing significant destabilization the country.

In a different realm of foreign policy, Kennedy was the first president to initiate security agreements with Israel. Presidents Truman and Eisenhower had both supported Israel's right to exist but had refused to supply weapons to Israel and even placed an embargo on them. Kennedy was the first president to sell arms to Israel, declaring that the United States had a "moral" obligation to the Israelis.

Nearing what would be the end of his time in office Kennedy also signed the 1963 Nuclear Test Ban Treaty with the Soviet Union, which outlawed the testing of nuclear weapons above ground. The treaty and the space program he initiated were the crown jewels of his administration. His promise to land a man on the moon before 1970 would be realized in 1969, after his death.

Camelot

In 1955, John Kennedy became the first president to receive a Pulitzer Prize, winning it for *Profiles in Courage,* a volume of biographies on exceptional U.S. senators. He was also the nation's first Roman Catholic president.

Kennedy's years in the White House became known as "Camelot," a mythical and idealized era of happiness and heroes. And while Kennedy was able to inspire a generation of Americans to become more active in civic life—and to join his initiative, the Peace Corps—when he declared: "Ask not what your country can do for you, but what you can do for your country," Camelot was mostly a construct of his widow, Jackie, and of his admirers. This is not to say that Kennedy was not a significant figure, especially for the generation of his time, but his presidency was problematic from its beginning. He did not have the legislative skills to move on civil rights, had a difficult time dealing with the southern wing of his party, and made poor choices in foreign policy. His assassination on November 22, 1963, in Dallas, Texas, plunged the entire nation into deep mourning and disbelief, and brought Vice President Lyndon Baines Johnson to the White House.

Lyndon B. Johnson
(1963-1969)

"Until justice is blind to color, until education is unaware of race, until opportunity is unconcerned with the color of men's skins, emancipation will be a proclamation but not a fact."

Introduction

Lyndon B. Johnson was born in Stonewall, Texas, on August 27, 1908. His father, Samuel Johnson, had been a Texas legislator, and his grandfather had been an important Texas politician as well. In fact, when Johnson was five, they moved to the city named after his grandfather, Johnson City. Despite his family's renown, Johnson grew up poor. His father had speculated in the markets and lost everything, and although he did eventually regain some of his fortune, Johnson learned the value of hard work and the reality of poverty early in life.

Johnson graduated high school and then spent a year living a somewhat Bohemian lifestyle and drifting from job to job. A year later Johnson returned to his hometown and began doing manual labor—an incredibly grueling job. Despite the demanding physical work, Johnson enjoyed working prior to attending college. He worked as a janitor to pay his tuition at Southwest Texas State Teacher's University and even had to take a year off to earn some additional money in order to finish. During that year he taught poverty-stricken Mexican students, often paying for their school supplies and recess equipment.

After graduating from college in 1930, Johnson took a teaching job that was interrupted when he was invited to Washington to work for Congressman Richard Kleberg. Johnson took the job and spent three years observing the art of politics and witnessed Franklin Roosevelt's historic first 100 days as president. Johnson also met his wife, Claudia Alta "Lady Bird" Taylor, in 1934 on his way home from Washington. He asked her to marry him on their first date—which scared her a little at first—and they married two months later.

In 1935 Johnson took advantage of an incredible opportunity. FDR had setup the National Youth Administration in Texas, and Johnson applied for the job as director and was miraculously accepted. He became the youngest director of the NYA. In 1937, when Congressman James P. Buchanan died in office, Johnson ran for his seat in a special election. Unlike his opponents, Johnson was unapologetically in favor of Roosevelt and the New Deal and won a solid victory because of it. Roosevelt rewarded Johnson, meeting with him privately. LBJ then went on to meet the man who would be his early mentor in politics, Texas Congressman Sam Rayburn—an old friend of his grandfather and Speaker of the House of Representatives. As a congressman, Johnson was successful in obtaining electric power for his rural district, making him so popular that he ran unopposed for three terms. Despite his district-wide popularity, when Johnson ran in a Senate special election, he narrowly lost. Days following the Pearl Harbor bombing, Johnson volunteered to serve in any way possible—the first congressman to do so—and was stationed in the Pacific. On one flight his single plane was surrounded and attacked by the enemy over New Guinea, putting Johnson in grave danger. His plane managed to return to the base, and he was awarded the Silver Star for his "gallantry in action."

In 1948 Johnson decided to try for the Senate again, using a helicopter—nicknamed the "Johnson City Windmill"—to fly quickly to all the Texas districts, vigorously campaigning. People were amazed by his helicopter—a rarity in those days—and he spread his message faster than his opponents could ever have imagined. Johnson closed the gap between him and his principle opponent, and the primary election went into a runoff. Johnson won the runoff by eighty-seven votes out of hundreds of thousands in an election that was contested by his opponent. People still debate whether there was foul play. After winning the primary, Johnson went on to win the general election by a sound margin.

Upon entering the Senate, Johnson remarked that "the size was just right." He had difficulty establishing himself as a congressman, but he felt his style of politics was just perfect for a small group of 100 powerful men. Johnson's path to power is astounding, because at that time the only way to rise to a leadership positions in the Senate was by seniority, by years served. Johnson broke this tradition and shattered the seniority system. In 1951 he became the youngest Senate whip with his ability to gather votes. In 1953, after campaigning for Adlai Stevenson in his home state of Texas, which ultimately went for Eisenhower. He became the youngest floor leader in history. Then, in 1955 his leadership skills and focus on compromise won him respect and he became the youngest majority leader in history. His leadership in the Senate—from 1958 to 1964—marked years of compromise with the Republican Party, which actually helped the Democrats maintain congressional power.

Johnson's career almost came to end in 1955 because of a massive heart attack, but he resolved to quit smoking and changed his diet. In 1960 he decided to run for the presidency, his true goal throughout his life, but was beaten by the Democratic nominee by John Kennedy. Even worse, Kennedy offered him the position as the vice presidential nominee—the weakest position in government. Johnson, a man obsessed with wielding power, fell into a deep state of depression. When Kennedy won in 1960—very much in part to Johnson's political skills, which won the Democrats key parts of the South—he was exiled by the Kennedy administration. The president didn't even solicit his political advice. Johnson was a man of political mastery that might appear once in a generation—sat idly by as a lack of political leadership, skill and will, caused civil rights and liberal initiatives to stagnate. For Johnson, his political career and presidential aspirations—his life—seemed over...until 1963.

Coming to power and the politics of pressure

Lyndon Johnson was sworn in as president on Air Force One following John Kennedy's assassination in 1963. Immediately after becoming president, Johnson decided it would best for him to use Kennedy's legacy to help him begin the troublesome task of passing civil rights legislation. One of his first speeches used Kennedy as the subject and asked the American people to help him to continue the Kennedy vision.

Johnson also retained Kennedy's cabinet, most likely because he was afraid of dismantling the "Camelot" imagery of the past presidency. However, many historians say that Johnson fell into the trap that most presidents face when succeeding to the office through death; not clearing out the predecessor's cabinet.

One of Johnson's strongest talents as a politician was his power of persuasion. It has been called by historians "the treatment." Johnson, standing at 6'5", could tower over his colleagues. He would often lean over people and stare directly into their eyes while discussing a pending bill in the Senate. Often he would yell, then laugh as if they were longtime friends, threaten, cajole, tell stories, and could often even be crude to get his way.

Civil Rights Act

Johnson's premier piece of legislation, the Civil Rights Act of 1964, was a tough sell to the House and more so to the Senate. Democrats had held a stronghold in the South, and this was largely because Democrats, during the Great Depression, had powered much of the South with electricity; and many senators made up a "solid south" regime in the Democratic Party. That sector of Democrats was happy to pass progressive legislation relative to whites in America, but reluctant to do so for African Americans. Johnson had to do what Kennedy could not, that is, to bridge the gap between southern and northern Democrats and pass the Civil Rights bill.

Johnson played on his southern roots, swaying his former mentor and powerful Democratic leader Richard Russell of Georgia and other southern allies into believing that Johnson himself was not in favor of civil rights, but simply trying to please northerners. At the same time, Johnson was busy convincing northern progressive leaders like Hubert Humphrey of Minnesota to concede on certain aspects of the bill to help Johnson win southern votes. After numerous filibusters and fighting, Johnson held on to enough southern votes to enable passage of the Civil Rights Act.

The effects of the Civil Rights Act for African Americans and women were unmatched by any other piece of legislation since the days of Lincoln 100 years prior. Although race relations would still be rocky in the South throughout the 60s, 70s, and 80s, desegregation eventually occurred, and Title 7 of the Civil Rights Act allowed minorities and women to secure jobs—which they could not obtain prior to the act.

The political consequences were not as positive for Democrats. Johnson was well aware that the Civil Rights Act meant the destruction of the powerful Democratic coalition. Johnson even said to his White House staff assistant Bill Moyers, "We just delivered the South to the Republican party for a long time to come." And as usual, LBJ knew what he was talking about. By the 1980s, the Democrats lost their grip on the South. Today, the South is solid only towards Republicans and has not voted for a Democratic president since 1976, when it swung to the Georgia native Jimmy Carter.

Great Society

Johnson—who grew up a poor young man in Texas—had seen suffering first hand and wished to do his best to help alleviate poverty. In 1965 Johnson called for the creation of a "Great Society"—its main goal and purpose to help all Americans rise from poverty, regardless of race, ethnicity, disability, or gender. Through massive amounts of legislation, Johnson established many programs that attempted to do just that. However his eagerness to quickly pass legislation caused the creation of many bureaucratic agencies that were sometimes wasteful. Many of those acts were eventually defunded, but the Great Society acts that still remain in place today have been, in some ways, invaluable to Americans. Lyndon Johnson called for a "War on Poverty," and fought it with all his strength. In 1959, more than 20% of Americans lived in poverty—that's nearly 40 billion people. In 1970, just after Johnson left office, that percentage had fallen to almost 11%, decreasing the numbers in poverty to 10 million. Since 1965—the year Johnson introduced the Great Society—the poverty rate has fallen, approaching 10%, and stayed there through the- mid-1970s until the rate picked up again during the 1980s; it has yet to go beyond 15%.

In this Great Society, Johnson also envisioned a country where all people could vote. Jim Crowe laws in the United States had created literacy tests, poll taxes, and other methods of keeping minorities from voting. Johnson passed the Voting Rights Act a year after the Civil Rights Act to remedy the problem of voter discrimination. The act guaranteed every citizen the right to vote and has, since 1965, received overwhelming support by both parties and enfranchised millions of voters; but even in current times new restrictions have been enacted to limit voter access, e.g., requiring photo ID, proof of literacy, etc.

Finally, in order to address one of the leading causes of poverty in the United States, Johnson devised a program to deal with medical care. Illness could be debilitating and often led people, especially the elderly, to fall into poverty. Johnson's Great Society created Medicaid—a program that guarantees low-income families and individuals and the disabled access to healthcare—and Medicare to help manage that problem. In 1960, the poverty rate for the elderly was over 28%. Today, the poverty rate for the elderly is down to 9.1%, but without the Great Society programs it's estimated that elderly poverty would skyrocket to 41%.

Vietnam War

The Vietnam War tested Johnson's last bit of strength. Initially not wanting to intervene in the Vietnam conflict, Johnson felt pressured to do something because of advice from cabinet members Robert McNamara, Dean Rusk, and the Joint Chiefs. Moreover, the public was more "Hawkish" then "Dovish," and since Johnson followed polls closely, this had an effect on his decision making. In 1964 Johnson had defeated ultraconservative Barry Goldwater—who was practically ready to drop nuclear bombs on Vietnam. Johnson felt his policy of intervention, one of

containment, would be the middle ground between Goldwater's militarism and the liberals' dovish nature.

Later in 1964, off the Gulf of Tonkin in Vietnam, an American battleship was struck by a North Vietnamese cruiser. A month later, another incident occurred in the gulf, but this occurrence was probably the result of false radar imaging. After speaking to Defense Secretary McNamara, Johnson took the precautionary measure of asking Congress to give him authority to expand America's presence in Vietnam. The Senate passed the Gulf of Tonkin Resolution with only two dissenting votes, giving LBJ the power to use military force without requiring a declaration of war from Congress.

In 1965, Operation Rolling Thunder escalated the war, through systematic sustained air strikes and bombing runs on Vietnam. As the war raged on, the military continued to deliver reports that seemed positive. The public initially assumed that the military effort in Vietnam was succeeding, as the number of reported enemy deaths was high. However, people began to question the accuracy of the death counts. By 1967 the military as well as the Johnson administration were losing much of their credibility, as only a minority of the public continued to believe the exhibited reports.

The final blow to Johnson's credibility came in 1968, when North Vietnamese forces launched surprise attacks against American forces in a campaign called the Tet Offensive. Americans suffered thousands of loses, and the news at home reported the brutal attacks without much censorship. Americans watched the South Vietnamese die on their TV screens and witnessed U.S. servicemen returning home in coffins. By 1968—the single bloodiest year of the Vietnam War—the majority of Americans, seeing the death toll rise were opposed to continuing the war.

Rioting broke out in Detroit in 1967, as many in the black community rebelled against what they saw as white aggression: Dr. Martin Luther King Jr. had been assassinated and the fact that most of servicemen returning in coffins were black. Johnson took the riots quite personally, wondering how "Blacks" could treat him in such a way after he had signed into law the Civil Rights Act. Antiwar demonstrations, sometimes violent, multiplied around the country on college campuses. Such events highlight some of the reasons for the backlash, both Black and White, against Johnson, as southern Democrats also began to abandon him.

Vietnam Peace Conference and not seeking reelection

Amidst the staggering death toll in Vietnam, Johnson became increasingly depressed and sickened about the insufferable loss of his boys—his paternalistic reference—in Vietnam. Seeing that the war was nearly hopeless, and stuck between following the advice of the Joint Chiefs to use nuclear weapons, or continuing McNamara's dreadful Rolling Thunder scheme, Johnson took matters into his own hands and attempted to negotiate peace.

In order to avoid any political meddling at the peace conference, Johnson decided not to run for reelection in 1968 and announced his intention on a national broadcast. Some historians contend that Johnson was aware of his declining health and didn't believe he would be able to endure another term. (Johnson passed away only days before his would-be "second term" would have ended.) Or perhaps Johnson felt that he lost all his political capitol after anti-war candidate Eugene McCarthy challenged him in the 1968 democratic primary and almost beat him in New Hampshire.

The peace negotiations were doomed from the start, as Nguyen Van Thieu— president of South Vietnam— refused to take part in them. Johnson had paused the bombing runs in Vietnam in 1968 in order to bring the North Vietnamese to the negotiating table, but he was unable to get Thieu to join. Only a few weeks before the 1968 election, the Johnson administration discovered that Richard Nixon and John Mitchell—the head of the Nixon campaign—had been contacting the South Vietnamese government, telling them not to join Johnson's peace conference, but instead to hold out for a better deal when Nixon won in 1968. Thieu then absolutely refused to join into negotiations. The war continued for nearly four more years, and Johnson was unable to achieve peace due to the Nixon camp's meddling.

The end of a giant

Lyndon Johnson may well be one of the greatest tragedies in the history of the presidency. He had everything laid out to realize his Great Society; a House and Senate ready for change and a culture in the United States that was overwhelmingly prepared to go forth with his vision. But by 1966 all that would be set aside to fight a war that would break the country's morale for years and its preconceptions of American supremacy. As Johnson said, "I knew from the start that if I left the woman I love—the Great Society—in order to fight that bitch of a war, then I would lose everything. All my programs. All my hopes. All my dreams."

There is the part of LBJ that championed one of the most important pieces of legislation in 100 years since Lincoln's death—the Civil Rights Act of 1964—that helped generations of Americans enjoy life without racial barriers. There is also the other part of LBJ that pursued the

Vietnam War. In between was the man who wanted a "great society," neither black nor white, respected by the left and still very much distained by the right. Moreover, in 1968 Johnson was probably one of the most threatened presidents in history, so much so that he could not even give public speeches. Given the resentments and the debates over his legacy, Johnson remains one of America's most controversial presidents. One thing can be said however, no president was ever as effective and as skillful in the art of legislating.

Richard Nixon
(1969-1974)

"Sometimes I have succeeded and sometimes I have failed....I am confident that the world is a safer place today, not only for the people of America but for the people of all nations, and that all of our children have a better chance than before of living in peace rather than dying in war."

Introduction

Richard Nixon was born on January 9, 1913, in Yorba Linda, California. He came from a family of Quakers, both his mother and father were very devout. They moved around but eventually settled in Whittier, California in 1921. Nixon's father owned a general store, and Nixon began learning the importance of hard work from an early age.

Nixon's studiousness in school got him accepted into Ivy League colleges, but since he wasn't sure if he could afford them, he ultimately settled on Whittier College. He was a good student and was active in politics; he led a group that was against the exclusive university fraternities and secret societies. He attended Duke University School of Law and after graduating, returned to California and passed the bar. He also met his future wife, Thelma Catherine Ryan—nicknamed Pat—whom he wanted to marry. However, she turned him down for two years before she finally accepted.

When the United States joined World War II, Nixon initially did legal work for the military. He could have used his Quaker religion to exempt him from the draft. However he worked his way into serving in combat and became a lieutenant commander in the navy, serving in the Pacific.

After the war, Nixon decided to run for Congress. He was swept into the House on the 1946 Republican wave. Nixon, a supporter of the Taft-Hartley Act, which was enacted to counteract the power of the unions, became a devout anti-communist. Before Taft-Hartley passed over Truman's veto, Nixon actually debated the merits of the bill with another young congressman, John Kennedy. However, Nixon did break ranks with Republicans when he served on the Herter Committee, which investigated the need for the Marshall Plan. Nixon toured Europe and believed foreign aid to be necessary and became a supporter of foreign aid the rest of his life.

The assignment that mattered most in Nixon's career was being named to the House of Un-American Activities Committee —which investigated allegations of communism. A woman named Elizabeth Bentley, a Soviet agent working in New York, testified that the *Time* magazine writer and editor Whittaker Chambers was a communist. Chambers in turn accused Alger Hiss, a respected Democrat, of espionage with the Soviet Union. Nixon sunk his teeth into Hiss and never let go. For months the media attacked Nixon for wrongfully pursuing Hiss, but after a year things turned out Nixon's way, and Hiss was proven to have been a Communist agent. The entire episode gave Nixon the credibility to run for the Senate, winning his race by further red-baiting accusations against his opponent Democrat Helen Gahagan Douglas, ruining her political life although she was innocent.

Nixon took his Senate seat in 1950 and less than two years later was asked to join Dwight Eisenhower on the Republican ticket of 1952. Nixon agreed, but was almost dropped from the ticket when accusations of embezzling money emerged. Nixon survived the accusations, saying that there had been mismanagement of some campaign money, and that he would be willing to return it all, except for the money spent on his dog—Checkers—which he had bought for his daughter. The Checkers speech worked well and allowed him to continue on the ticket. He spent the rest of the campaign as a fighter for Eisenhower, giving speech after speech attacking Adlai Stevenson, the Democratic candidate. As vice president, Nixon played mostly a diplomatic role, meeting world leaders. He also stepped in for Ike when the president had health issues and when he had heart surgery. And perhaps Nixon's most famous diplomatic event occurred when he went to Russia and visited a replica of an American kitchen with Nikita Khrushchev and debated American and Russian ideologues; Nixon bested the Russian president.

In 1960 Nixon ran for president against John F. Kennedy. Nixon lost and felt he had been cheated by the Kennedy campaign, that they had played dirty tricks and had a never-ending supply of money. The election of 1960, coupled with Nixon's loss for governor of California in 1962, soured him. The Nixon after 1962 was much more of a politician set on winning than playing fair. He had toured the entire country in 1960, giving stump speech after stump speech. However in 1968, he calculated the number of speeches he needed to give in person, stuck to television, and revealed very little about his actual feelings on policy.

Peace with not so much honor-Vietnam

Nixon's first order of business after taking office was to find some resolution to the Vietnam War. Nonetheless he escalated the conflict. The peace talks between the Johnson administration and the North Vietnamese had fallen apart, yet Nixon and his advisors felt the war could not be won. They decided to pursue a policy of "Vietnamization," which was to replace American soldiers with South Vietnamese soldiers in order to slowly withdraw U.S. troops. Instead of bringing the

war to a close in 1968, the Vietnamization process continued the war until 1973. However, the majority of American troops had returned home by 1970-71.

The fighting was not isolated to Vietnam. Nixon committed the air force to dropping massive amounts of bombs on Cambodia and Laos to break up supply lines to Communist North Vietnam and to destroy the Khmer Rouge, a name given to the Communist party in Cambodia and that ruled the country. The Khmer Rouge and Communist party leader Pol Pot were responsible for the horrifying genocide in the middle to late 1970s, and in an effort to centralize Cambodia's farming, they annihilated one-quarter of the country's population. Many suggest that Nixon's bombings in Cambodia were intended to prevent the Khmer Rouge and Pol Pot from gaining control there. As this plan clearly was not successful, many historians debate whether Nixon's actions in Cambodia were well-founded in at least trying to stop the rise of Pol Pot and Khmer Rouge or were in fact contributing factors to their rise to power.

In 1971, activist and U.S. military analyst Daniel Ellsberg discovered the Pentagon Papers which were the Defense Department's private history of the war in Vietnam. The details of the papers show that the Johnson administration had lied to both the public and to Congress about the extent of the bombings, while also showing that the war had been expanded under Nixon into Cambodia and Laos. Ellsberg released the papers to the *New York Times,* which published large amounts of the secret administrative details.

Nixon shocks, the energy crisis, and the EPA

Nixon's first term wasn't just preoccupied with foreign wars, he had a heavy focus on the economy too. At an economic summit at Camp David, the presidential country retreat near Washington, D.C., Nixon and his advisors discussed how they would handle the economy. In 1971, inflation was creeping up, and Nixon knew that voters more or less voted with their wallets on issues like the economy and foreign policy.

Nixon decided to institute price controls and wage freezes. These measures did keep inflation in check until 1972 (just in time for the election) but caused some major economic problems later in the decade during the Ford and Carter administrations. But the main economic consequence of the Nixon shocks to the economy came when he and his under-secretary of the treasury, Paul Volcker, devised a plan to take the United States off the gold standard, thrusting it into a new age of free-floating currency, one not tied to gold. Nixon made this decision without informing any of the foreign interested parties, who were naturally "shocked" by his action.

This policy had short-term failures, but long-term successes. Initially, the policy caused more inflation, as the Federal Reserve was able to print more money unchecked, enabling some people to extend their credit line and artificially raise prices. The long-term effect was that the free-floating currency helped contribute to the multiple economic post-Nixon booms like the ones in the 1990s. However, more economic problems were right around the corner. In 1973 an energy crisis occurred, causing gas rationing in the North and price jumps. A growing concern for the environment, problems of pollution and more awareness of the preciousness of energy inspired Nixon to create by executive order the Environmental Protection Agency (EPA).

Détente

One of the most interesting changes to presidential foreign policy during Nixon's administration was détente. Unlike his predecessors—going all the way back to Harry Truman—Nixon felt that arms races and combative tactics with the Soviet Union were not only dangerous but antiquated and ineffective. Nixon decided that the best way to avoid another Vietnam—or another situation such as the Cuban Missile Crisis, which nearly brought about worldwide destruction—was to relax tensions between the United States and the Soviet Union. This policy was called détente. Many historians believe that only Nixon could have pursued

this policy, as his rise in politics was solely because of his rabid anti-communism and that people trusted him on the anti-communist issues. People believed that Nixon hated communism, and so when he proposed the idea of coexistence with the Soviets, people accepted his word that it would not lead to the end of world. It is possible that if anyone else attempted such a feat he might have faced serious opposition.

His first act was to "relax tensions," *détente,* between the U.S. and China. Since World War II, the United States had refused to acknowledge the People's Republic of China. Mao Zedong had unified mainland China under Communist rule, while his rival—Chiang Kai-shek—maintained a nationalist government on the island of Taiwan, which the United

States acknowledged as the official government of China. Nixon was determined to break down the wall between the Mao's China and the United States. So in 1972, he became the first American president to visit and recognize the existence of the People's Republic of China.

Then, by the end of the year, the war in Vietnam was essentially over. Most of the troops were home and a sense of normalcy seemed to exist in America. The Paris Peace Accords were signed on January 27, 1973 essentially ending direct U.S. military combat and stopped the fighting between North and South Vietnam. His other major display of détente occurred when Nixon met with Soviet leader Leonid Brezhnev and negotiated the Anti-Ballistic Missile Treaty between the U.S. and the USSR.

Nixon had signed the first Strategic Arms Limitation Treaty (SALT I) with the Soviet Union in 1971, and the treaty helped to relations with the Soviet on arms controls. Brezhnev declared that the treaty was a start of a "peaceful coexistence" between the two nations.

NIXON IMPLICATED

Haldeman, Ehrlichman, Kleindienst & Dean Are Out

Watergate

In 1972, five burglars were caught inside the Watergate office complex, where the Democratic National Committee headquarters were located. The burglars were searching for information about the democrats and confidential information that could help Republicans have a leg up in the 1972 election. When the burglars were brought to court, one of the five was actually found to be from the CIA. After serious investigation, two reporters from the *Washington Post*—Bob Woodward and Carl Bernstein — relentlessly pursued the story.

Over 1972 through 1974, Bernstein and Woodward, with strong support throughout the media, uncovered the extent of Nixon's participation in the scandal. In 1973 Nixon was accused of being involved in the Watergate break-in and was impeached by the House of Representatives for lying about it. Nixon quickly began dismissing and firing close advisors and aids, trying to protect himself from associations with anyone who had participated in the planning of Watergate. However, these same allies he fired when called to testify under oath said that the White House was involved in a cover-up, and that there were White House tapes to prove it.

Nixon was ordered by the Supreme Court to provide the tapes as evidence to the House. Historians are still unsure why Nixon did not burn the tapes, but surely enough, the House found the "smoking gun" tape that revealed Nixon's involvement in the cover-up.

Resignation

Amidst mass protesting against him, losing the support of the House and Senate, and fearing being removed from office by impeachment, Nixon felt it would be best for the nation if he were to resign.

Nixon delivered his resignation speech on August 9, 1974. After the speech, Nixon walked out of the White House and onto the helicopter that would take him away from all he had worked his entire life for. His final act was to raise both his hands and flash two peace signs; maybe done to invoke memories of Churchill and the V for Victory, perhaps to try and be remembered as a peacemaker or maybe just to anger the hippies. Whatever the reason, the iconic photo is the last one of Nixon as president.

The bitterness that grew out of 1960 stayed with Nixon, possibly until 1974, when he resigned. After leaving the White House, he retired to quiet life in California, and became a historian, writer, and commentator on foreign policy, somewhat healing his reputation.

Gerald Ford
(1974-1977)

"History and experience tell us that moral progress comes not in comfortable and complacent times, but out of trial and confusion."

Introduction

Gerald Ford was born as Leslie Lynch King, Jr. on July 14, 1913, in Omaha, Nebraska. His parents divorced in 1915, and his mother moved with Ford to Michigan. There she met and married Gerald Rudolph Ford, Sr. She also had her son's name changed to Gerald Rudolph Ford—not telling young Jerry that Gerald Sr. was not his real father. Ford's stepfather was a successful businessman and gave him and his mother great financial security until the Great Depression, which wiped out Ford Sr.'s investments and hurt his company. To make things more difficult for the young Ford, when he was seventeen, his real father approached him while he was working at a sandwich shop and revealed what his mother had hidden for so long. Ford was shocked and confronted his mother.

Amazingly, amidst the depression and family issues, Ford was a good student and realized some athletic ability in high school. He was less interested in books than in sports—at least during his youth—and excelled at football, which earned him a scholarship to the University of Michigan. The scholarship itself wasn't enough though, and Ford had to work his way through school. Michigan's football team was not very good, but Ford still stood out as a good player. He received professional football offers but turned them down—back then they paid very little. Instead, Ford wanted to switch his focus to academics and decided to apply to Yale Law School. He got in, coaching football to pay his way, and graduated in 1941. He returned to Michigan and went into a law partnership, but that was interrupted by the war.

He volunteered for military service and was initially made a physical education instructor but later served on board the USS Monterey in the Pacific. He took part in the island-hopping carrier strikes campaign in 1943 and became a lieutenant commander in the Naval Reserve Training Command. Ford returned home and entered politics, fighting for low-cost housing for returning servicemen. Later, in 1948, Ford ran for Congress against an incumbent conservative. Ford canvassed his district, meeting as many people as possible and even worked with farmers in the field while explaining his policies. When Ford was unsure of his stance on a certain issue he would promise to do more research— usually getting back to his voters quickly. His modesty and honesty won him the election. Before he left for Congress he married Betty Bloomer Warren.

Ford's congressional tenure was quiet. He did his best to represent the people in his district and was a loyal Republican. He turned down a possible Senate run in 1952, preferring to be in the House, aiming to become Speaker one day. Almost ten years later, Ford was asked by President Johnson to chair the Warren Commission to investigate the Kennedy assassination, and in 1965 he took a big step toward his goal of become Speaker and was chosen by the Republicans to be minority leader. In 1970 Ford made his first commotion in the House by trying, unsuccessfully, to impeach Supreme Court Justice William O'Donnell, attacking him for his "liberal opinions." However, during most of the early 70s and Nixon's tenure in the White House, Ford was a loyal supporter of the president's agenda and earned the respect of many fellow Republicans.

When Nixon was in dire straits in 1973 and without a vice president, he turned to Ford, who had a reputation for integrity. Ford reluctantly accepted the vice presidency and eventually took on the presidency when Nixon resigned.

After taking the oath of office on August 9, 1974, Ford remarked:

> "I am acutely aware that you have not elected me as your President by your ballots, and so I ask you to confirm me as your President with your payers. And I hope that such prayers will also be the first of many.... "If you have not chosen me by secret ballot, neither have I gained office by any secret promises. I have not campaigned either for the Presidency or the Vice Presidency. I have not subscribed to any partisan platform. I am indebted to no man, and only to one woman—my dear wife—as I begin this very difficult job."

Rebuilding the Presidency

As Gerald Ford stepped into office he made the remarks:

"My fellow Americans, our long national nightmare is over.....
As we bind up the internal wounds of Watergate, more painful
and poisonous than those of foreign wars, let us restore the gold-
en rule to our political process, and let brotherly love purge our
hearts of suspicion and of hate.... God helping me, I will not let
you down."

In 1974 the American presidency was facing one of its greatest
challenges. The office had been seemingly desecrated and a president
had just resigned. The intense faith that Americans had in the presidency
was in crisis. Gerald Ford had to restore that faith in the presidency and
in the American system.

His first step on that long journey came as a surprise to the nation.
On September 8, 1974, he announced his unconditional pardon of
President Nixon—an act that received almost universal criticism. The
House and Senate were appalled that he had not contacted them prior
to his decision. Ford owned his decision and fought to prove that
what he had done was nonpartisan and had nothing to do with his
relationship with Nixon. Some began to speculate whether Ford had
made a deal with Nixon, and even lifelong friends and close allies felt
betrayed. Ford agreed to appear before a congressional subcommittee—
one of only two presidents to do so, the other being Abraham Lincoln—
and answered every single question in regard to the pardon, proving
his sincerity.

While the decision to pardon Nixon was unpopular in 1974, there
are many who now tend to credit Ford for the wisdom for this act. And
at the time, pardoning Nixon allowed the nation to move on beyond
Watergate and return to dealing with important issues beyond the
resignation. Moreover, it allowed the nation to begin to heal.

Recession, inflation, and conservatism

Nixon had shaken Americans' trust in government by his
participation in the Watergate cover-up, but Americans were in for
another surprise from Nixon long after he left the White House. The
Nixon administration's economic policy during the early 1970s had
been crafted to bolster his reelection but caused major turmoil during
Ford's years in office. The price controls, wage freezes, and monetary
policy of the FED had guaranteed that the economy would stay strong
in 1971 and 1972, but their effects on the middle and late 1970s proved

disastrous. When Ford came to office he faced the largest recession since the Great Depression. Unemployment reached 9%, inflation was on the rise, and the public was, as expected, very unhappy.

Ford initially advocated for a tax increase and a stimulus program but a year later switched to a policy of tax cuts and cuts in government spending. The inconsistency in his fiscal policy confused his supporters and business leaders alike. As inflation continued to rise, the administration devised a grassroots campaign to be fiscally responsible in order to beat inflation. "WIN!" (Whip Inflation Now!) buttons were part of the campaign, but it was largely unsuccessful, and the media constantly attacked the slogan throughout Ford's tenure.

When dealing with the tough economic climate, Ford acted much more like a president of the Founding Father's era than of his time. He called for a very limited domestic agenda and let the House of Representatives take the lead on legislation. He used his veto power extensively to block the House from passing inflation-contributing spending, pork barrel spending, and acts Ford believed were unconstitutional. In Ford's two years in the White House, he used the veto a staggering sixty-six times—a considerable amount compared to Ronald Reagan who, for example, used the veto twelve more times than Ford despite being in office more than twice as long.

Ford's Achilles heel

While Ford followed his conscience on domestic policy and fought inflation, he felt less confident on foreign policy and delegated much of that agenda to Henry Kissinger, national security advisor and secretary of state to Ford and Nixon. Ford's distance from his own foreign policy—and Kissinger's radical policy—damaged the president's image on the world stage and in the 1976 election.

A blow to his presidency came on April 30, 1975, when Saigon, the capital of South Vietnam, fell to the North Vietnamese Communists. With this final assault on the South Vietnamese, the war in Vietnam was officially over. While Ford's foreign policy was the first in years to be free of Vietnam, American morale took a slight dip. And in an attempt to better relations between the United States, Europe, and the Communist Bloc, Ford joined in the negotiations of the Helsinki Accords in 1975. The most controversial part of the accords was the recognition of the Soviet Bloc's border expansion due to its annexation of several eastern European countries. Even though the Helsinki Accords were not binding, many Americans believed that détente had gone too far, conceding too much to the Soviet Union. This resolution split much of the moderate and conservative factions of the Republican Party.

Meanwhile Kissinger was focused on the 1973 Yom Kippur War between Egypt and Israel. He had taken a role in the Middle East, using a term dubbed "shuttle diplomacy." Ford himself had become skeptical of the success of Kissinger's diplomacy. The major achievement that Ford made in the realm of Middle East foreign policy was the good relations he formed with Egyptian President Anwar Sadat—a man who would be vital in the coming years to the Carter administration.

Healer

With only 895 days in the White House, President Gerald Ford had one of the shortest presidencies. However, his impact on the office was one of the most important of all the presidencies of the postwar era. After the national nightmare of Watergate, Ford was able to restore a positive image of the presidency, which Nixon had destroyed. With Ford, few worried about his integrity, as the flurry of accusations about the Nixon pardon lasted only a short period of time; and Ford's appearance before Congress helped to affirm his honesty. Moreover, Ford was fiscally conservative and disliked the idea of bailing out cities, vetoed reckless congressional spending—more so than any president since Grover Cleveland—and advocated personal responsibility. Unfortunately for Ford, he was somewhat a victim of his time. The middle and late 1970s experienced the aftershock of the Nixon economic policy—as well as other coinciding world events—which plunged the economy into inflation chaos.

Jimmy Carter
(1977-1981)

"War may sometimes be a necessary evil. But no matter how necessary, it is always an evil, never a good. We will not learn how to live together in peace by killing each other's children."

Introduction

James Earl Carter, Jr., was born October 1, 1924, in the small town of Plains, Georgia. He was the fifth generation to be born there, and his father James Earl Carter, Sr., owned a small farm with no electricity or running water. His father was a stern conservative and segregationist, while his mother, Lillian Gordy Carter—a nurse who provided healthcare to even her poor neighbors and joined the Peace Corps in 1966—was very much the opposite, a liberal. Carter's ideology stems much from the divide of his parents, adopting some of the fiscal conservatism of his father and the social liberalism of his mother.

Carter grew up next to the families of black children, divided by a fence and learned that there was no difference between black and white. Carter also learned about hard work and responsibility by working on the farm with his father from a young age, observing farming techniques and acquiring business skills.

Carter wanted to go to college but his family had little money to spare. He decided to apply to and was accepted at the U.S. Naval Academy in Annapolis in 1943, graduating with good grades in the top ten percent of his class in 1946. That same year he married Rosalynn Smith, who also became his partner in politics, campaigning for him and also serving as an envoy during his presidency and was the only first lady to sit in on cabinet and policy meetings in the White House. Two years later Carter was assigned to submarine duty on the USS *Pomfret* and later was reassigned to the experimental K-1 submarine. He took graduate courses in nuclear engineering at Union College and even helped to disassemble an exploded reactor in New York. And in 1952, when the government began constructing and testing nuclear subs, Carter was assigned to the USS *Sea Wolf.* He requested leave in 1953 to be with his father who was terminally ill.

After his father's death, Carter felt that life in Plains was more fulfilling, and important than the navy. Carter returned to Plains to work on the peanut farm again in 1953. They initially lived in low income housing while he took classes on business and farming techniques and slowly made his peanut farm profitable. In 1954, after *Brown v. Board of Education,* when a white citizen's council formed in Georgia, Carter refused to join. They boycotted his peanuts, but he kept his business going. In 1955 he entered local politics, sitting on the Sumter county board of education. Then, in 1962 he decided to run for the Georgia senate. Carter, in the primary against an opponent supported by the Georgia political machine who had rigged the election using fictitious voters, originally lost the election. Carter contested the results and after a recount was declared to have gotten the most votes, won shortly before Election Day. He had managed to pull off a victory and became a state senator.

Carter witnessed the power of lobbies and special interests when he joined the state senate and was appalled by it and felt his position was not powerful enough. He then decided he would need to become governor in order to effect change. He declared his candidacy in 1966, running against segregationist Lester Maddox. Carter came in third during the primaries—impressive for an unknown state senator—while Maddox became governor. Carter returned to his farm but also began getting ready for his next run for governor in 1970. He and Rosalynn divided up their campaign events and estimated that they had shaken over half a million hands during the 1970 campaign.

After winning, Carter surprised both Georgia and the nation by stating in his state inaugural address: "I've traveled the state more than any other person in history and I say to you quite frankly that the time for racial discrimination is over. Never again should a black child be deprived of an equal right to health care, education, or the other privileges of society." He was the first southern governor to take such a stance.

Carter had a successful term as governor of Georgia, heavily reforming the state. His popularity is attributed to beating back the Wallace and Maddox politicians and paving a new way for southern progressives to rise. He appointed more African Americans to important positions, consolidated over two hundred and fifty state departments to make the government more efficient and handed the state a $200 million surplus through a conservative approach called "zero-based" budgeting. He also became the chair of the Democratic Governor's Campaign Committee in 1972 and the chairman of the National Democratic Party Campaign Committee in 1974. He was kept from running for reelection because of term limits in Georgia but continued to support Democrats in key positions until he launched his national campaign for the presidency in 1976. The American public chose the relatively unknown Jimmy Carter over the unelected Gerald Ford.

Inauguration

On January 20, 1977, Jimmy Carter—wearing a Georgia-made tailored suit bought right off the rack—was sworn into office and gave his inaugural address. He opened the speech by shining the spotlight on his predecessor, Gerald Ford. "For myself and for our Nation, I want to thank my predecessor for all he has done to heal our land."

Carter also used the inauguration to begin a long line of reforms to the president's image. The Carters walked to the White House from the inaugural ceremony instead of being driven. Moreover, Carter held no inaugural balls, carried his own luggage to the White House, and cut the size of the White House staff by a third. The presidential

yacht was sold shortly after entering office and the role of chief of staff was minimized. Carter wanted to make it clear to the people that the imperial presidency—which had grown in power since the 1950s—was gone with his entry into the office.

Carter's first order of business was to give unconditional amnesty to draft dodgers and evaders who did not fight in Vietnam. Although Carter was told by his advisors that it was a politically dangerous step—and even after meeting large opposition from congressional Republicans and Democrats alike—Carter simply believed it was the right thing to do and took a dip in the polls for it.

At odds with Congress

Carter had been a successful governor but state politics was not like the politics of the House, Senate, or the presidency. The Democrat controlled House and Senate were equally skeptical of the new Southern President, fearing he would be more conservative. The power players in the Congress during the late 70s were Democrats Robert Byrd—the Senate majority leader—and Tip O'Neil, the Speaker of the House.

Being a reformer and fairly conservative Democrat, Carter seemed to refuse to play the Washington game of pork barrel spending which appropriated large sums of tax money for the legislators' own district. One of the first bills that crossed his desk was the Rivers and Dams Bill—rampant with backroom pork deals and wasteful spending—and Carter refused to sign it. He responded with a modified version of the bill that gutted 301 of the dams, which would have saved taxpayers more than $5 billion dollars.

President Carter again used the veto against pork barrel spending measures, such as the Energy and Water Bill of 1978, where he stated: "I, along with the people of our country, am tired of seeing the taxpayers' money wasted, and I am determined to see the fight against inflation succeed. That's why I'm going to veto this unreasonable bill." In fact, among one-term Presidents who were in power with both chambers controlled by their own party, Carter ranks third in amount of uses of the veto behind Calvin Coolidge and William Howard Taft. In fact, Carter was able to champion and achieve many things with the Congress. He stopped the building of the B-1 Bomber in 1977, which saved taxpayers over $50 billion; passed a tax reduction and simplification act, the Humphrey-Hawkins Act of 1978, which formalized and expanded Congress's roll in the economic process; and bailed out Chrysler in 1979 when they were under threat of going out of business.

The underlying problem with Carter's relations with Congress was that Congress still represented an out-of-date liberalism that simply could not function with high levels of inflation. Carter represented a new school of progressive thinking, endorsing fiscal conservatism in order to combat inflation while trying to preserve the Roosevelt safety net through balanced budgets. The House and Senate, both controlled by Democrats, were still focused on an older left-wing mindset of using the government to obtain full employment and expanding the government in any way possible. What ultimately resulted in this divide was a failure to pass key parts of Carter's agenda such as welfare reform and the consumer protection agency, which were abandoned by political leaders by 1979.

Healthcare—the liberal and conservative split

President Carter subscribed to a conservative remedy to healthcare reform. He believed that switching to a centralized system would be burdensome, expensive, and overly complicated, and simply not pragmatic.

In 1978 Carter proposed a reform to the healthcare system that would lower and control the inflated medical costs of the 70s. Carter was highly reluctant to go beyond that measure because inflation was on the rise, and he believed that liberal reforms would increase spending and cause inflation to worsen. Senator Ted Kennedy opposed Carter's measure on the grounds that it didn't go far enough to reform the system and keep costs down.

With Carter (and most of the conservative Democrats and Republicans) refusing to endorse Kennedy's centralized system—and with the liberals refusing to compromise with Carter—the healthcare reform debates ended. However, Liberals did get their way shortly after the healthcare debates when Carter created the Department of Education.

Commitment to human rights

Jimmy Carter's first action regarding foreign policy was a commitment to taking action on human rights. Prior to the Carter administration, the majority of the foreign policy community were centered on the support of most non-Communist governments despite the often savage treatment of their own people. Carter attempted to change the direction of foreign policy by showing that a commitment to human rights was a strong foreign policy and a more effective way to combat communism than supporting dictators. Carter was able to use the commitment to human rights as a weapon against the Soviet Union. While initially it was perceived as a weak policy, the Soviets soon realized that Jimmy Carter's commitment was more combative than Nixon's détente. This was because Carter began to publicly denounce the Soviet Union, a policy that slowly drove the United States to follow a more hawkish line.

Carter's persistent criticism and highlighting of Soviet crimes against its people only bolstered the good image of the free West as opposed to the Soviet East. The only divergence from this new aggressive policy was SALT II, which Carter wanted to ratify. SALT was an arms-reduction treaty with the Soviet Union which was initially very unpopular, however, despite its failure to pass in the Senate, the Soviet Union and the United States actually followed its terms until 1986.

Unsurprisingly, Carter had to compromise on his commitment sometimes. His meeting with the Shah of Iran—which all the presidents before him since Eisenhower had done—was an example of this, as the Shah was in no way a defender of human rights. For the most part however, Carter remained fairly consistent and decreased the amount of weapons being sold to nations oppressing their people. And, in many nations such as Nicaragua, Carter changed the policy of supporting dictators such as Somoza in 1977, when Carter withdrew aid.

With a policy of human rights established, Carter turned to China, where he would continue to pursue long-term relations. While Richard Nixon opened up China, Carter established long-term relations with the Chinese government. Part of the new initial agreement was that China had to allow at least a limited amount of religious freedom. The result was that Christianity and the Bible were permitted in the country, and China would have a stronger diplomatic connection with the United States.

Panama Canal Treaties

In 1977 and 1978 President Carter surprised the nation by initiating a process that gave sovereignty back to the people of Panama. The United States had leased the Panama Canal and completed construction during the administration of Theodore Roosevelt, and the zone provided the U.S. with an incredibly important piece of strategic value during both World Wars I and II, and at the same time guaranteed the U.S. stature as an international power. However, Carter believed that by 1978 it was time to restore sovereignty to the Panamanian people who had been controlled by the United States for too long. Theodore Roosevelt had been proud of leading the charge on the construction of the Panama Canal, but even he did not envision the United States holding onto it for so long.

Carter and Panamanian leader Omar Torrijos entered negotiations over the return of the Canal Zone in 1978. The American people, as well as the majority of American politicians, totally opposed the idea, fearing that Communist countries would try to gain control of the canal. Carter was in an uphill battle but was relieved to receive support from many conservatives on the issue. Staunch Republican and conservative icon, John Wayne, was one of the first to come out in favor of Jimmy Carter's initiative in Panama. The conservative champion William F. Buckley even debated Ronald Reagan in 1978 and supported Jimmy Carter in his effort to give Panama back to its people. By 1978, Carter had built up a coalition of moderate senators, and the Senate ratified the treaties to return Panamanian sovereignty.

Camp David Accords

When Carter became president, he wanted to do something about the turmoil in the Middle East. Like Theodore Roosevelt, Carter would risk it all in mediation in order to settle problems in the Middle East between Egypt, Israel, and Palestine.

The mediation that Carter championed resulted in the Camp David Accords which was an agreements signed by of Egyptian president Anwar Sadat and Israeli Prime Minister Menachem Begin. Carter brought the two together at Camp David, the president's country retreat. The Camp David Accords accomplished three key things.

1) Established diplomatic relations between Egypt and Israel;

2) Ended Israeli occupation of the Sinai Peninsula in Egypt, thus ending thirty-one years of war;

3) Called for Israel to have further open debate over the Palestinian question.

However, getting the accords signed was not easy. Sadat and Begin were at odds the entire time. Their relationship was so strained that often Sadat and Begin would refuse to leave their rooms and speak with one and other, forcing Carter to run messages to each one. Through days of negotiation Carter was able to arbitrate this massive agreement, the first of its kind to bring calm to the chaos in the Middle East. In 1978 Sadat, Begin, and Carter shook hands. Both Sadat and Begin eventually received the Nobel Peace Prize for their actions.

Deregulation and breaking up the AT&T monopoly

Much of Carter's legislative agenda in 1978 was to deregulate parts of the market where previous administrations, such as the Nixon administration, had over regulated it. Carter was able to deregulate four industries; the airline, trucking industry, the rail industry, and beer companies.

Carter's deregulation of the airline industry took off most government controls over pricing, but left the safety regulation of airlines totally intact. Many studies have shown that since the Airline Deregulation Act of 1978, air travel has been made possible for more than just wealthy Americans. The deregulation of the trucking and rail industries were due to the Nixon administration's placement of price and wage controls on trucking. Another goal of Carter's was to help bring inflation down by making it cheaper to ship commodities as well as oil. Many of these industries had an economic resurgence in the 1980s due to deregulation.

In addition to the deregulatory policy, Carter used antitrust laws to break up the AT&T monopoly that controlled the telecommunications markets throughout the 1970s. The telecommunications titan was eventually broken up, which in part led to the competition that has given us the huge advances in telecommunications that we have today, e.g., smartphones and cellular data.

Iranian Hostage Crisis

In November 1979, more than sixty Americans were taken hostage at the American Embassy in Tehran, Iran's capital. The Iranian Revolution, which began in 1977, was what triggered the hostage crisis. Students in Iran were protesting Shah Mohammad Reza Pahlavi, whom they perceived to be a puppet installed by the Allies in 1953. The Iranians began to revolt and attempted to overthrow the Shah, as they had done in 1951. The Shah had close ties to the United States and had shaken hands and come to the United States to meet every president since Eisenhower. And in 1977, it was Carter's turn, meeting him on New Year's Eve 1977 which angered the students in Iran.

In 1979, student unrest occurred once again and forced the Shah to flee. However, the Shah was terminally ill with cancer and asked permission to enter the United States and receive treatment. Carter was briefed by the State Department as well as Henry Kissinger and David Rockefeller, both who advised the president that allowing the Shah entrance was the diplomatically and morally right thing to do. Carter allowed the Shah to enter.

With the Shah's entry into the United States, some Iranian revolutionaries began to believe—mistakenly—that America was planning another coup in Iran. In an attempt to take the upper-hand, the student movement broke into the U.S. embassy and took sixty-five Americans hostage. Thirteen of the hostages were let go due to illness. For 444 days the hostages were brutalized. Carter was determined to free the hostages, but through peaceful measures only;—he was unwilling to go to war in the Middle East. In 1980, with the Americans still held hostage, Carter sent a rescue unit to take them back by force; however the task—which was called Operation Eagle Claw—failed due to a surprise storm that hit at the worst possible time, destroying the helicopter.

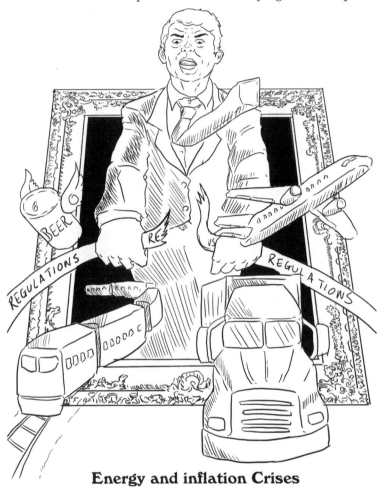

Energy and inflation Crises

Iran was not the only crisis for Carter in 1979. That same year an energy crisis hit the United States. OPEC propped up the price of oil because of the Iranian revolution, and the amount of oil the United States imported decreased significantly. The combination of higher oil prices and lower reserves caused a shortage of oil in the northern, western and Midwestern regions of the United States. Gas lines and rationing were put into effect by state governments, and inflation only continued to rise due to the crisis.

The Carter administration issued a wide variety of measures to end the crisis. The first and the most successful was the deregulation of the oil markets that had been put in place by the Nixon administration. By deregulating oil production in the United States, the amount of oil produced domestically rose and the price of oil started to go down. The second policy was to place a windfall profit tax on oil companies. Over half of the American people believed that OPEC was artificially raising prices on oil due to speculation on problems that could occur in the Middle East. Carter believed that if his administration was going to deregulate oil—which, while alleviating the crisis would also bring even more profit to oil companies—the excess profits should include some tax benefits that would give something back to those afflicted by the crises. While Carter was able to deregulate oil, many conservatives and even some liberal economists refused to back Carter on the windfall profit tax, and so he was unable to get Congress to pass the tax bill.

As if 1979 could not get any worse for Carter and the American people, inflation hit an all-time high of 13.3% (later bested in 1980 by 14.8%). The inflation rate was coupled a period of "stagflation," i.e., when the inflation rate is high, economic growth falls and unemployment rises. And in 1979, for the first time in the Carter administration, GDP growth fell and unemployment rose.

Why did inflation rise? Much of the rise in inflation had been due to the policy of the Nixon administration. Nixon's appointee to the Federal Reserve, Arthur Burns—under pressure from the president to help keep employment near 4%—used the FED to funnel money into the economy. This unnecessary stimulus, coupled with the lowering of interest rates in an already steady economy, caused people to borrow and spend in an unhealthy manner. Burns continued this policy from 1974 to1978. When Carter appointed a new FED chairman in 1978, G. William Miller, Miller continued Burns' policy to the end of that year. Carter repeatedly told Miller to raise interest rates, but the FED ignored the administration. Carter forced Miller to resign as FED chairman, changing his position to treasury secretary. Additionally, economies all around the globe suffered from recession and inflation. Moreover, the energy crises stifled growth and led to more unemployment and shook the American economy, adding even more inflation.

Carter was again faced with the task of appointing a new FED chairmen. He personally interviewed all of the nominees and was most interested by Paul Volcker, who had been frank with Carter in their interview, stating that he would need independence at the FED and would use shock therapy to alleviate the high inflation. Carter was told by his advisors and cabinet members that Volcker would be a poor choice for chairman, but ultimately Carter decided to go with him anyway.

Going into office, Volcker increased interest rates from 1979 to1982. By the time Carter left office in 1981, the high 14.8% inflation rate of 1980 would come down to 11%. By March 1981, only two months after Carter left office, inflation was under 10%; and by the end of 1982, the inflation rate would be stabilized due to Volcker's manipulation of interest rates.

Soviet invasion of Afghanistan, Operation Cyclone

In December of 1979, the Soviet Union invaded Afghanistan. The reason for their invasion, however, relates to the foreign affairs of 1977 and 1978. In 1977 the Soviet Union setup a proxy government in Afghanistan under the guise of the "Democratic-Republic of Afghanistan." In 1978, a rebel group formed to oppose Soviet rule, a group called the Mujahideen. The Soviets did not fear the Mujahideen as a major threat until 1979, when the Carter administration launched Operation Cyclone.

When the administration got wind of the Soviet control of Afghanistan, debate arose among Carter's foreign policy team as to what should be done. Within Carter's foreign policy team there was a long-lasting standoff between the hawkish National Security Advisor Zbigniew Brzezinski and the more dovish Secretary of State Cyrus Vance. Akin to the polarity of the Jefferson vs. Hamilton debates, these two men, who disagreed with each other on almost every issue, dominated foreign policy

Brzezinski felt that supporting the rebels in Afghanistan was not only the most important piece of Middle East diplomacy, but that it was also the strongest card to play in cold war diplomacy. If the Soviets went into the Middle East uncontested, there would be a domino effect, and Soviet expansion could continue. Siding with Brzezinski, Carter began aiding the Mujahideen in their fight against the USSR.

The Unites States used a strategy that would eventually break the Soviet Union. The Afghanistan war forced the Soviets into bankruptcy and destroyed whatever morale was left in the Kremlin. Moreover, the United Nations and more than 100 nations condemned the Soviet Union, and as a result, the Soviets lost trade agreements, economic support, and their world image further crumbled.

Crisis of confidence

Nearing the end of 1979, President Carter was ready to once again address the American people about energy problems. Instead, he decided that it was more important to talk to the American people about deeper problems afflicting the nation. At the time the speech was said to be "politically off tone," but many now see Carter's Crisis of Confidence speech as an accurate depictions of the problems afflicting the United States in the post-Watergate era.

Final acts in 1980

In the chaos of 1980, Carter's final budget was the first balanced budget since 1957. Raising military spending and cutting some liberal programs, he met some opposition to his budget, but it was successfully passed. This was the last balanced budget to be submitted and passed by Congress until 1998. However, Carter made a risky move in 1980 by boycotting the Olympics. The boycott was in response to the Soviet invasion of Afghanistan. Along with sixty-two other nations, including Canada, Israel, and Japan, the Olympic Games were left fairly empty. Before the end of 1980, Carter passed one last large act which was the Alaska Conservation Act, protecting more than 103 million acres of land.

End of the Iranian Hostage Crisis

January 19, 1981, a day before Carter left office, Deputy Secretary of State Warren Christopher negotiated the Algiers Accords. The accords guaranteed the release of the American hostages in Iran. On Carter's final day in office, the hostages were on their way home. On January 21, as President Carter was flying home to Plains, Georgia, the hostages were also flying home—back to the United States.

Few presidents in the modern era have come into office burdened with such a wide range of complex issues. The transitioning economy, cultural divide, and heating up of the cold war would require a Herculean effort from any president. Although not seen that way at the time, historical opinion of Carter is changing, showing that Jimmy Carter did meet many of the challenges of the late 1970s.

Carter, as his record shows, was not an exactly a liberal. In fact, Carter's balanced budget, his vast deregulation and rejection of full employment liberal policies, pork barrel public works projects and over stimulus of the economy makes Carter one of the last conservative Presidents. Although defeated in 1980, his economic legislation and policies would bring inflation down; many of his former cabinet members and appointees in economics, such as Paul Volcker and Zbigniew Brzezinski, were reappointed or utilized by Ronald Reagan because of their stellar job performance.

Carter could often be indecisive and often relied too heavily on round-table discussion to solve problems. He could have benefitted from Truman's more direct, no-nonsense leadership style, which would have saved him from appearing less-than-presidential and helped him in his dealings with Congress. Jimmy Carter was a man of high morals who evinced a sense of compassion and common decency— and toughness. In 2002, he was awarded the Nobel Peace Prize for his "decades of untiring effort to find peaceful solutions to international conflict...and prompt economic and social development."

As for foreign policy, celebrated Cold War historian Martin Walker has said: "The real historical legacy of Jimmy Carter [is] as one of the men who won the cold war. He was the president who really set in train the mixture of policies which the Reagan administration then pursued."

Ronald Reagan
(1981-1989)

"Government exists to protect us from each other.
Where government has gone beyond its limits is in
deciding to protect us from ourselves."

Introduction

Ronald Reagan was born on February 6, 1911, in Tampico, Illinois. When he was a boy, his father, Jack Reagan, nicknamed him "Dutch," as he looked like a "little Dutch boy," and the name stuck. The Reagans moved around for a few years before settling on Dixon, Illinois. There Ronald went to high school and graduated with fair grades and afterward became a lifeguard for six years while attending Eureka College.

Reagan graduated from Eureka in 1932 and applied to work at radio stations. He was hired by the University of Iowa and worked as an announcer for the Chicago Cubs baseball team. He learned the art of quick-thinking oratory when reporting the games with a delay. He often had to predict events or come up with ways to keep the flow of the game going. He traveled with the team through much of the United States, eventually ending up in Hollywood, where he applied for work with Warner Brothers. The studio signed Reagan to a contract, and he mostly appeared in B movies. He acted in a series of films, one of the more famous being his role in *Knute Rockne, All American*, a movie where he played a character named George, the "Gipper," Gipp—a name that became synonymous with Reagan throughout his political career. Reagan's movie career was interrupted when he joined the war effort after Pearl Harbor. He never went overseas but served stateside in a motion picture unit in public relations. After the war, Reagan returned to Hollywood.

Reagan was a registered Democrat and an ideological liberal during his time in film. He led the Screen Actors Guild and supported unions. In the 1940s he married actress Jane Wyman, and they divorced in 1948. His ideological switch to the Republican Party would not occur until he met and married another actress Nancy Davis (her screen name). It was also around this time that Reagan reluctantly spied for the FBI on Hollywood actors.

In the 1950s Reagan became more interested in politics. He had supported Harry Truman in 1948, but switched to Eisenhower in 1952. By 1964, Reagan had made a full ideological turn-around, becoming a member of the very far right. He enthusiastically supported the presidential candidacy of ultraconservative Barry Goldwater, giving a speech titled "A Time for Choosing" that warned of the dangers of the left.

Reagan successfully ran for governor of California in 1967 against what he called "welfare bums" and a promise to end the sometimes violent anti-Vietnam protests at UC Berkley He served for two terms and had a controversial tenure, raising taxes, allowing no-fault divorce, signing a pro-abortion bill, and using the National Guard to end the protests against the Vietnam War. Despite Reagan's less than conservative tenure as governor, he was elected for a second term.

In 1976 Reagan went for the presidency, attempting to replace the incumbent, Gerald Ford for the Republican nomination. The Reagan campaign attacked Ford and hurt him badly, but the moderates in the party gave Ford the nomination but destroyed Ford's chances for reelection. Reagan spent the next four years preparing for 1980, staying in the spotlight.

Bringing Camelot back

Reagan came into office with many promises to fulfill. He had told America that he would alleviate the woes of a country that had fallen on hard times, and by 1984 he would announce that it was "Morning in America." Everything started with his economic plan.

Reagan put into place his preferred brand of economic policies, dubbed "supply-side economics," with the approval of the 1981 budget. It drastically reduced taxes as well as alleviated a problem called "bracket creep"—where inflation pushes income into a higher tax bracket without an increase in purchasing power.

The idea behind supply-side economics was that if people were taxed less by the government, they would have more money in their pocket to invest back into the economy. With the influx of money into the economy, markets would be able to handle the economy better than the government. In fact, many of the Reagan budgets that passed began phasing out social programs for health, food, drug rehabilitation programs, and housing.

Many Democrats, who still controlled the House, were highly skeptical of supply-side economics, believing that the average person would not benefit; but that CEOs and business owners would benefit from the financial deregulations. Money would not be put back into the economy, but into the pockets of the already rich and powerful.

Overall, Ronald Reagan only managed to lower taxes for the average person by a small percentage. Reagan cut taxes significantly in 1981 and brought the top tax bracket from 70% down to 28% by 1986. However, taxes as a percentage of GDP growth only decreased around 1% from 19.6% in 1981 to 18.2% when Reagan left office in 1989, with the majority of taxes being raised on the payroll tax and social security. Another part of Reagan's supply-side economics was deregulating the financial markets. Reagan was able to do this with the passing of the 1982 Garn-St. Germaine Depository Institutions Act that deregulated savings & loans banks so that they could make adjustable mortgage rate loans and exceed existing interest rate ceilings. Herein lies the power of presidential imagery. Reagan was brilliant at the podium, and he slowly became known as the "Teflon" president, immune to any discredit or criticism sticking to him.

His command of presidential power hit new heights when in 1982 the air traffic controllers union went on strike, demanding higher wages and better working conditions. Reagan had said on the campaign trail that he would not stand for a strike by federal employees and threatened to dismiss the controllers if they continued to strike. The controllers were threatening the safety of the airport and the economy. The union did not give up their efforts, and Reagan dismissed 11,345 strikers, replacing them with supervisory staff, air force personnel and other employees. The airports got up and running again—a major success for the tough image he wanted to portray.

All this eventually led to Reagan being able to consolidate his popularity and power. Reagan began pursuing legislation that would start the buildup of the military and commit to fighting the war on drugs.

Deficit spending—something the conservatives were not comfortable with in the 1970s—became acceptable, as Reagan championed it as a means to bolster the American military. Reagan's increase in military spending was planned to out run the Soviet Union in an arms race and also to create new technologies that the Soviet Union lacked. Reagan's two major programs were STAR WARS—or SDI, the Strategic Defense Initiative—and innovations in stealth. SDI was a program that attempted to create a defensive shield that would intercept enemy missiles and destroy warheads in space. Although the program was unsuccessful in creating the shield, it did help advance some laser technology. Reagan's more successful innovation was stealth, which the Soviets were unable to achieve. In total, however, the United States debt quadrupled during Reagan's presidency.

Israel and Lebanon and the Beirut catastrophe

Reagan's first dabbling in diplomatic affairs had gone well for him in 1982 when British Prime Minister Margaret Thatcher asked him to assist her in rallying support for Britain's war in the Falklands Islands. However, later on in the year things became more troublesome for Reagan.

Israel invaded Lebanon in an attempt to eliminate the Palestine Liberation Organization—the PLO. The PLO had been attacking Israel from their bases in Beirut, which led to Israel's shelling of Beirut. The international community intervened in the fighting and temporarily convinced Israel to stop until the PLO was moved from Beirut into Jordan and Tunisia. However, Israel disregarded the international community and occupied Beirut with a green light from the Reagan administration and Secretary of State Alexander Haig. The result of the invasion was a prolonged fight that caused the massacre of hundreds Palestinians in refugee camps. Reagan was forced to fire Haig and to replace him with George Schultz.

In 1983, with more turmoil in Beirut, Reagan sent troops to Lebanon in hopes to ease the tensions of their civil war. Later in that year, a suicide bomber killed 231 American Marines and wounded 50 more. With the American public growing more and more resistant to the U.S. presence in Lebanon, Reagan pulled the rest of the united forces out of Lebanon soon after.

Two days after the bombings in Beirut, in 1983, the Reagan

administration ordered the invasion of Grenada. The prime minister of Grenada had been assassinated by pro-Marxist rebels, and Reagan invaded, citing his concern for the 1,000 American students on the island. However, the island was a commonwealth of Great Britain, and Margaret Thatcher vehemently opposed Reagan's action. Moreover, the United Nations attempted to pass a resolution citing the invasion as "precipitous and unnecessary," which was unsurprisingly vetoed by the United States in the Security Council. The Marxists rebels were no comparison to the United States troops and were quickly put down. While Americans largely supported Reagan, many believed Grenada to be a political smokescreen for the incident in Beirut, which had badly damaged Reagan's reputation.

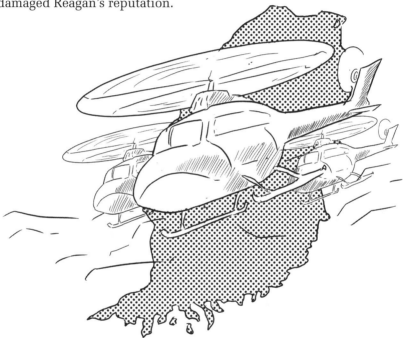

Chink in the armor.

What would eventually be known as the Iran-Contra affair began Reagan's first experiences with troublesome relations with the House and the Senate. In 1982 and 1984, the House passed amendments sponsored by Democratic Representative Edward Boland that prohibited the United States from aiding the Contras in Nicaragua. The Contras were a rebel group, formed and trained by the CIA in 1981, which opposed the Socialist Sandinista government that was in power.

In 1986 it was revealed that Reagan decided to violate the Boland Amendments and sold arms to Iran—a nation on which the United States had placed an embargo—and used the illegally secured money to fund the Contra operation. All this was done without telling the Congress or the American people. The plan was in part orchestrated by Oliver North, a military advisor on the National Security Council; and for his participation in the event, North, as well as twelve other members of the Reagan administration, were indicted or imprisoned. Although the Iran-Contra affair could have led to an impeachment, Congress most likely did not want to go through another impeachment nightmare and eventually let the scandal die.

Playing all sides of the field

Part of Reagan's success in passing legislation was his ability to seemingly cater to all views without alienating his conservative base. When Reagan passed an immigration reform bill that gave amnesty to

3 million illegal immigrants he placated conservatives with more tax breaks. When Reagan cut corporate tax rates he hiked up Social Security benefits to placate liberals. He also got his way with some unorthodox appointments such as the notable appointment of Alan Greenspan, who replaced Paul Volcker as FED chairman in 1987.

However not everyone was swayed by the charismatic Ronald Reagan. Farmers were at odds with him throughout the 1980s. The last time a president had really pleased the farming community was during the 1930s and 1940s with Franklin Roosevelt's herculean effort to reform the United States agricultural policy. However, after FDR, no president really focused on the issue of agriculture.

Reagan, however, attempted to impose his free market ideology on the agricultural community during the 1980s. His administration intended to reduce price supports for farmers and also lower trade barriers. This policy was coupled with the new reality that the farmers of the 1980s faced—debt. During the 1970s farmers had benefited from exemplary trade with the Soviet Union and easier lending policies due an agricultural boom that brought above-average incomes to them for almost an entire decade. However, as technology became more expensive and necessary while landownership became more competitive because of the rise of big agricultural business, farmers began to spend more and go deeper into debt. When interest rates jumped in 1980 and 1981, farmers had a difficult time borrowing money—which farmers tend to rely on doing—and continued to go into higher levels of debt. Also, in 1980, the year-long embargo on grain trade with the Soviet Union caused exports to fall, giving farmers less income.

Reagan initially moved to lessen government subsidies to farmers and to allow privatization to work its magic. Thus during his first term an unprecedented number of small farmers went out of business and had their land purchased by large agricultural businesses or insurance companies. By 1983, Reagan had a 35% approval rating with small farmers. So Reagan passed an expensive farm bill that year, amounting to a staggering $51 billion, which boosted his approval rating back to 51% among farmers by 1984. However, in 1985—after being safely reelected—the Reagan administration sponsored the Food Security Act, which once again attempted to refocus agricultural policy towards market orientation. Moreover, the administration required farmers to reduce their acreage, which only made farmers try and produce more with less acreage and allowed larger farms and businesses buy up their land. Once again,

Reagan's approval rating among farmers fell into the 30 % range in 1985. Thus, the 1980s began with the disappearance of the family farm and the rise of big agricultural business. Nixon's secretary of agriculture Earl Butz takes some blame here too, as he moved the government towards a policy of corporate farming and encouraged farmers to "get big or get out," causing them to rapidly expand by incurring debt.

End of the Teflon President

John Kennedy and Ronald Reagan have a lot in common, but one of those most interesting things they share is that their loyalists got out in front and created an atmosphere that has kept both men held high in the public's esteem. While Reagan's name has become synonymous with tax cuts, he left office with a tax rate almost at the same level as that in the last year of the Carter administration with the majority of the tax cuts going to corporations or wealthy citizens. The Reagan administration clung to the belief that the debt did not matter—the justification being that all this money that quadrupled the deficit was necessary to destroy the Soviet Union. The deficit actually rose from $997 billion to $2.8 trillion alongside an expanded government bureaucracy. For the average business owner in America regulations stayed the same. President Reagan, however, deregulated only parts of the financial market; deregulating the financial market led to the Savings and Loans Crisis that occurred during Reagan's final years.

Ronald Reagan is not without his achievements. His firm stand against the air traffic controller union in 1982 was risky but ultimately solved the problem with dividends, reaffirming the Taft-Hartley Act. Moreover, Reagan's continuation of Carter's Operation Cyclone in Afghanistan— supporting Afghan Rebels—contributed to the fall of the Soviet Union and their eventual withdrawal in 1987.

Intellectual Anglo-American Christopher Hitchens summed up Reagan best when making a contrast between him and Margaret Thatcher: "Mrs. Thatcher wanted to be respected; Ronald Reagan wanted to be loved." Margaret Thatcher was harsh, often uncompromising and spoke of sacrifice, but her leadership changed Britain despite the disdain she received from not only her opposition but from her own party. Ronald Reagan's legacy is vexing. He spoke of conservatism but gave the American people policies that were truly neoconservative, promising everything for nothing.

George H. W. Bush
(1989-1993)

"We are a nation of communities... a brilliant diversity spread like stars, like a thousand points of light in a broad and peaceful sky."

Introduction

George H. W. Bush was born on June 12, 1924, in Milton, Massachusetts. His father, Prescott Bush, was a Wall Street banker and a U.S. senator from Connecticut. Prescott moved the family to Greenwich, Connecticut and like him, his son attended private schools in Connecticut and in Massachusetts.

H. W. Bush distinguished himself during World War II. He had postponed college and enlisted in the navy at the age of 18. He became a naval aviator and flew a bomber during the war. On one occasion his plane was hit and burst into flames though he completed his bombing run before abandoning the plane. He floated for hours in the water until he was rescued. After the war, he studied economics at Yale, where he joined the exclusive secret Skull and Bones Society—as his father

Prescott had done before him. He met Barbara Pierce of Rye, New York and married her in 1945.

After graduating from Yale, he moved to Texas and entered the oil industry. From the 1950s to the mid-1960s   Bush spent most of his time developing oil companies and became a millionaire. However, in 1964 Bush decided to enter politics. He took a congressional seat in 1964 as a moderate Republican. He supported the Civil Rights Act of 1968 and even voted in favor of allowing birth control, despite conservative opposition. After serving for three terms, Bush set his sights on becoming a senator. President Nixon asked him to run against incumbent Texas Senator Ralph Yarborough—a Democrat and a man who was anti-Nixon to his core—and Bush abandoned his congressional seat to challenge the senator. Bush lost, but Nixon returned the favor and made him U.S. ambassador to the United Nations. Bush did his job well and continued to rise through the ranks of the Republican Party, becoming chairman of the Republican National Committee in 1973—a tough time to be a Republican.

Bush supported Nixon throughout 1973 and 1974 until the last few days of the Nixon presidency, when Bush strongly suggested that it would be best for Nixon to resign. Bush's loyalty once again paid off; Gerald Ford—the new president—appointed him envoy to China in 1975. Relations with China, even after the Nixon visit, were still not normalized, and so there was no ambassador. In 1976 Ford again called upon Bush and appointed him as the director of the Central Intelligence Agency (CIA); however, it was short lived because Ford lost the election in 1977. Bush spent the next few years, from 1977 to1979, working at the first international bank council and for the Foreign Relations Committee and decided to run for president in 1980. While Ronald Reagan represented the far right of the Republican Party and John Anderson represented the far left of the liberal Republicans, Bush was at the center. He called Reagan's economic policy "voodoo economics" and tried to appeal to the old moderates who had elected Eisenhower and Nixon. However, the climate was not on Bush's side. 1980 was gearing up to be a radical year, and Ronald Reagan's brand of politics had become more palatable. Bush lost the primary as a presidential candidate, but became the vice presidential nominee.

After winning in 1980 with Ronald Reagan, Bush served for eight years as vice president, taking a less active role than his predecessor, Vice President Walter Mondale. Bush mostly was sent overseas to political events, attending so many funerals that he got the nickname the "grim reaper." However in 1988 the Republican Party was finally ready to accept him as long as he ran on Ronald Reagan's policies and avoided calling them "voodoo economics" again.

Leading in his own way

George H. W. Bush had large shoes to fill when he came into office. Reagan had proven to be one of the most popular presidents of the postwar era and conservative and blue dog Democrats alike expected Bush to follow the Reagan agenda. However, H. W. Bush was a different man and held a different ideology. When he first ran for president in 1980 against Reagan in the Republican primary he had mocked "Reaganomics." However he had promised his electorate during the 1988 campaign: "Read my lips. No new taxes." He promised to be tough on taxes and continue what Reagan had started in terms of governance.

His promises became difficult to carry out though, because he was faced with a series of major crises. The first was the Savings and Loans Crisis, resulting in Bush and the Congress bailing out the failing banking institutions. Then there was the U.S. invasion of Panama, which was intended to dismantle the government of Dictator Manuel Noriega. Bush sent 2,000 troops to Panama in 1992, the same year that Noriega lost his election to Guillermo Endara, who refused to give up power. While suppressing protestors and Endara supporters, Noriega killed a U.S. serviceman. Bush seized the opportunity to send in 24,000 troops and successfully overthrew the Noriega regime.

By 1990, when a new budget was being debated, Bush realized that a compromise would have to be reached on the question of taxes and revenue. He had promised on the campaign trail in 1988 that he would not impose any new taxes on Americans; however Democrats in the Senate refused to pass any Republican budgets without tax hikes. Far right-wing Republicans refused to compromise even though Democrats had a majority in the both the Senate and the House. Bush knew that he would have to compromise, and after negotiating with Democrats, was able to get them to lower their original demand regarding the proposed tax hikes. In the end, the aim was to reduce the 1990 federal budget by $492 trillion while increasing tax revenue by $140 trillion. With the signing of the compromise Bush had broken his 1988 campaign promise. Many far-right Republicans such as House minority whip Newt Gingrich revolted against Bush for the rest of his administration.

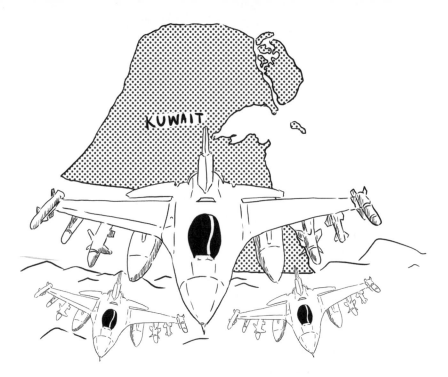

Fall of the Soviets and the Gulf War

While things were rocky domestically, Bush had some major successes in foreign affairs. It was also foreign policy that maintained and brought his approval ratings up. In 1991, the Soviet Union dissolved after Mikhail Gorbachev stepped down as premier. Advisors close to Bush told him to take this chance to boast about American exceptionalism and claim victory over the Soviet Union, but Bush felt that the fall of the Soviet Union was a moment for Russia and all of the Eastern Bloc. Bush largely isolated himself from the event, letting the citizens of the former Soviet Socialist Republic bask in their freedom. Although the public wanted Bush to do more than just sit back and nod, he felt it would not be proper.

Then there came the Gulf War. In 1990, Saddam Hussein, the tyrannical leader of Iraq, invaded and annexed Kuwait, a neighbor that controlled large sums of oil deposits. Hussein claimed that Kuwait was traditionally part of Iraq. Bush saw Hussein's aggression as violation of international law and took military action against Iraq. With the United Nations and authorization from Congress, Bush launched the First Gulf War—aka Operation Desert Shield—in which the United States pushed Hussein back into Iraq. In line with United Nations guidelines, Bush stopped the war effort once Hussein had fled Kuwait, although many advisors and the American public felt he should have ignored the rules and gone after Hussein.

The war boosted Bush's approval ratings to 89% and dispelled the "Vietnam syndrome" that had settled in the American mindset after the Vietnam War. Although the war successfully followed UN guidelines, it was not without its consequences. Americans had been sold on the war in Kuwait (i) because of propaganda that equated Hussein with the likes of Hitler, and (ii) because the war was internationally televised on the nightly news, thus the nickname *Video Game War*. When Bush decided not to pursue Hussein into Iraq, the American people had felt that the mission was unresolved.

In the mid-1990s Bush and his National Security Advisor Brent Scowcroft commented on why they did not invade Iraq and force Hussein out of power. Both men had agreed that chasing Hussein and deposing him would have led to destabilization of the Middle East, and that despite Hussein's reputation as a ruthless dictator, it made little sense to disturb an entire region for one man.

Recession and NAFTA

Bush's 80% approval ratings did not last long. By 1991 the economy had fallen into a recession, with unemployment reaching 7.8%. The reason for the recession was largely due to the typical boom/bust of the economy. Many people started using bumper stickers and wearing buttons that said things like "Saddam still has his job. I don't have mine." They felt that Bush was out of touch on economic issues.

Bush did use 1992 to begin negotiations over the North American Free Trade Agreement (NAFTA), which created the largest free trade zone in the world. He signed the agreement in 1992, although it did not pass in the Senate until he left office, in 1994.

Election of 1992

In the beginning, 1992 seemed to be another election year that would have a clear cut and simple outcome. The Republican incumbent during a recession would lose to a Democrat running on a platform of change from the status quo. However, by February of 1992, that expectation crumbled. The Republican incumbent had received a challenge from his own party, the Democratic sweetheart had been nearly brought down by an alleged affair, and out of nowhere came one of the most successful dark-horse, third-party candidates—Ross

Perot. Bill Clinton—the young governor of Arkansas with a history in the Democratic party—battled for the nomination against Iowa senator Tom Harkin and California governor Jerry Brown. Harkin, a running quasi-populist campaign, was quickly forced out by Clinton; and the race focused on Clinton and Brown. Despite the romantic scandal that hurt Clinton in the early primary races, he clinched the nomination.

President Bush had opposition at the Republican convention. Because he broke his promise not to create any new taxes, Bush faced a challenge from journalist Pat Buchanan, a far-right Republican candidate. Despite some strong support for Buchanan, Bush won the nomination anyway.

Enter Ross Perot, the independent and dynamic Texas billionaire set on changing the election. Perot entered the race without running a single campaign ad or spending a single dime on getting his name out and was instantly neck and neck with Clinton and Bush in the polls—a feat never before achieved. Much of Perot's support came from Americans who were weary of the status quo and felt that in prior elections they had not been presented with a real choice. Perot received much of his support from labor, as he was a powerful businessman and a protectionist who attacked NAFTA—which both Clinton and Bush supported. For Perot, NAFTA was the most harmful job-losing agreement in American history. He famously stated that NAFTA would create a "large sucking sound," as it sent American jobs to Mexico. He was also a reformer and dedicated much of his campaign rhetoric to lowering the national debt.

Surprisingly, Perot pulled out from the race in the summer of 1992, when some pollsters had him at 39% in polls. Although he was fairly ambiguous as to why he quit the race at the time, Perot later said that he was threatened by Republican operatives. For whatever reason, he had quit, causing him to lose a large chunk of popular support when he eventually jumped back into the race weeks later.

The presidential debates gave Clinton a huge boost and damaged Bush and Perot. Bush seemed out of touch and probably did not win any voters by checking his watch during the debates. Perot's energetic debating style and eccentric personality took some points away from him when he was matched up with Clinton, who came off as calm, knowledgeable, and someone who could "feel your pain."

Clinton won the election, securing most of the North and key parts of the South. Some poll sampling indicated that Perot may have hurt Bush's chances, but Perot siphoned off an equal number of votes from Democrats as well as Republicans. Perot showed the best third-party performance since Theodore Roosevelt's progressive run for the White House in 1912.

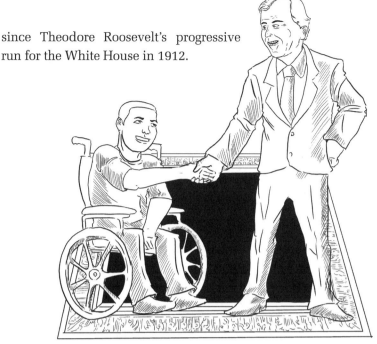

The quiet champion

In the 1988 campaign the media initially labeled Bush the "wimp factor." However, Bush's foreign policy was truly among the most successful of the 80s, 90s, and 00s. He embodied Theodore Roosevelt's "speak softly but carry a big stick." When the Soviet Union fell, Bush behaved with his usual restraint, and, remained quiet, allowing the rest of the Western world to triumph over having beaten Russia. In Kuwait, the military operation was quick and successful in following the rules of the United Nations and in creating an international coalition. It was also Bush who led the way for the American's with Disabilities Act. Yet Bush lacked the charm and the image that the American public had grown used to with Reagan. His natural reserve did not endear him to the media or to the public.

While Reagan was able to compromise and maintain his popularity within the Republican Party and among the voters with spin, Bush let his compromise stand for itself. Moreover, while Bush stayed fiscally conservative and refused to use stimulus to alleviate a boom/bust cycle recession, it was not enough to sway the radical conservatives in his party who challenged him in the Republican primary. The economy seemed to be in decline, though it was recovering by the time Clinton came to office. Despite Bush's strong record and 56% high approval ratings, an economy in recession can end presidential tenure.

Bill Clinton
(1993-2001)

"There is nothing wrong with America that cannot be cured with what is right in America."

Introduction

Bill Clinton—William Jefferson Blythe III at birth—was born in Hope, Arkansas, on August 19, 1946. His father died three months before Clinton was born. Clinton spent his earliest years with his grandparents, as his mother, Virginia Dell Cassidy, left home to finish her studies. She returned in 1950, when Bill was four, and married Roger Clinton, changing her son's name to Bill Clinton His stepfather was an alcoholic and was abusive to Clinton's mother and half-brother. Clinton said that he had to intervene and threaten violence to force his stepfather to mend his ways.

Clinton was a good and popular high school student. The most important part of those years for Clinton occurred in 1963, when he shook hands with President Kennedy—a moment caught on video and played during his 1992 campaign. Kennedy's rhetoric resonated with Clinton, and he went to the Georgetown School of Foreign Service with scholarships. He was active in student government and politics and did well in his studies, graduating in 1968 and winning a Rhodes scholarship, which enabled him to attend Oxford University in England. When he returned to America, he entered Yale's Law School and participated in antiwar rallies. Clinton got a taste of politics when he became active in George McGovern's 1972 presidential campaign in Texas. At Yale, Clinton met Hillary Rodham and fell in love. After graduating from Yale in 1973, he moved to California for a short time to be with her, and they married in 1975.

Clinton decided to enter politics in 1974 with a run for the House from Arkansas. He lost but was determined to win another position. He ran for attorney general and won. The position elevated him, giving him a public image in Arkansas and allowed him to run for governor in 1978. He won, becoming the youngest governor in the country at the time. With the worsening economy and the growing turmoil in Arkansas over Cuban refugees and his proposed rate increases, Clinton lost his reelection bid in 1980 but redeemed the loss in 1982 with a victory that secured him the governor's mansion for a decade.

From 1982 to 1992, though Clinton had a successful tenure as governor, he had some personal issues in the office. He made some poor investments in Arkansas real estate and allegedly made some deals that would come to haunt him during his presidency. Clinton also thought about a presidential run, but decided against it—possibly to settle his personal affairs. However, the overall improvement of education and of the economy in Arkansas gave him a good base to run on in the 1992 presidential election.

High hopes and gridlock

Bill Clinton's presidency offers an interesting look at the modern political arena. Elected by less than a majority in a three-way contest, Clinton took office with a moderate amount of support as well as a democratically controlled Congress. However, the Democrats in Congress had lost seats in the 1992 election, signaling the fact that the country was still interested in the conservative message. Two years after Clinton took office, the Democrats would lose both the House and the Senate to the Republican Revolution. Georgia representative Newt Gingrich would take over as Speaker of the House, relentlessly opposing the president's agenda and causing significant gridlock. Sound familiar? But Clinton was adept with a fair amount of compromise as president to accomplish passage of some of his agenda.

Clinton's first major negotiation in the White House was over NAFTA. With help from Democrats and Republicans alike, he passed the North American Free Trade Agreement, which lowered or abolished tariffs with Mexico and Canada. The effects of NAFTA have been extremely controversial. Perot's accusation of NAFTA causing jobs being sent to Mexico has been somewhat vindicated during this time, as manufacturing plants and factories were closed and jobs were shipped to Mexico. The United States also went from having one of the highest trade surpluses to one of the worst trade deficits with Mexico. Blue collar workers were less than thrilled by the legislation, but many corporations and Republicans applauded the agreement. Clinton then used some of the political capital to try and reform the healthcare system.

The goal was to obtain universal healthcare. Clinton set up a task force, in part led by First Lady Hillary Clinton, to sway the public in the debate on healthcare since it met opposition in Congress. Ultimately the Clinton task force was unsuccessful, and the House rejected the Clinton healthcare reforms. Democrats broke ranks with Clinton and Republicans united against them.

Despite the loss on healthcare, in 1993 and 1994 Clinton passed a legislative agenda that aimed to combat crime in the United States. The crime level had been steadily rising to an obscene level during the 80s. While the gun control and death penalty provision of Clinton's criminal reforms received some criticism, Clinton's crime initiative went forward successfully. When Clinton came to office crime rates had reached a near historic high in the 1980s, and by the time of his departure from office they reached record lows.

Government shutdown

In the 1994 midterm elections, Republicans took control of the House of Representatives for the first time since 1952. Battling with Clinton, Republicans shut down the government rather than pass the budget that Democrats presented to the House in 1995. The government was shut down for five days, but eventually Clinton and Republicans came to an agreement on a new budget. In addition, Clinton was put into a corner on many things such as gay rights. Due to the political climate he signed into law the Defense of Marriage Act (DOMA) and Don't Ask, Don't Tell policy.

Despite the partisan fighting Clinton's last four years in office saw the passage of four balanced budgets that came about during a time of economic growth. The surplus that Clinton acquired in 1998—the first

since 1969—was revenue from the balanced budgets used to pay down some of the public debt. While the 1990s sustained some of the best economic stability and growth in American history, surpassing both the 1980s and 1950s, it should be noted that Clinton's presidency coincided with a gigantic tech boom, which caused the stock market to surge to insane levels but eventually burst in late 1999.

Although some compromise is necessary in any presidential administration, it can go too far. This is made most clear near the end of Clinton's presidency. He had signed a compromise bill, the Gramm-Leach-Bliley Act in 1999, which deregulated financial markets and removed one of Franklin Roosevelt's pillars of the New Deal; the Glass-Steagall Act of 1933, which separated investment banks from savings banks. Many economists, such as Paul Krugman, say that this deregulation led to the 2007 subprime mortgage and 2008 financial crises.

Monica Lewinsky scandal and impeachment

In 1998, Linda Tripp, a friend of White House intern Monica Lewinsky, volunteered information to the independent counsel investigating Clinton improprieties dating back to Arkansas. The allegation was that Ms. Lewinsky and President Clinton had a sexual affair from 1994 to 1996.

Clinton denied having "sexual relations" with Lewinsky, but the investigation produced evidence convincing the public to think otherwise. Although Clinton repeatedly stated; "I did not have sexual relations with that woman," he finally admitted that she performed oral sex on him. The House voted to impeach, the Senate refused to convict him, and Clinton was acquitted. Bill Clinton left the White House in 2001 with a polarizing legacy. He had presided over the largest economic peacetime expansion in American history, balanced the budget, and also reduced crime across the nation with early initiatives. However, scandals have perhaps damaged his image as president. Moreover, labor is still dealing with the effects of NAFTA on American workers, and many foreign policy buffs have questioned how strong Clinton's foreign policy truly was and if the government should have been more active in the Middle East and in rooting out terrorist groups.

One thing is for sure however. Bill Clinton remains immensely popular in public opinion polls. He left office with high approval ratings and has become a highly esteemed representative not only of the Democratic Party but of the country.

George W. Bush
(2001-2009)

"Terrorist attacks can shake the foundations of our biggest buildings, but they cannot touch the foundation of America. These acts shatter steel, but they cannot dent the steel of American resolve."

Introduction

George Walker Bush was born in New Haven, Connecticut, on July 6, 1946. His father is the 41st President of the United States, George H. W. Bush. George W. Bush was raised in Texas and educated in Massachusetts. He attended public school in Texas for a while and eventually went to the Phillips Academy in Andover, Massachusetts. After Phillips, Bush went to his father and his grandfather's alma mater, Yale University. He graduated in 1968 after earning himself an interesting reputation as he was a cheerleader, a member of the Skull and Bones secret society, and as president, in his senior year, of Delta Kappa Epsilon fraternity. His education continued in 1973, when he entered Harvard Business School—obtaining an M.B.A.

In 1968 Bush was commissioned into the Texas Air National Guard and learned to fly and was eventually honorably discharged in November of 1974. In 1977 Bush married Laura Lane Welch, a librarian and a school teacher. Bush credits her with helping him to overcome his alcoholism; he quit drinking in 1986.

Bush started his political life in 1978, when he attempted to win a seat in the House of Representatives. He lost to Kent Hance, and instead of politics Bush went into the oil industry. He founded Bush Exploration and was active in the oil business throughout the 1980s until his father moved the family to Washington, D.C., where Bush worked on his father's 1988 campaign. After his father won, Bush returned to Texas and bought a share in the Texas Rangers baseball team, bringing him over $14 million in profits.

After once again helping his father's campaign in 1992, which his father lost, Bush ran for governor of Texas in 1994. He ran against the popular Democratic incumbent Ann Richards but was able to beat her with help from Karl Rove, who orchestrated a campaign that utilized the issue of gun rights—Richards had vetoed a concealed weapons bill—and also circulated rumors that Richards was a lesbian.

As governor, Bush cut taxes—using the surplus that the preceding administrations had accumulated—signed pro-gun legislation and made Texas a leading power in wind energy. Bush won reelection in a landslide, which helped propel him to become the Republican presidential nominee in 2000. Bush ran against Clinton's vice president, Al Gore. Bush won fewer of the popular vote than his opponent— presenting a constitutional crisis– but was ultimately rewarded the presidency by the Supreme Court.

Start of the Bush presidency and the 9/11 attack on the Twin Towers

When George W. Bush stepped into office in 2001 the doomsday clock was nowhere close to midnight in America, for the country had just gone through a prosperous decade and felt financially secure. W. Bush had a domestic agenda to enact, but just as he got the Bush tax cuts secured—a large reduction of taxes for the wealthy and corporations— the country's outlook changed fundamentally, for his presidency would have to focus on foreign terrorism.

On September 11, 2001, airplanes flew into each of the Twin Towers of the World Trade Center in New York City's financial district. The perpetrators, members of Al-Qaeda, an Islamic terrorist organization headed by Osama Bin Laden, claimed responsibility, and a debate was launched in the United States over how to combat terrorism in the future.

America changes

One of Bush's first acts after declaring the War on Terror was to seek passage of the Patriot Act, a piece of legislation that was intended to help the federal government crack down on suspected terrorists domestically and abroad.

Another measure to combat terrorist threats at home was the creation of the Department of Homeland Security, established in 2002 to stop terrorist attacks and to respond to any potential threats to or disasters in America.

The Defense Advanced Research Project Agency (DARPA) was established to gather and to gain total information awareness in the United States. Surveillance, tracking systems, enlarged government bureaucracy, and expanded powers became prevalent in the government. If older historians referred to Nixon's White House years as the "imperial presidency," then the new presidency could be called "the enhanced imperial presidency."

The end of peacetime

In 2003 Bush initiated the Operation Enduring Freedom invasion to root out the Al-Qaeda terrorist organization that had a significant presence in Afghanistan. Then Bush called for an invasion of Iraq, claiming that the Saddam Hussein regime and the Iraq government were in possession of Weapons of Mass Destruction (WMD). Bush demanded that Colin Powell, his secretary of defense, bring the debate to the United Nations, as the president was trying to receive international support to invade. The UN sent inspectors and found no evidence of WMDs in Iraq and refused to join the Bush administration's venture.

Bush used the "self-defense" claim, which justified attacks on our perceived enemy. With approval from Congress, Bush invaded Iraq. The invasion was immensely expensive, costing $1.7 trillion.

Mission accomplished?

On May 1, 2003, Bush emerged onto an aircraft carrier wearing a flight suit to declare not only our success in the Iraq war, but to tell the nation that the major combat operations in Iraq were over, and that the mission was accomplished. Despite these claims, the majority of the casualties in the war occurred after the "Mission Accomplished" speech, and tensions escalated throughout his second term, 2004 to 2008. Nevertheless, Bush won reelection against Massachusetts senator John Kerry.

By late 2003, the Bush administration was caught in its own web of lies about the Weapons of Mass Destruction, as the only weapons found in Iraq were old decommissioned chemical armaments that were no longer a threat to anyone and had been catalogued nearly a decade earlier.

The remains of the Bush domestic policy and "No Child Left Behind"

Bush, along with Senator Ted Kennedy –a Massachusetts Democrat-- passed massive educational reform legislation called "No Child Left Behind." NCLB increased the government's role in the public education system by offering more federal funding to schools to improve test scores in teaching English, Math, and Reading.

The bill has been heavily criticized for forcing public schools to focus less on content and more on teaching a narrow line of subject matter that prepares students to take standardized tests in each state. History, the sciences, and the humanities have been systemically curbed, as English and math are more heavily promoted. The United States had drastically fallen behind in international educational competition since the implementation of NCLB. Bush attempted Social Security reforms too. He and the Republicans wanted to privatize it. Democrats in the House opposed Bush's efforts, and even after his sixty-day tour of the country advocating for his reforms, the Republicans could not pass it.

There was also the issue of illegal immigration. Over eight million immigrants had illegally crossed the border and were living in the U.S.. Bush called for immigration reform and stronger defenses at the Mexican border. The Republican Party split over the bipartisan immigration reform bill of 2007, conservatives believing the bill to be offering amnesty to illegal immigrants. The bill died in the Senate after cloture could not be reached.

Economic crisis of 2007-2008

In 2007 the major banks in the United States failed, and the economy went into free fall. Millions of people lost their jobs, homes, and savings. The United States fell into what has been called the "Great Recession," but what caused this crisis?

The crisis was caused by far more than just policies pursued and enforced by the Bush administration. Beginning with the Reagan administration, with the passage of the Garn-St. Germain Depository Institutions Act of 1982, which deregulated mortgage rate loans and led to easier adjustable rates, a mixture of government policies as well as government deregulation poisoned the financial markets.

Deregulation

RONALD REAGAN: Garn-St. Germain Act: deregulated banks, loosening government oversight of mortgage rates.

ALAN GREENSPAN: While Chairman of the Federal Reserve, he kept derivatives market unregulated.

BILL CLINTON: Gramm-Leach-Bliley Act deregulated financial systems by repealing Franklin Roosevelt's Glass-Steagall Act, which barred investment and savings banks from merging.

GEORGE W. BUSH: Encouraged continued deregulation and ignored calls for oversight and regulation of hedge funds and massive banks.

Government policy

BILL CLINTON: Through amendments to the Community Reinvestment Act, banks were forced to give more lenient rates on mortgages and had incentives to give loans to less than desirable home owners.

GEORGE W. BUSH: Encouraged irresponsible home ownership, encouraged banks to give out loans to practically anyone.

Irresponsible markets

The government alone is certainly not responsible for the economic crises, Wall Street, Banks, investment firms and other private institutions share some of the blame. Through irresponsible market tactics such as Credit Default Swaps (CDCs), Shadow Banking and overleveraging, the markets failed to act in behalf of their customers and the citizens of the United States.

Shadow Banking is a new system that has risen in the financial markets, where institutions act like banks but do not fall under the same regulations and traditional roles as proper banks do.

Subprime Mortgage is a mortgage that was given to someone who may not be able to pay back the mortgage on a reasonable time table and has poor credit history.

Overleveraging happens when people have too much debt but are able to purchase a mortgage by putting down a payment that is obscenely low in comparison to the actual mortgage cost and price tag of the home.

Credit Default Swap is a contract, close to that of an insurance contract, between two institutions that guarantee money. In relation to the financial crises, banks and private institutions purchased large amounts of stocks, and like a car, had them insured by other banks and institutions, essentially getting rid of their "risk" factor in owning the stocks. The problem was, that all these institutions became entangled in so many insurance schemes, that when the stock market crashed, nearly all the banks went bankrupt, as no one had the funds to insure all the failed stocks and bonds.

Collateral was used in insuring credit default swaps by using a sum of money as a guarantee in the CDC contracts that deals would be made whole. If the collateral could not be paid or was used because of a failure to keep a deal whole, the credit rating of the institution guaranteeing that collateral would go down.

So what happened? After the 2006 peak in home ownership, new homeowners and people who had purchased Subprime Mortgages and were overleveraged were unable to make payments on their mortgage. The interests on the mortgages, which had provided the nation with economic growth and a boom in markets, had been heavily invested in by Wall Street and other private firms. The investments made by Wall Street were then insured by Credit Default Swaps, where institutions glued themselves together by insuring each other's loans and taking away risk. When the market became unstable in 2007 due to the failure of homeowners to come through on payments, the stock market took a hit and the investors became skittish about their insured loans. Investors made runs on each other's insurance, and when the web of CDCs started to tighten, the investors ran out of money with which to pay the collateral, since they had invested too much money in the market. Unable to pay collateral and keep their deals whole, their credit ratings decreased. This was the case with AIG, where their credit rating of AAA rapidly decreased. The fall in credit rating forced the companies to provide even more collateral, which in turn made the companies lose more money, deepening the crisis. Finally, in a rapid short period of time, companies and banks such as AIG decided to cut their losses and liquidate their assets, throwing the economy into free fall.

Bank bailouts

In response to the failure of the banks and the financial markets, President Bush called for a bank bailout package, which was passed by the House and Senate under the acronym TARP. The Bush administration, with almost full support of both houses of Congress, appropriated $700 billion to fund to the failed banks and requested the banks to consolidate and repay the government loans. By 2009, only four major banks dominated the markets: JP Morgan-Chase, Citigroup, Wells Fargo, and Bank of America.

While we all want to declare that a mission is accomplished, it is often not the case; in fact, it can be premature. Declaring the Iraq war a "mission accomplished" is prime example. Despite good intentions, the goal of getting Americans to acquire homes—without having any financial resources or collateral–was not a way to accomplish a better life for them.

George W. Bush left the White House in 2008 with low approval ratings and returned to his home in Texas.

Barack Obama
(2009-2017)

"There is not a liberal America and a conservative America - there is the United States of America."

Introduction

Barack Hussein Obama II was born on August 4, 1961 in Honolulu, Hawaii. His mother, Ann Dunham, was from Kansas and his father, Barack Obama Sr., from Kenya. His parents separated just after he was born when his mother moved to Seattle to finish her degree. Obama's father finished his undergraduate education at the University of Hawaii and then went on to Harvard Graduate School to study economics. His parents were divorced in 1964.

In 1965 Obama's mother remarried to an Indonesian graduate student she met at college, Lolo Soetoro. She and Lolo relocated to Indonesia with Obama in 1967 where they stayed until 1971. In that same year young Obama returned to Hawaii to live with his maternal grandparents while his mother remained in Indonesia. During Obama's stay in Indonesia he had received some education in Indonesian schools, but much of his education came from his mother in the form of homeschooling. When Obama moved to his grandparents he began attending private school with the assistance of a scholarship. His mother returned to Hawaii in 1972, with her second child, and stayed until 1975, but when she returned to Indonesia with his sister Obama decided to stay in Hawaii with his grandparents.

Barack Obama completed his high school education at Punahou School in 1979 and enrolled in Occidental College in Los Angeles the same year. There he attracted much attention after delivering a speech calling for Occidental's divestment from South Africa. This helped him transfer to Columbia University where he majored in political science.

He graduated from Columbia in 1983 and spent a year working for the Business International Corporation and then the New York Public Interest Research Group. In the mid-1980s Obama decided to move to Chicago and do something to contribute to the community. He became a community organizer working with local parishes and focused on creating programs that aided in job training and college prep, among many other things. It was during this period that Obama picked up some important skills that eventually helped him to become President, running a campaign based on "organizing for action." In 1988 Obama entered Harvard Law School and got national attention when he became President of the *Harvard Law Review* in his second year. He graduated with a J.D. *magna cum laude* in 1991 and began teaching constitutional law at the University of Chicago.

From 1992 to 2004 Obama was a professor but he was also a writer and state senator. He wrote and published in the early 90s *Dreams from My Father*, his now famous book about his father, Barack Obama Sr. One year after the book was published, his mother died from ovarian cancer and since Obama had lost his father in 1982, he was now on his own.

From 1997 to 2004 Obama was a state senator and reformer. He made reforms in the state welfare system, enacted death penalty reforms and fought for tax credits for low-income workers. He gave running for the House of Representatives a shot but lost the 2000 primary. However, after meeting and hiring David Axelrod in 2002 he decided to run for the Senate. He won the Senate race in a year in which Democrats retook Illinois, and made a name for himself. His recognition was bolstered most by a speech he gave at the 2004 Democratic Convention. It was a year when people were dissatisfied with polarization and both of their choices for President—George W. Bush and John Kerry; Obama's speech about unifying the country and bringing a better image to politics made people turn their heads.

His tenure in the Senate was also impressive. He served on a series of committees including the powerful Senate Foreign Relations Committee and proved himself to be more than just a good speaker but an able statesman.

The Great Recession and the busy first two years

When President Obama was inaugurated in January of 2009, the unemployment rate had been steadily rising and the economy had contracted in the greatest economy crises since the Great Depression. By April in 2009, the unemployment rate hit 9%, peaking at 10% in October. The GDP fell by 16.1%, Americans were more in debt then they had ever been and the world economy was in free fall.

Obama acted quickly and in early 2009, as the unemployment rate soared, President Obama secured passage of the American Recovery and Reinvestment Act the largest stimulus package in American history. The stimulus injected a large amount of investments and economic assistance into the economy, building infrastructure, granting tax relief and credits to businesses and encouraging the use of green technology around the nation.

While it faced huge opposition from conservatives who argued that the Keynesian policy of stimulus would not work in combating the Great Recession, the economy relapsed from free fall during the second quarter of 2009, when the stimulus went into effect. Progressive Democrats argued that the stimulus was imperative in order to raise

GDP growth following 2009, heal unemployment numbers and end the recession. Many Conservatives believe that the stimulus actually prolonged the recession and that the numbers were coincidental.

The downside to the stimulus was the way that Obama passed it. During his first hundred days in office he relied on passing the majority of his legislation with only democratic support. Republicans felt excluded from the process and the legislature remained very partisan.

In addition to the stimulus President Obama endorsed a bailout of General Motors and Chrysler. The bailout, which loaned money to the two bankrupted car manufacturers, helped revitalize the auto-industry as well as improve regulation standards for new cars, such as required fuel efficiency standards and "greenness" of the cars manufactured in the United States. As of 2012, both General Motors and Chrysler are self-sufficient and have paid back the loans to the United States government, with interest, which was key to improving economic conditions after the crisis.

Affordable Care Act: Obama's crown jewel or curse?

With the stimulus passed and the economy no longer in free fall, Obama was determined to do what no other president had done—reform the healthcare system. The Affordable Care Act (ACA) was a centerpiece to Obama's campaign against Hillary Clinton and John McCain, the largest healthcare reform since the passage of Medicaid and Medicare. The Affordable Care Act's purpose was to provide health care for more people at a cheaper price while improving the quality of the healthcare service given to people. The Affordable Care Act set caps on the price of health insurance; prior to the passage of the ACA, health insurance prices had been steadily skyrocketing. Insurance exchanges would be a catalyst for newly insured people under the ACA to acquire private health insurance. The most controversial aspects of the ACA, the individual mandate, which requires people to sign up for health insurance or be penalized was put in place to combat what is called an insurance death spiral. The spiral happens when people wait until they are sick to get a premium, which in turn causes insurance companies to jack up premium prices greatly affecting everyone in the healthcare system. Although challenged in the Supreme Court, the court upheld the mandate 5-4.

One of the cornerstones of the bill was to end discrimination due to pre-existing condition. People were originally unable to become insured due to preexisting conditions, but the Affordable Care Act prevented insurers from refusing to insure people or charge higher prices when there are preexisting conditions, regardless of history.

While the ACA had some great benefits for people it became the rallying point of opposition to Obama. Republicans used it to sweep to a massive victory in 2010 and it continues to be a contentious issue today. And such criticisms are not unwarranted. The ACA covered more people but the price of healthcare continues to rise.

Banking reform

The final act of Obama's busy first two years in office was banking reform. After the economic crises in 2008, many economists and politicians called for stronger regulations on Wall Street, similar to the response of the Franklin Roosevelt administration after the Great Depression. Many people agreed that something had to be done about toxic credit default

swaps, shadow banking and the extremely neglectful eye on banks and Wall Street. The Dodd-Frank Act, at a staggering 2,300 pages, is the bill that began the regulating of Wall Street. The central achievements of the Dodd-Frank Act is the oversight council that was created because of the bill, which checks the financial stability of banks to make sure that they do not become too big to fail and breaks them up if such a thing were to happen. Although, there were people who argued that banks are already too big to fail. The Dodd-Frank Wall Street Reform and Consumer Protection Act of 2008, more familiarly known as Dodd-Frank, also gives the government regulatory power over hedge funds, which was very limited before the passage of the bill.

The most important aspect of the Dodd-Frank Act is the Volcker rule, created by Jimmy Carter's appointee to the Federal Reserve, Paul Volcker. The rule essentially ends banks' ability to use credit default swaps by barring them from using private equity funds, hedge funds and other such investment instruments as profit making tools in the marketplace.

A House Divided: War and Tea

President Obama suffered from the same afflictions that dismayed Woodrow Wilson in 1914 and Bill Clinton in 1994—a sweeping loss of the House of Representatives in 2010. This was somewhat unavoidable due to the Obama administration's legislative etiquette which was governed by a mindset of swiftness. The Democrats had two supermajorities in both the House and Senate when Obama first came into the White House. With that immense power they passed bill after bill without much Republican consultation. Thus there grew a reaction movement, known as the Tea Party—a staunchly right-wing branch of the Republicans. The Tea Party was the death of any of the last standing moderate Republicans left over from the days of Gerald Ford and Nelson Rockefeller and had quasi-loyalty tests for politicians to represent the new conservative wing. The Tea Party movement began as a protest movement in Washington, directly in opposition to all the policies of the Obama administration. It grew quickly into a political movement that crushed the Democratic supermajority in the Congress and weakened the Democrat's control of the Senate.

More than just a political movement, many of the Tea Party politicians seem to have a deep seated hatred of President Obama, as many of them, such as minority leader in the Senate Mitch McConnell, swore to oppose anything Obama did solely to keep him a one term President. The divided house that appeared in 2010 would lead to six years of gridlock and indecision and complicate Obama's presidency and change the way he used executive power.

The effect of the new makeup of the house and senate was seen immediately. A crisis arose as early as 2011 regarding defaulting on the national debt, and the debt ceiling. The debt had been growing exponentially since the 1980s due to increased spending on the military, increased social benefits, multiple bailouts over the years and the disagreements over how to deal with the large amount of debt.

Republicans threatened to allow the debt to default if spending wasn't cut, and Democrats refused to cut spending without seeing a decrease in military spending. Nearing the deadline, a compromise was proposed which created a sequestration. Sequestration would take effect if a compromise couldn't be reached in 2012 over the debt-ceiling, where military and social spending would be cut. In return for halting sequestration, the Republican house passed the Budget Control Act, raising the debt limit, along with the Democratic Senate and President Obama's signature.

Every year since the 2012 crisis the same story unfolds. The crisis appears before each budget is submitted and so far the country continues to pass large spending bills, the most recent of which was $4 trillion dollars.

Executive Powers

With a divided government so engrossed in gridlock, the House of Representatives became the most unproductive in history. President Obama reacted to the stalemate by using executive orders and privileges to continue parts of his agenda. Many of his uses of executive order and privilege have been in the area of immigration, social issues, legal reform and wage reforms. Although legal, the opposition in the house has been riled up by the break in the tradition of executive power. Although the President is elected by the people, he must still work with Congress to pass legislation. Although some emergency situations warrant the use of executive power it has been very seldom used in the way Obama has managed it today. For example, President Obama has used executive action to reform or modify numerous things such as (to name just a few): immigration reform—particularly around deportations—gun control, civil liberties, Guantanamo Bay and issues regarding same-sex couples.

The Middle East Quagmire and the Russian Standoff

The domestic economy was in the process of repair but the wars being fought in the Middle East raged on during Obama's first term. In 2011, President Obama finished the troop withdrawal in Iraq and ended the Iraq War—the same year Osama Bin Laden was killed. Moreover, in an attempt to heal the image of the United States after the Iraq War President Obama attempted to close Guantanamo Bay but was unable to complete the shutdown due to gridlock in the House.

As the U.S. left Iraq the Middle East continued to become more unstable. 2010 was an explosive year for the Middle East, as rioting, revolution and religious tumult increased. The Egyptian government was overthrown and replaced by Mohamed Morsi and the Muslim Brotherhood, violence increased in Iraq and Afghanistan, and fundamentalist Muslims grew stronger. This was true of Iraq as well, where radical Muslims slowly gained more power, eventually forming ISIS.

Obama adopted a policy in the Middle East that relied heavily on drone warfare and small interventions. Drones were used more often in Afghanistan and Obama intervened in the Libya to depose Muammar Gaddafi. As always intervention is not without its blowback. The destabilization of the Middle East, Syria and Libya would eventually lead to an influx of refugees to Europe and the United States which has pushed the West into the period of identity crisis it now faces.

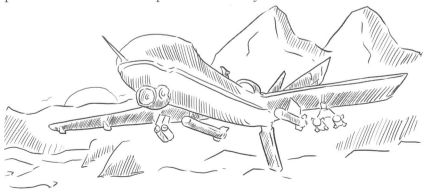

The American Drift

Political divisions throughout the country and in the chambers of government held back Obama from passing an extensive legislative agenda after 2010. However, even without the government being active, the political and cultural landscape of America changed drastically during the Obama years. In politics, both parties evolved and moved farther away from one another ideologically. The Democrats, who in 2010 still had Robert Byrd—a southern senator who originally opposed the civil rights act and supported the war in Vietnam—became a party that adhered to strict liberalism and had few moderates or southerners that represented the old guard. Likewise, the Republican Party expelled or alienated the majority of moderates and fully embraced the neo-conservatism of the Bush years.

Much of the drift in American political and social culture can be associated with the growing prevalence of social issues being pressed during the final term of the Obama presidency. Of course many of these issues surfaced during previous years, as far back as the 1960s, but the rapid cultural change beginning in 2010 was quite explosive compared to the preceding two decades. By the end of 2015 people found themselves living in a country that had legalized same-sex marriage, bolstered affirmative action programs, increased support for transgenderism, opposition to the confederate flag, heightened adherence to political correctness, and showed a strong divide between races evidenced by violent clashes between police and African Americans. Moreover, the way people experienced the federal government changed as the cyber age became more advanced. The NSA was caught spying on private online information, Russians were hacking into American corporations and life became increasingly more tied to the internet. There was also the issue of gun control which came back into the spotlight due to a terrible string of massacres that occurred at an alarming rate, starting with the Sandy Hook Massacre in Newtown, Connecticut. All these issues and more caused increased chaos in the American psyche, polarizing conservatives and liberals. President Obama was never shy and weighed in on nearly every major issue and event. As he commented on social issues such as the Black Lives Matter movement—a group that started in response to an increase in African American deaths by police officers—it often became clear that although Obama could not act legislatively in response to these events, such as with gun control, he could voice his opinion or support for certain groups which separated him even more from already skeptical American conservatives.

By 2016 the cultural landscape of the United States had changed so drastically that the Republican right-wing split and formed a movement separate from the neo-conservatives that often had liberal social views, and from the Tea Party members that had a strong focus on taxation and economics. This new group believed in preserving American traditions and culture and attacked political correctness. Their interest in economics was far more nationalistic than economic, as seen with the Tea Partyers. They did not necessarily believe that free trade was always a good thing, nor did they believe that what's good for US corporations is good for all Americans.

There is no question that the liberal side of the Democratic Party got its way on social issues by the end of the Obama administration. However, as the clock ticked to the end of the Obama presidency, the country was nearing polarization levels not seen since the 1960s. Americans also faced an identity crisis, and with the rapid changes of the Obama years how would America proceed both domestically and on the world stage? Would the United States embrace the enlarged and empowered federal government along with the new globalist world that did not adhere to traditional institutions and structures? Or would the conservative stalwarts hold onto the America that existed before the transformations of the 2000s? Even with the 2016 election decided and the new president chosen, we will not know the answers to these questions for some time.

The next decade will be a difficult period for the American Presidency, especially after the 2016 election which was not a proud moment for the country. The American people were asked to choose between two of most unpopular and divisive candidates in American history thus it was unsurprising that voter turnout continued to fall and the current president-elect, Donald J. Trump, managed only an Electoral College victory. (Trump's opponent, Hillary Clinton, won the majority of the popular vote.) For the first time in American history a sitting president will have been elected with no prior political experience and no military service to substitute for the lack of political savvy. Where do American politics go from here?

As stated in the foreword, the history of the presidency is akin to that of the most dramatic of theater presentations. The center stage has always brought uniquely qualified individuals to its glare and those who managed to take on the lead role defined their era of American history. However one has to now wonder if we are living in an era of reality TV rather than theater. An era defined by a decadent celebrity president who leads a decadent country. Edward Gibbon noted in *The Decline and Fall of the Roman Empire* that the grandest empire of its time fell because "the leaders of the [fallen] empire gave into the vices of strangers, morals collapsed, laws became oppressive, and the abuse of power made the nation vulnerable to the barbarian hordes." If the presidency—the heart of America, the organ that perfuses all the vital processes of our great democratic-republic—falls to the same level of decadence that claimed all the other empires now laid to rest, the United States will find itself broken and defeated.

Despite all the anxiety and fear that engulfed the election of 2016, any new administration at any point in history must be given a chance to succeed despite how one might feel towards the president. The most important thing to remember for those who study the presidency is this: the president is the leader and representative of the strongest empire in history, and is the role model for many of the next generation. The responsibilities of this office were described by Truman as being akin to having "the moon, the stars, and all the planets falling on [you]." That office is sacred and all of us should remember that it does not belong to the loudest, the wealthiest, or the most well connected. It belongs to the average citizens of this country and sometimes the best performers on the grand stage of the presidency are simply the few good men and women who want to do right by their god, their family, and their fellow countrymen.

Bibliography

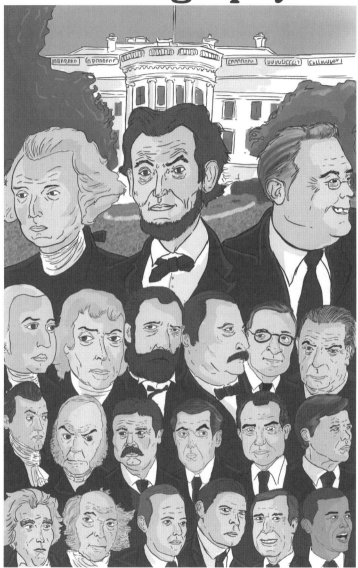

So many Presidents, so many references—too many, in fact, to list here. You can find the full bibliography at www.forbeginnersbooks.com/american-presidency and click on "Reference Guide" to download a pdf file to use in your classroom or for your own personal reference.

THE FOR BEGINNERS® SERIES

ABSTRACT EXPRESSIONISM FOR BEGINNERS:	ISBN 978-1-939994-62-2
AFRICAN HISTORY FOR BEGINNERS:	ISBN 978-1-934389-18-8
ANARCHISM FOR BEGINNERS:	ISBN 978-1-934389-32-4
ARABS & ISRAEL FOR BEGINNERS:	ISBN 978-1-934389-16-4
ART THEORY FOR BEGINNERS:	ISBN 978-1-934389-47-8
ASTRONOMYFOR BEGINNERS:	ISBN 978-1-934389-25-6
AYN RAND FOR BEGINNERS:	ISBN 978-1-934389-37-9
BARACK OBAMA FOR BEGINNERS, AN ESSENTIAL GUIDE:	ISBN 978-1-934389-44-7
BEN FRANKLIN FOR BEGINNERS:	ISBN 978-1-934389-48-5
BLACK HISTORY FOR BEGINNERS:	ISBN 978-1-934389-19-5
THE BLACK HOLOCAUST FOR BEGINNERS:	ISBN 978-1-934389-03-4
BLACK PANTHERS FOR BEGINNERS:	ISBN 978-1-939994-39-4
BLACK WOMEN FOR BEGINNERS:	ISBN 978-1-934389-20-1
BUDDHA FOR BEGINNERS	ISBN 978-1-939994-33-2
BUKOWSKI FOR BEGINNERS	ISBN 978-1-939994-37-0
CHICANO MOVEMENT FOR BEGINNERS:	ISBN 978-1-939994-64-6
CHOMSKY FOR BEGINNERS:	ISBN 978-1-934389-17-1
CIVIL RIGHTS FOR BEGINNERS:	ISBN 978-1-934389-89-8
CLIMATE CHANGE FOR BEGINNERS:	ISBN 978-1-939994-43-1
DADA & SURREALISM FOR BEGINNERS:	ISBN 978-1-934389-00-3
DANTE FOR BEGINNERS:	ISBN 978-1-934389-67-6
DECONSTRUCTION FOR BEGINNERS:	ISBN 978-1-934389-26-3
DEMOCRACY FOR BEGINNERS:	ISBN 978-1-934389-36-2
DERRIDA FOR BEGINNERS:	ISBN 978-1-934389-11-9
EASTERN PHILOSOPHY FOR BEGINNERS:	ISBN 978-1-934389-07-2
EXISTENTIALISM FOR BEGINNERS:	ISBN 978-1-934389-21-8
FANON FOR BEGINNERS:	ISBN 978-1-934389-87-4
FDR AND THE NEW DEAL FOR BEGINNERS:	ISBN 978-1-934389-50-8
FOUCAULT FOR BEGINNERS:	ISBN 978-1-934389-12-6
FREEMASONRY FOR BEGINNERS:	ISBN 978-1-939994-56-1
FRENCH REVOLUTIONS FOR BEGINNERS:	ISBN 978-1-934389-91-1
GENDER & SEXUALITY FOR BEGINNERS:	ISBN 978-1-934389-69-0
GREEK MYTHOLOGY FOR BEGINNERS:	ISBN 978-1-934389-83-6
HEIDEGGER FOR BEGINNERS:	ISBN 978-1-934389-13-3
THE HISTORY OF CLASSICAL MUSIC FOR BEGINNERS:	ISBN 978-1-939994-26-4
THE HISTORY OF OPERA FOR BEGINNERS:	ISBN 978-1-934389-79-9
ISLAM FOR BEGINNERS:	ISBN 978-1-934389-01-0
JANE AUSTEN FOR BEGINNERS:	ISBN 978-1-934389-61-4
JUNG FOR BEGINNERS:	ISBN 978-1-934389-76-8
KIERKEGAARD FOR BEGINNERS:	ISBN 978-1-934389-14-0
LACAN FOR BEGINNERS:	ISBN 978-1-934389-39-3
LIBERTARIANISM FOR BEGINNERS:	ISBN 978-1-939994-66-0
LINCOLN FOR BEGINNERS:	ISBN 978-1-934389-85-0
LINGUISTICS FOR BEGINNERS:	ISBN 978-1-934389-28-7
MALCOLM X FOR BEGINNERS:	ISBN 978-1-934389-04-1
MARX'S DAS KAPITALFOR BEGINNERS:	ISBN 978-1-934389-59-1
MCLUHAN FOR BEGINNERS:	ISBN 978-1-934389-75-1
MORMONISM FOR BEGINNERS:	ISBN 978-1-939994-52-3
MUSIC THEORY FOR BEGINNERS:	ISBN 978-1-939994-46-2
NIETZSCHE FOR BEGINNERS:	ISBN 978-1-934389-05-8
PAUL ROBESON FOR BEGINNERS:	ISBN 978-1-934389-81-2
PHILOSOPHY FOR BEGINNERS:	ISBN 978-1-934389-02-7
PLATO FOR BEGINNERS:	ISBN 978-1-934389-08-9
POETRY FOR BEGINNERS:	ISBN 978-1-934389-46-1
POSTMODERNISM FOR BEGINNERS:	ISBN 978-1-934389-09-6
PRISON INDUSTRIAL COMPLEX FOR BEGINNERS:	ISBN 978-1-939994-31-8
PROUST FOR BEGINNERS:	ISBN 978-1-939994-44-8
RELATIVITY & QUANTUM PHYSICS FOR BEGINNERS:	ISBN 978-1-934389-42-3
SARTRE FOR BEGINNERS:	ISBN 978-1-934389-15-7
SAUSSURE FOR BEGINNERS:	ISBN 978-1-939994-41-7
SHAKESPEARE FOR BEGINNERS:	ISBN 978-1-934389-29-4
STANISLAVSKI FOR BEGINNERS:	ISBN 978-1-939994-35-6
STRUCTURALISM & POSTSTRUCTURALISM FOR BEGINNERS:	ISBN 978-1-934389-10-2
TESLA FOR BEGINNERS:	ISBN 978-1-939994-48-6
TONI MORRISON FOR BEGINNERS:	ISBN 978-1-939994-54-7
WOMEN'S HISTORYFOR BEGINNERS:	ISBN 978-1-934389-60-7
UNIONS FOR BEGINNERS:	ISBN 978-1-934389-77-5
U.S. CONSTITUTIONFOR BEGINNERS:	ISBN 978-1-934389-62-1
ZEN FOR BEGINNERS:	ISBN 978-1-934389-06-5
ZINN FOR BEGINNERS:	ISBN 978-1-934389-40-9

www.forbeginnersbooks.com